PRESUMED
GUILTY

PRESUMED GUILTY

The Tragedy of the Rodney King Affair

SGT. STACEY C. KOON, L.A.P.D.
with Robert Deitz

Regnery Gateway
Washington, D.C.

Library of Congress Cataloging-in-Publication Data

Koon, Stacey C., 1950–
    Presumed guilty : the tragedy of the Rodney King affair / Stacey
C. Koon with Robert Deitz.
        p.   cm.
    Includes index.
    ISBN 0-89526-507-9 (alk. paper)
    1. Police—California—Los Angeles—Complaints against—Case
studies. 2. King, Rodney. 3. Afro-Americans—California—Los
Angeles—Crimes against—Case studies. 4. Police training—
California—Los angeles. I. Deitz, Robert, II. Title.
HV8148.L552K66   1992
363.2'3'092—dc20
[B]   92-29422
                                                         CIP

Published in the United States by
Regnery Gateway
1130 17th Street, NW
Washington, DC 20036

Distributed to the trade by
National Book Network
4720-A Boston Way
Lanham, MD 20706

Printed on recycled, acid-free paper

Manufactured in the United States of America

10 9 8 7 6 5 4

To Mary, Matthew, Gregory, Alicia, Kimberly, and Jennifer.
You've believed in me through everything difficult.
Especially Mary.

19.95

Acknowledgments

First, I must acknowledge all of the magnificent street cops it was my privilege to learn from and serve with on the Los Angeles Police Department for almost fifteen years. There are so many that it would require a complete chapter to name them all. But you know who you are. Thanks, to all of you.

Thanks, too, to the Los Angeles Police Protective League and to Cliff Ruff, a director of that organization. The League furnished strong moral and financial support to sustain me and my officers through a long legal process that is not yet over.

Besides my wonderful, supportive, loving, and very smart wife, Mary, two other people have been especially helpful in providing me with both spiritual and practical comfort in getting through the personally difficult ordeal that has followed the night of March 3, 1991.

The first is my attorney, Darryl Mounger. He is brilliant. Clarence Darrow could not have surpassed his competence in conceiving and executing a stunning courtroom strategy for the defense based upon the truth. The second is Father Robert Rankin—"Father Bob"—of Our Lady of Perpetual Help Church. His wisdom and patience have nourished the spiritual determination required to confront adversity.

Alfred Regnery at Regnery Gateway is a courageous publisher, and I am indebted to him and his associates, Jennifer Reist, Megan Butler, and Patricia Bozell, my editor, for taking on this project and seeing it through to conclusion. Alfred

Regnery is a brave and daring man, who was willing to undertake this publishing project despite almost universal hostility in the media toward our cause.

Al also enlisted the assistance of Robert Deitz, an author, reporter, and editor for thirty years. Bob has done a fine job in helping organize the manuscript and getting it ready for publication. It is a delight to have made a new friend, as well as a new professional associate. In addition, he added to my understanding—if not my total acceptance—of how the American media operate today.

Finally, I am deeply obliged to my parents, Helen and Larry Koon, and my brother, Dana. They all were essential in providing the moral training and support that has sustained my perception of right and wrong, and the ethical strength to do what I have believed is right even when challenged by seemingly overwhelming opposition. More immediately, they were excellent editors and a loving, but discerning, sounding board in the preparation of this manuscript.

Thanks, folks. I love you.

STACEY C. KOON
Los Angeles
August 1992

Contents

Foreword

On March 4, 1991, people in Southern California who had tuned in to the 10 P.M. news on KTLA-TV in Los Angeles were horrified by selected parts of an eighty-two-second videotape that showed four Los Angeles Police Department officers circling a suspect and delivering a torrent of blows to his body with their metal batons.

By the next day, the videotape had been distributed by KTLA to Cable News Network. The horror spread worldwide. What people saw was this: An edited clip of a twelve-minute videotape, about one minute and twenty-two seconds in all, of what seemed to be mindless cruelty to a stopped motorist by four LAPD officers commanded by a sergeant. The sergeant stood to the left of the scene directing the officers' actions. He was clearly in charge.

I was that sergeant.

For the eighty-two seconds of edited tape, the officers, following my orders, would strike the suspect, then back away only to return moments later to beat him again. To the casual observer, it seemed as if they were taking turns. At one point in the videotape, it appeared as though one officer stepped forward to kick the suspect. Finally, mercifully, the suspect got to his knees and raised his arms in what seemed to be a pleading gesture of docile submission. He was then handcuffed by the officers. His ankles and feet were secured to his wrists in what's customarily called a "hog-tie" hold. Then he was taken

11

to the side of the road to await an ambulance that had been called to take him to a hospital.

To the casual viewer, it appeared that the police officers were methodically, systematically brutalizing a helpless, innocent black man who lay prone upon the ground. It seemed they were beating a defenseless suspect who was unable to protect himself and was seeking desperately to crawl away from the blitz of blows from police batons. The portions of the videotape that were shown resurrected all of the painful memories of police brutality to innocent minorities, especially black people, that stir so uncomfortably in the American conscience.

The picture of unjustified police brutality is untrue, grotesquely so. In fact, nothing about the Rodney King incident could be more false than that image.

If you are like most Americans, you will never be able to forget that videotaped picture of police batons swinging down to strike Rodney King repeatedly.

Even so, regardless of what you think you saw, it was not what actually happened. This book will *not* ask you to put aside the image that lingers in your mind. Neither is it an apology for what happened on a darkened San Fernando Valley street in Los Angeles shortly after midnight on March 3, 1991. Nor is it an examination of the social policies that might have led Rodney King to a brutal confrontation with the law.

No, you will not be asked to suspend belief. You will not be asked to forget what you saw on the videotape, now commonly referred to as the George Holliday videotape.

All that will be asked of you, the reader, is to look at the evidence from a different angle, to examine some evidence that has gotten far less media exposure than the dramatic videotape. Try to recall the image in your mind as if you were on the scene at the time, as the police officers were.

You will be asked to try and cast yourself in the role of what the officers knew and what they didn't know. Throughout this book, try to relive our previous experiences as police officers, especially in the arrest and detention of suspected felons and "dusted" offenders,[1] who are a police officer's worst nightmare. Try to consider the facts the officers had to work with at the time. These are indisputable facts that provided the basis for what had to be split-second decisions which, if wrong, could endanger the lives of other law enforcement personnel on the scene, innocent civilian bystanders, and, not coincidentally, Rodney King himself.

Do this, learn about the policies and procedures of the LAPD that will be explained in the context of the King arrest, and you will come to understand something extremely important about this incident:

The Simi Valley, California, jury that found me and three other officers innocent of wrongdoing arrived at the only reasonable conclusion that could be reached. It was the only verdict possible, based upon the evidence. We were rightfully judged innocent despite almost universal presumption of our guilt both before and after the trial. That presumption was fed by the media.

All of which means, of course, that the public revulsion and bloody, costly Los Angeles riots that followed the verdict were a tragic, avoidable reaction. They were the response of a misguided public that had been deceived by the Los Angeles police, municipal officials, and community leaders. They were the reaction of an ill-informed public denied information by news media that had an agenda in which truth and full disclosure were not factors. The Los Angeles riots were the grim reward for a public that had been whipped into a hysteria of primitive anger by cynical, self-serving politicians and community leaders pandering to minority interests, politicians who had private reasons for keeping hidden their own culpability in creating the policies and arrest procedures that made the Rodney King incident an inevitable event, a bomb waiting to explode.

But these are not the only reasons why the Rodney King

---

[1] Drug abusers on PCP, phencyclidine, or "angel dust," as it is known on the streets. A powerful hallucinogenic anesthetic developed for use with animals, PCP gives humans extraordinary strength and imperviousness to pain. At the LAPD Academy, you're taught that if a dusted suspect grips you by the arm or neck, it's a death grip.

affair will go down in history as one of the greatest tragedies in the American experience of law enforcement and race relations. There are other compelling reasons, too.

One is the devastating impact the affair and its ghastly aftermath have had on so many lives. Beyond the irreparable destruction of the careers of four dedicated, competent police officers, the King episode has damaged thousands of other people.

The list of victims is a long one. Begin with the police officers and their families, who must undergo the ordeal of another trial on federal civil rights charges that constitute de facto if not de jure double jeopardy. Then move to the unfairly condemned Simi Valley jurors. Worst of all are the people who died in the riots and, of course, their loved ones. Then add the thousands of people who were injured or lost property and jobs from the destruction of whole neighborhoods of Los Angeles. Include former LAPD Chief Daryl Gates. His refusal to stand behind the legal actions of his officers—a denial that can be explained only by the ruthless, scheming politics of the Los Angeles police department—will be a matter of conscience that Chief Gates must deal with for the remainder of his life.

Yet another victim, ironically, is Rodney King himself. As this book is being written, Rodney King lives the life of a virtual prisoner, under twenty-four-hour protection, and, according to at least one published source, tranquilized as his attorney seeks to extract a multimillion dollar ransom from the city of Los Angeles for suffering King only brought upon himself through his own uncontrolled actions the morning of March 3, 1991.[2] He reportedly leaves his home only to run errands. And, one might add, get arrested, something that has happened three times since March 3, 1991. Still, King and his attorney insist on being compensated for the injuries he brought upon himself. If

---

[2] In an excellent article in the July 1992 issue of *Vanity Fair* magazine entitled, "The Selling of Rodney King," reporter Peter J. Boyer says King is "shut away in a safe house . . . wrapped in the arms of pharmaceuticals, and under the twenty-four-hour watch of a private security team led by (of all people) a former L.A.P.D. cop," as his attorney negotiates a deal with the city of Los Angeles and marketing wizards who would make King "a mythic symbol of denied justice. . . ." Peter J. Boyer, *Vanity Fair*, Vol. 55, No. 7, July 1992, pp. 78–83, 158–161.

King collects his ransom from the city of Los Angeles tax-payers, as he almost surely will, it will be a travesty of justice, if not a minor tragedy by itself.

Nor do these tragedies end with just the identifiable victims like King, Gates, the police officers, the jurors, and the dead and injured in the Los Angeles riot. Truth has been another casualty. The news media have been the perpetrators of this ugly injustice.

This is because the news media, particularly television and the nation's most influential daily newspapers, have methodically withheld or given little or no attention to facts that might have led the American people to a conclusion that is 180 degrees distant from the George Holliday videotape. The media nurtured that picture by repetitious replays of the edited clip—not the entire videotape, especially the part showing Rodney King attacking an officer—thousands of times. It was a videotape screened on prime-time television for months on end, before another side of the story could be told. Why the media performed in this fashion can only be surmised; those suppositions will be explored in this book.

Finally, what would appear to be the last tragedy of the Rodney King incident is that it didn't have to happen. If the city of Los Angeles had followed the urging of the LAPD a decade ago, or adopted the restraint-by-force policies of many other large urban police departments, the Rodney King affair could have been avoided.

But even this is not the worst of the story. No, the ultimate tragedy of the Rodney King incident is that neither the public, the city of Los Angeles, nor police officials appear to have learned from the episode. Nothing of substance has changed in the policies of the Los Angeles Police Department, reputed to be the best in the nation, if not the world.

Because, you see, what happened in the dark, early morning chill of March 3, 1991, can happen again. In fact, it almost certainly *will* happen again. And the next time it occurs, more people are likely to die. That's the final catastrophe of this painful drama, a misunderstood tragedy whose final scenes have yet to be played out.

Prologue

Monday morning, March 5, 1991, was a typical Southern California day in early spring. At 6:30 A.M., the moon was suspended against the pale blue background of an early morning sky in stark relief over the Santa Clarita mountains. It was like a surrealistic painting, almost as if the moon had been hung from an invisible wire. The weather was cool. Southern California's smog hadn't yet settled in a smothering blanket over the valley.

I was laid back that morning. It was "monkey-slapping" time, as cops call it. Actually, "monkey-slapping" originally meant masturbating. "Slapping the monkey" was an old military expression that described sexual self-gratification. But that was before females came on the police force and into the military. When finally forced to do so, macho cops and military men had to clean up their language, or the intent of that language, at least.

So, over the years, among cops "monkey-slapping" came to be a euphemism for relaxation time, time off the job, time to kick back and take it easy for a while. That's why I hadn't fast-walked my usual two and-a-half miles up and down the Santa Clarita hills that morning. It was my second of two consecutive days off, and I wanted to relax. Instead of cooking breakfast for the kids like I usually did on the days when I didn't have duty, I went out to buy doughnuts.

It had been a good weekend, neither particularly easy nor especially hard. The weekend was unusual in only one respect.

Shortly after midnight Saturday, or early Sunday morning, my last workday of the week, we'd had an incident that was rare only because it had required an infrequent use of multi-officer force on a felony suspect. I had told my wife of nineteen years, Mary, about it on Sunday while we were driving to church with our five children.

"We had a bitchin' arrest last night," I'd said in the car. "Bitchin'," a Valley-girl cliché meaning "good" or "excellent," had become an unwelcome part of my vocabulary since starting to work in the Foothill Division of the San Fernando Valley one year earlier. I didn't like using the word, but it had become a habit. Not a bad habit, like smoking or drinking, both of which I shun. Language is a minor verbal vice. "Bitchin'." It means good. I can live with the flaw.

"Had to use some big-time force on this guy," I continued with the story to Mary as we drove to church. "He was dusted. A huge guy, maybe six-two, six-three, 240 pounds or so. Super-human strength. It took me and four other guys to get him cuffed. But we didn't hurt the guy too badly."

I was proud of that. Proud that when we had gotten to the hospital we'd found that the suspect wasn't badly injured. The emergency room examination showed that he had suffered only some bruises and minor lacerations, even though we'd had to hit him hard, repeatedly, before he'd respond to our commands to be cuffed. It was remarkable that he hadn't been hurt worse. In fact, at one point I'd even had to order the officers to cripple this guy. That was because the only other alternative was to shoot him. Our objective was to take him into custody using minimum necessary force. But he'd re-sisted our best efforts. Finally, we had to power-stroke him in the joints—wrists, ankles, elbows, knees. By doing so, he might have had trouble walking later. But he wouldn't have been dead. That was the plan: take him into custody without killing him, regardless of his repeated refusal to obey a lawful order. And do so despite his continued efforts to rise and assault an officer as he did at the beginning of the incident.

This guy wasn't Mister Innocent Citizen, either. Not by a long shot. He had been driving around one hundred miles per hour-plus for almost eight miles before he was forced to stop. After exiting the freeway where he'd first been observed driving in an extremely dangerous fashion, he broke the law and endangered other motorists by running red lights and stop signs, interfering with cross-street traffic, weaving, and generally driving with a total disregard for safety. He had even made a right turn across at least three lanes of expressway traffic at eighty miles an hour. That's serious traffic danger. And it happened at midnight on a weekend.

Then, when he did stop, it was at a place known as a graveyard for corpses who'd lost in drug deals gone bad. That park, only about two miles from the Foothill Division police station where I was a supervisor, had a bad reputation. Bodies were found there. When the suspect had been forced to stop in front of that park because of a cable across the entrance, we'd all thought that maybe we were getting lured into something. It's happened before. How many times have you read about a cop getting killed after stopping somebody for a speeding violation?

This question was fresh in all of our minds that night. In just the past few weeks, North Hollywood officers had been involved in two shootings brought on by carelessness in dealing with felony suspects. In the first situation, the officers had elected not to prone out a stopped suspect. Then, as one officer approached, the suspect became belligerent. The partner officer, believing assistance was needed, left his place of concealment and advanced on the scene. The officers, both out in the open, didn't even have time to break leather—pull their guns from their holsters. The suspect whirled and opened fire with a .44 magnum. The officers dropped to the ground and began shooting. When it was over, both officers were seriously wounded, but alive. The suspect was dead.

The second incident was worse. It was a simple drinking in public investigation. The driver officer got out of his vehicle. The partner officer, a probationer, sat in the passenger seat communicating the black-and-white's (the police car's) location. She did not see the suspect approach. Or, if she did, she did not have time to react. In an instant, the suspect was at her window firing a gun. Her partner quickly dumped the suspect with a volley of shots, but it was too late. The probationer was mortally wounded. She was the first LAPD female officer killed in the line of duty.

We had been reminded of these incidents repeatedly at roll call over the past two weeks. And our suspicions and cautions were heightened this night because there were two other suspects in the car that was fleeing the pursuit. It wasn't just the driver; there was another guy sitting shotgun and a third in the back seat. That made it an even more difficult situation. To be sure, I didn't see the two passengers at first. I saw them later, after King had been subdued. But I learned that the other two had gotten out quickly, following officers' commands, and allowed themselves to be cuffed. No problem there. That's why I didn't know about it. My problem was the driver.

That's because he was different. First of all, he was big. Very big. Then, shortly after getting out of the car, he had assaulted an officer. It quickly became evident that he was on something, alcohol or drugs. At the time, I believed it to be PCP. Later tests at the hospital for PCP usage were inconclusive. But other tests showed that Rodney King was intoxicated, with blood and urine tests revealing a .094 for alcohol; .08 is legally drunk. And these samples were taken almost six hours after the incident in Foothill. Take that back to the time of the incident, calculating King's height and weight, and you get an indicated blood/alcohol content of .19 when the arrest took place. Which means, of course, that Rodney King was more than twice the level required for being legally drunk when he was stopped.

This might explain in part why, when he finally did stop and got out of his car, King kept trying to get up while we were ordering him to prone out on his belly, hands behind his back so we could put on the cuffs. From our view, and based on what he already had done, Rodney King was trying to assault an officer, maybe grab a gun. And when not moving, he seemed to be looking for an opportunity to hurt somebody, his eyes darting this way and that. Not for escape; he'd already had that chance and blown it. So we knew Rodney King wasn't trying to run away.

We couldn't afford to let him get up, because then he'd either go after a cop or try to escape, as unlikely as the latter alternative seemed. Neither option was acceptable. We couldn't let him attack an officer again, because then somebody would get hurt, maybe—probably, even—killed. And we couldn't let him escape, because his hazardous driving patterns had already endangered innocent civilians as well as himself and his passengers.

Yet the guy just wouldn't respond to our orders. Once, after getting hit repeatedly with batons, he even turned over to get up and seemed to be reaching into the waistband of his trousers where weapons often are concealed. This was when Officer Ted Briseno stepped forward and stomped on King's back. On the videotape it looked like casual, unnecessary violence. But it was a perfectly proper procedure for subduing a violent suspect. It was a premeditated blow from Briseno intended to prevent King from reaching into his waistband and drawing out a concealed revolver, if he had one. We didn't know whether Rodney King had a weapon or not. We hadn't had a chance to cuff and search him. And we didn't want to find out the hard way.

So we'd had to use force to make him respond to our commands, to make him lie still so we could neutralize this guy's threat to other people and himself.

The force we used was well within the guidelines of the Los Angles Police Department; I'd made sure of that. And I was proud of my officers, proud of the professionalism they'd shown in subduing a really monster guy, a felony evader seen committing numerous serious traffic violations. And subduing this guy without the deadly force that all too often accompanies the arrest of a PCP-dusted felony suspect. My view has always been that a police officer should use proper tactics to avoid escalating to deadly force. An officer should resort to deadly force, the most common of which is the use of a gun, only after all other measures haven't worked. Police officers are sworn to serve and protect citizens—even those who are crazy on drugs and trying to kill other people, including the officers trying to save the life of the very person they're trying to arrest. Police officers are paid to save lives, not take them.

But we're getting ahead of the story here. Let's go back to Sunday, on the way to church, when I told Mary about the early morning incident.

Mary didn't respond to my abbreviated summary of what happened early Sunday morning. To her, it was just another cop story. She'd lived through plenty of cop stories. Later, Mary said her feeling was this: "So what? Just another night on the LAPD."

Just another night on the LAPD. That's what it had been.

And that's why, while driving to the doughnut shop about seven o'clock Monday morning to get breakfast for the kids, I wasn't particularly concerned to hear a radio report that the LAPD Internal Affairs Division (IAD) had begun an investigation into a reported incident of police using excessive force to subdue a suspect in the Foothill Division early Sunday morning. The radio report said the incident had been videotaped by a witness, and the IAD was looking into the matter.

An Internal Affairs investigation? Big deal. I knew that everything done that night was appropriate and well within LAPD guidelines. So in my mind an IAD investigation wasn't even important. All I heard was that the incident had been videotaped. And I knew that it was the only use-of-force episode that had occurred in the Foothill Division Sunday morning. So it must have been my arrest. And it had been videotaped!

"BITCHIN'," I thought. "This is great! They got it on tape! Now we'll have a live, in-the-field film to show police recruits. It can be a real-life example of how to use escalating force properly. Take it up and take it down. Watch what the suspect does. If he moves, control him. If he doesn't, cuff him. The guys are going to love this one. It's true stuff. Bitchin'."

Maybe it was naive, but it never occurred to me that the videotape, which I hadn't seen at the time, could be interpreted otherwise. But, then, the civilian who made the video-tape, George Holliday, and his camcorder were 150 feet away from the scene. Neither George Holliday nor his video camera could see what I saw shortly after midnight on March 3, 1991. Neither the videotape nor viewer could see what I had learned at the Police Academy and what I had seen in the previous fifteen years, most of them as a Los Angeles street cop—the experiences that determined how the Rodney King affair, as it has become known, would be handled.

Begin with that night. Then we'll fast-reverse this book to show how LAPD policies made the Rodney King affair an inevitable consequence of limitations on the LAPD's use-of-force procedures advocated by minority leaders and imposed by the political establishment of Los Angeles. After that, we'll look at some of my prior experiences as a street cop, which suggest that the affair couldn't have been managed any better than it was. And why, if it had to occur, I was the best officer to supervise on the scene. Finally, we'll examine the trial and go through the Rodney King videotape, second by second, so you can see through my eyes what you didn't see on the television screen in your living room. At the end, we'll examine the tragic consequences of the Rodney King incident.

You might not like hearing this, but Rodney King could be dead today because of his actions on the night of March 3, 1991. And he would be dead, if it hadn't been for the restraint my officers and I exercised in making his arrest, or if some other, more impulsive, cop had been in command.

You see, it was not a case of excessive force. To the contrary: it was a determined effort to *prevent* escalation to deadly force. At any time during the videotape you saw, certainly near the end, it easily could have escalated to a deadly force situation. I could have ordered an officer to use a chokehold or draw a weapon and subdue King with lethally dangerous force. But that would have been a poor tactic even if permissible under deadly force policies.

Try to keep an open mind. Remember, you're seeing this

through my eyes—not through the lens of an amateur camera-man shooting fifty yards distant from the incident, half the length of a football field, and at the darkest hour of the night. By itself, that should be enough to make you suspect what you saw. Or, at the very least, make you question what you *thought* you saw.

1

Force in the Foothills

The Pursuit

It was shortly before midnight on Saturday, March 2, 1991.

I had arrived at the Foothill Station a few minutes before the beginning of my 11 P.M.–7:45 A.M. morning shift to relieve the prior shift's watch commander so he could go home early. After getting to the station, I skipped off roll call. The roll call training that night was on the proper use of the PR 24 metal baton. The officers would be instructed on how to deliver power strokes to a suspect resisting arrest. The "suspect" was a wooden post covered with old rubber tires. I was familiar enough with the PR 24. Other supervisors were capable of refreshing the patrol officers on the proper techniques to employ.

One of the Foothill Division patrolmen during the training sessions had trouble using the PR 24 baton properly; he wasn't hitting hard enough. That was Officer Laurence Powell. Tonight he'd be given special attention at roll call. But he'd get it from somebody other than me. I needed to correct logs and do some of the other routine paperwork that street cops hate to do but that keeps a modern police department bureaucracy gainfully employed, drawing paychecks and awaiting retirement, while street cops do what they get paid to do out in the war zone.

Paperwork done, I was eager to get out in the field where street cops do their work. I was just leaving the station, walking out the rear door, when the California Highway Patrol pursuit went down. A CHIP unit had a major chase under way.[1] It was just a few miles away. The CHIPs had radioed a request for LAPD help. Two of my units had responded and an LAPD police helicopter had been dispatched to follow the action.

I got into my squad car and began paralleling the pursuit, based on what was coming over the police radio band. The chase was occurring about one or two miles away from where I was driving. It was happening fast, seventy, maybe eighty miles an hour and faster. But something didn't make sense. The CHIPs apparently didn't know the directions of the streets they were following. They kept saying they were headed south on a road that ran east-to-west, or east on a street that ran north-south. That was my first clue that this thing needed to be straightened out: the CHIPs didn't know where they were. Then there was something about a unit from the Los Angeles Unified School District Police (LAUSD) being involved.

The pursuit had begun about five miles away and a few minutes earlier. It had started as the CHIP cruiser approached the end of a long, steep descent of the 210 Freeway. The driver, Officer Melanie Singer, a three-year veteran of the California Highway Patrol, had first noticed the suspect vehicle's headlights in her rearview mirror. The headlights of the approaching car were rapidly narrowing the gap between it and the CHIP cruiser. That wasn't unusual, given the steep incline. Still, it looked to Melanie Singer as though the vehicle was traveling not just at an excessive speed, but at a speed that was unusually dangerous. She told her partner, Tim Singer, who was also her husband, about the approaching car. To get a handle on the vehicle's estimated speed, Melanie and Tim

---

[1] The California Highway Patrol is known as CHP to LAPD personnel. However, the CHP was popularized by the television show, "CHIPs," a designation that is more familiar to most general readers. For that reason, CHP will become CHIP in this book.

Singer decided to exit at the Sunland Boulevard off-ramp. Then they'd reenter the freeway immediately to gauge the suspect auto's speed. By the time the CHIP cruiser got back on the 210 Freeway, the suspect car had passed the off-ramp and was almost out of sight. To Officer Melanie Singer, that meant it had to be traveling at one hundred miles per hour plus. Melanie Singer floored the accelerator of the cruiser—the speedometer of her cruiser read 115 miles per hour—but she wasn't getting closer to the suspect, she wasn't narrowing the gap.

The suspect's vehicle began to get jammed up in traffic and slowed down. It was the break Officer Singer needed to close in on it. She neared to within a couple of car lengths of the speeding suspect, her speedometer now reading eighty miles per hour. She should have slowed to a safer speed and distance, but Melanie Singer was too wrapped up in the moment. It was a dangerous reaction, one that marks an inexperienced officer. She was eager, too eager, to turn on the lights and siren and force a traffic stop.

It was a poor police tactic. Stopping at that point would have put her partner flush against a freeway sound wall (a high wall intended to confine the din of traffic to the roadway). This would have made it difficult for her partner to get out of the cruiser. It would have limited his ability to move and defend himself, if the need arose. Besides, Officer Tim Singer wanted to run a status check on the suspect's vehicle to see if it was stolen or involved in a recent felony. It was the wise thing to do. Tim Singer waved his partner-wife away from forcing the suspect's vehicle to stop at that moment.

As they approached the 118 Freeway Interchange—about three miles from where they first noticed the speeding vehicle—Melanie Singer turned on the lights and siren. The suspect didn't stop. Instead, he exited the freeway at Paxton Avenue. To make the exit, he had to turn sharply to the right across at least three lanes of traffic—at over eighty miles per hour. At the end of the exit ramp is a stop sign, with a blind curve to the right on Paxton. The suspect ran the stop sign and turned left onto Paxton at thirty-five miles per hour, ignoring traffic signs and stop lights and pursuing police vehicles. By now the chase was in the Foothill Division of the LAPD. It was my territory.

Lights blinking and siren howling, the CHIP cruiser exited the freeway close behind the suspect vehicle. Melanie Singer was excited by the pursuit and her adrenalin was pumping. Tim Singer was giving information on his radio, but the information was inaccurate. CHIP assistance was rolling, but from a distance of twenty miles. The Singers needed help sooner. That's why they radioed for LAPD support. More help was on the way from two officers from the Los Angeles Unified School District Police who had observed the chase.

The suspect vehicle was making a large, horseshoe-shaped track of the city streets. Now it was paralleling the 210 Freeway on Foothill Boulevard. Melanie Singer had closed to within a car length and was staying on the suspect's bumper. At the intersection of Osborne and Foothill Boulevard, the suspect suddenly braked to a stop. Melanie Singer was caught off guard. She swerved to avoid a rear-end collision and stopped the cruiser alongside the suspect. Her partner-husband, Tim Singer, was directly beside the driver, whose name we learned later was Rodney Glen King (known to most of his friends as Glen, not Rodney). Officer Tim Singer and Rodney King stared at each other. Neither could fathom the other's intentions, although the CHIPs had made their wishes clearly known throughout the pursuit with lights flashing and siren howling.

The Stop

Melanie Singer realized she had made a serious tactical error. Her partner was exposed, dangerously exposed, to the suspect. They were only about three feet apart. The driver of the 1988 white Hyundai Excel could have raised a pistol and made Melanie Singer an instant widow. So she shifted the car into reverse and backed away. The suspect suddenly gunned his car forward, starting the pursuit all over again. But he drove only about fifty yards before rolling to a stop. His vehicle came to a halt on the right-hand shoulder of a curved portion of Foothill

Boulevard, only a few yards away from the foliage of Hansen Dam Recreation Park. He stopped because a cable was across the entrance to the park and he could go no further. The park, known as a very bad area for drug dealing and associated violence, was on the right in front of the gas station and liquor store. The park followed the curve along Foothill Boulevard and swept farther around to the right, almost enclosing the scene on two sides. It was the park that had us worried. Why had the suspect continued on to the park after stopping earlier? Were we getting set up?

Melanie Singer had stopped the CHIP cruiser directly behind King's car. The School District police pulled up and stopped to the right of and slightly behind the CHIP cruiser. An LAPD unit that had caught up with the chase just before the pause at the Osborne intersection pulled in to the left of the Singers' cruiser. The police helicopter was overhead, its dazzling spotlight illuminating a scene already made garish by the flashing lights of three police cruisers.

The officers got out of their cruisers, guns drawn, and took cover behind their car doors. Tim Singer, still in the patrol car, attempted to use the CHIP cruiser's loudspeaker to order the three suspects out of the car and onto the ground in the felony prone position.

"GET OUT OF THE VEHICLE. HANDS UP. GET ON YOUR STOMACH. PUT YOUR HANDS BEHIND YOUR BACK. NOW! MOVE IT!"

But the Singers' vehicle was only a couple of feet from Rodney King's rear bumper, causing a shrill feedback of the cruiser's public address system that made Tim Singer's commands unintelligible. Tim Singer dropped the microphone. It was useless. He stepped out of the car and began shouting commands over the noise of the school police's siren, which hadn't been turned off. The rotor blades of the LAPD helicopter overhead added to the pandemonium. Meanwhile, another LAPD unit pulled up. These officers also got out with guns drawn. They shouted at the school police to turn off their siren. It was quickly done.

Tim Singer now yelled a command for the driver, Rodney King, to get out of the car. King didn't move. Frustrated, Tim

Singer ordered the two passengers, later identified as Freddie Helms and Bryant Allen, out of the vehicle and into the felony prone position. Helms and Allen quickly obeyed, getting on the ground, where they were eventually handcuffed without incident.

Tim Singer again shouted for King to get out of the vehicle. Now, slowly, King complied. But it was obvious that something was wrong. King seemed to be under the influence of either alcohol or a much stronger chemical agent. He had his own agenda. He was making light of a dangerous, potentially lethal situation. He danced around. He waved at the helicopter. Worse, he reached into his pockets, an exceptionally dangerous action since he hadn't been cuffed and searched and the officers on the scene had no idea whether he was armed. Not only were eight officers now there, all with guns drawn, but a crowd of civilians from the apartments across the street had begun gathering to witness the real-life drama. Traffic was backing up a block behind the scene, as motorists tried to see what was happening.

Again, Tim Singer ordered Rodney King to get on his belly, face down, and put his hands behind his back. King ignored the order.

Initial Use of Force

That was the tense situation when I arrived at the scene. I braked to a halt, pulling my squad car directly to the side of King's vehicle at a 45-degree angle about twenty feet away. That put the engine block between me and the scene, providing some protection in case the suspect had a gun and wanted to start shooting. I got out of the car to survey what was going on.

This was when I made my first eye contact with Rodney King. He was by the open door of his vehicle, on his knees, swaying back and forth and from side to side. I estimated him to be a big man, very big, about six-feet, two-inches tall and maybe 250 pounds. Even though he wasn't standing up, I could tell that he was huge.

Not only that, but he was "buffed out." That means he had enormous upper-body muscles—his torso had been pumped up through rigorous, systematic exercise. It's a physical condition often associated with ex-cons, who have a lot of time to spend working out in exercise yards while they're in the slammer.

So my initial suspicions were that this guy was an ex-con and either drunk or on drugs. As it turned out, both hunches were correct. Rodney King was at the very least drunk. And later we learned he was an ex-con who, if convicted of the felony traffic offenses he'd been seen committing, could be returned to prison.[2]

Both of these were important suspicions—that the suspect was either drunk or on drugs, and that he was an ex-con. These were especially significant in view of what had gone on in the prior minutes of the chase. In fifteen years as an LAPD cop, thirteen of them on the street, I'd been involved in about fifty high-speed pursuits, most of them at night. Of these, only one or two had been a speeding offense only. All of the others had involved unrelated felony violations. Which means, of course, that this situation had to be approached as multiple traffic violations committed in connection with another, more

---

[2] At the time of this incident, Rodney King was on parole for robbery. In 1989 he had stuffed a two-foot-long tire iron into his jacket and used it as a weapon to rob a Korean storeowner in the Los Angeles suburb of Monterey Park. After buying a package of chewing gum, King ordered the storeowner to open the cash register, then struck him with a metal rod after he objected. King fled with about $200, but was quickly caught, tried, and convicted. He was paroled in December 1990 after serving half of a two-year term. Conviction for another offense would have meant a forced return to prison. Rodney King's prior record was less than clean. He was arrested in January 1989 for soliciting sex from an undercover Pasadena policewoman. Two years earlier, in 1987, he was sentenced to two years probation after pleading no contest to a misdemeanor battery charge filed by his wife. Earlier, in June 1983, at age eighteen, King was convicted of reckless driving after allegedly attempting to run over his future wife following an argument. And only two months later, in August 1983, he was convicted on a charge of trespassing, reduced from a theft charge, when he failed to pay for $251.87 worth of auto parts allegedly stolen from a Pep Boys outlet in Pasadena. Long before March 3, 1991, Rodney King was compiling a record as ugly as a mail-order suit.

serious crime, perhaps a burglary or, worse, an armed robbery or shooting incident. And remember this: my suspicion, based upon the evidence I had to work with at the time, was that this was an ex-con and therefore knew all the tricks to take out a police officer.

The lights from the cruisers and helicopter revealed that King was sweating. His muscular torso was beaded with perspiration that glistened in the artificial lighting from the helicopter and black-and-white headlamps. That was kind of weird. It was a cold night, yet this guy's sweating. Then he reached out, still on his hands and knees, and I thought he was going to go into the compliance mode for a felony cuffing. I thought he'd get on his belly, face into the pavement, hands behind his back.

But King didn't do that. Instead, he started patting the ground—not like he was going to get on his stomach in a felony prone position, but like he didn't know where the ground was, like he was feeling for something he couldn't quite reach.

That struck me as more than peculiar, too. "Why can't this guy find the ground he's kneeling on?" I thought to myself. Then he started talking gibberish. Not jabbering a real language, like English, Spanish, French, German, or any of the Asian tongues—Vietnamese, Laotian, Cambodian, or Thai—that I'd heard. Instead, it was a made-up language. He was mouthing unintelligible words, repeated over and over and over. I've seen it many times before. I'm beginning to get a bit concerned that we've got a "dusted" suspect here, not somebody just spaced out on booze or a drug like marijuana, but on something much more dangerous—like PCP.

What happened next increased my concern. What King now did was to crouch into the cocked position of a runner on the blocks or a football lineman getting in position to blitz an opposing tackle. I'm looking directly at this suspect, and he's looking at me—but he's looking through me. I've seen that look many times before. It's the look of somebody who's under the influence, specifically the influence of PCP. Now the suspicion that he's dusted gets stronger. But it still hasn't been confirmed.

King gave no hint that he was going to comply with the officers' orders to spread on the ground with his hands behind his back. But I had a backup plan for that. So I reached into my squad car for a TASER,[3] an electronic stun-gun that can fire two cassette cartridges, each capable of jolting a suspect with fifty thousand volts of low-amperage electricity through wires that connect into clothing or skin with small darts. The manufacturers of the device have a film of the TASER in action. One cassette is shot into an adult bison and BOOM: the bison falls like it's been poleaxed.[4] I'd used a TASER hundreds of times, especially when on duty as a sergeant in the jail where you're not allowed to carry a weapon or tie up physically with a prisoner. In the jail, a TASER was our only defense against prisoners. It is a formidable, nonlethal tool.

I unholstered the TASER and returned to my position behind the engine block. Melanie Singer decided her command presence was required. She shouted at King to show her his hands. Recognizing the voice as female, King grinned and turned his back to Melanie Singer. Then he grabbed his butt with both hands and began to gyrate his hips in a sexually suggestive fashion. Actually, it was more explicit than suggestive. Melanie Singer wasn't so much fearful as offended. She was being mocked in front of her peers. She was a female officer and she would be damned if a suspect was going to make fun of her and be so blatantly disrespectful in front of other officers, one of them her husband. Control and common sense were cast aside. Melanie's Jane Wayne and Dirty Harriett hormones

---

[3] The acronym stands for "Thomas A. Swift Electric Rifle," a wry use of the name of a fictional juvenile-book hero of inventive nature.

[4] At the trial, one of the attorneys suggested that we use this film as evidence. But my attorney and I feared we might have an animal-rights lover on the jury who might resent seeing a buffalo being TASED. As it turned out, we did have an animal lover on the jury. So the film showing a bison falling to his knees after getting TASED with one fifty thousand-volt charge and then toppling over like a bag of bricks was never screened for the Simi Valley jurors.

kicked in. She drew her pistol, and advanced to within five feet of the suspect.

Had she proceeded, either she was going to shoot Rodney King, or he was going to take her gun away and shoot her. If not her, then he might shoot some other officer or a civilian bystander. By drawing her gun and advancing on the suspect, Melanie Singer was unnecessarily raising the level of force. I don't know what CHIP training is, but the LAPD won't permit an advance on a suspect with a gun. The idea is to de-escalate before pulling your gun, if possible. So I ordered her to stop, telling her that we would handle the situation. Although the CHIPs had initiated the pursuit, my two cruisers were the primary and secondary units on the scene. And the incident was now on LAPD territory. As far as I was concerned, LAPD was in charge, not the CHIPs.

That's when I got involved. I had to. It was a dangerous situation. Until now, I had just been observing. The cops seemed to be handling it without a problem. There were eight of them with their pistols drawn, including Melanie Singer, and all were crouching behind their patrol-car doors. But then Melanie Singer had started to advance on the suspect, weapon drawn, and there were just too many targets. The situation had to be de-escalated, immediately. It was moving, quickly, toward something ugly and deadly. There were too many guns out, too many people around (by now a crowd of civilian gawkers had arrived). It was neither the time nor the place for a shoot-out at the OK Corral. I quickly formed a tactical plan.

"PUT YOUR GUNS AWAY. PUT YOUR GUNS AWAY!" I yelled.

The officers, all that I could see, holstered their pistols. The first part of my tactic, to take this suspect into custody without violence, was working. Now deadly force was not imminent. Now we could implement the next stage of my tactical plan, formed in the first seconds of my arrival on the scene.

I shouted at Melanie Singer to back away, to put away her pistol. What she was doing was a lousy tactic, a very lousy tactic. She was injecting a gun into a situation that didn't call for a gun. I was the ranking officer on the scene, and she prudently obeyed my orders. Now, before using a TASER, I could go to the next part of my plan: a "swarm" on the suspect.

Only four LAPD officers were on the scene at this time. I had designated Larry Powell as the shooter, if needed. His job was to shoot to kill the suspect if he grabbed an officer or an officer's weapon. But I had only four LAPD officers on the scene. So I had to relieve Powell as designated shooter and take that responsibility on myself. That was because I needed at least four officers to swarm the suspect.

Through body language and verbal commands I ordered the four LAPD officers nearest Rodney King to surround him. The idea was to force him into the felony prone position through what's known as a "swarm." That means two officers would each grab an arm, and two others a leg. The suspect is then slammed down face first into the ground, his arms twisted behind the back, and the handcuffs put on. The "swarm" is a police device that has proved useful with thousands of violently reluctant suspects—white as well as black, brown, or yellow; women as well as men; and any combination of race or gender in between. It's a technique that is neither racist nor sexist. And it was within LAPD policies governing the use of force.

The question occurs: Why weren't more than four officers directed to take King down? In the first place, we had a dangerous tactical situation. The suspects were in two groups: Rodney King on one side of the car, the other two suspects on the other side. So we had to split our forces. The CHIPs and school police could handle the suspects who were already complying; I would employ the LAPD officers on the resisting suspect.

But, just as importantly, when more than four or five officers are used to swarm a suspect, the extra bodies increase the danger of getting tangled up with the person you're trying to arrest. Then you might lose a wrestling match for a weapon. That's how somebody gets hurt, maybe even killed. It's why the LAPD has a stay-away policy for subduing violent suspects:

you don't get physically entangled with a suspect unless it's absolutely unavoidable. Under LAPD rules, you can use up to seven officers for a swarm. I had only four, not an ideal ratio, and the suspect was potentially violent. Now was the time to use a swarm.

Powell and the three other officers had formed a semicircle around King. I indicated for them to flank this guy from the rear, for them to swarm him. But I specifically ordered them to back off if he resisted. Then I'd TASE the guy. I didn't want my cops tangling with this big guy who I suspected was an ex-con and dusted with PCP.

The officers moved forward on King, who was in the runner-on-the-blocks position. Powell grabbed King's left arm. On the legs—I didn't know it at the time, but I do now—were Officer Ronaldo Solano who took the left leg and Officer Timothy Wind who took the right one. On the right arm was Officer Ted Briseno.

Officers Powell and Briseno were attempting to pull King's arms apart, but his arms were very rigid, straight in front of him like a couple of steel poles. Finally, King shoved his arms voluntarily. Then he went down, WHAM SPLAT face-first into the asphalt. Later evidence demonstrated that this may have been when Rodney King broke his cheekbone, an injury falsely ascribed to officers' batons. It's hard to tell precisely when King's cheekbone was fractured, because he went face-first into the asphalt three different times.

At this point Rodney King did kind of a twist. Powell had his knee on King's back and was trying to twist his left arm back to be cuffed. Briseno was struggling to get King's right arm back for the cuffs. Officers Solano and Wind were on his legs.

Then something happened that really scared me.

Because what happened then is that Powell gets thrown off. Then Briseno gets thrown off. Now Rodney King's arms are out in front of him. He's thrown off two officers. He's kind of weaving left and right. It's moving quickly now—all of this happens in split seconds—then Rodney King shakes his legs and throws off Solano and Wind. I think to myself, "Oh shit! He's turned into the Hulk!"[5] The situation has turned deadly serious now. My officers are in immediate danger. No question of it.

Now Rodney King's on his knees, and I order the officers: "BACK AWAY, BACK AWAY!"

That's part of the game plan, the tactic I had developed. If the guy starts to fight, back away, don't tangle up with him. That's how somebody gets hurt. Just back away and I'll TASE him. That's my tactic.

So we go to the next part of the plan. Now I *know* that the suspect is under the influence of PCP. If I had a suspicion before, now the suspicion is confirmed. It's not just a single piece of evidence but an accumulated body of knowledge, based on thirteen years as a street cop.

It's not just the chase. That's over. It's not just the sweating on a cold night. I remember that, and how weird it is. It's not just the bizarre behavior, the dancing around, waving at the helicopter, shaking his butt at Officer Melanie Singer. That's all just part of the picture. It's not the glassy eyes, the gibberish he's been spouting. It's everything. Put it all together with the superhuman strength to throw off four cops—they're not small cops, either—and bingo: you've got a PCP suspect. Now it's confirmed. He's got this Hulk-like strength. And you don't find all of this with somebody who's not on PCP. I can't throw off four officers, and I don't know many people who can. And I'm getting scared.

Now I order all the officers away and I try to talk to Rodney King, I give him verbal commands. Verbalization—giving orders by voice—is an essential part of the LAPD policy on using force. So I tell Rodney King to get down, get down in felony

---

[5] Some minority leaders have criticized my description of a PCP suspect as having "Hulk-like" strength. They have suggested it has racial overtones. As I recall, Lou Ferrigno, the star of "The Incredible Hulk," is Caucasian, and his color was a greenish-blue tint when transformed into the "Hulk." If there is a racial connotation here it escapes me.

prone position, get on your belly and your hands behind your back, or I'm going to TASE you. "GET DOWN. LIE [sic] ON THE GROUND. GET YOUR HANDS BEHIND YOUR BACK! DO IT NOW OR I'LL TASE YOU!" I shout.

But he doesn't seem to hear. Instead, his torso's up, his legs are cocked, it looks like he's getting up to come after me or one of the other officers. And this is just after he's had his face slammed into the pavement and then thrown off four cops. "GET DOWN, LIE [sic] DOWN!" I shout again. "GET DOWN OR I'M GOING TO TASE YOU!"

But he kept moving up. And so I TASED him. Got him right in the back. A nice spread with the darts. They don't have to touch the skin. All they have to do is hang up in the clothing. I've TASED people hundreds of times, and I know this TASER's working. I can see the darts hanging in his shirt, I can hear the activity of the TASER. It's zapping him with fifty thousand volts. Rodney King is on his knees. He's kind of grimacing and making a bear-like groan. He sags briefly, then he starts coming up again. He has overcome the first TASER.

This thing isn't working like it's supposed to, like they teach you at the academy, and like I'd seen with hundreds of suspects. You TASE a guy and he's supposed to fall down like a bag of potatoes. That had mostly been my experience. Except with two kinds of people. One is a psycho and the other is somebody who's dusted on PCP. If I had any doubts about this guy's drug of choice, all of those doubts were gone now. Rodney King was wired better than the TASER.

But I didn't have anything else to work with in that split second. Now he's up on his knees again, he's turned 180 degrees and I order him again:

"GET DOWN OR YOU'RE GOING TO GET TASED!"

It's like talking to that bag of potatoes. Because Rodney King's up again. He's groaning like a wounded animal, and I can see the vibrations on him. I know the TASER's working, and he knows it's working, too. So I TASE him again, this time in the left side. The barbs strike King's torso. The TASER's rapid clicking sound begins. Another fifty thousand volts, enough to put down a second buffalo. And this time the TASER's working again, too. I can see the vibrations, I can hear the sound of a TASER emitting its electrical discharge. Now Rodney King's down on the ground, and I'm thinking that maybe this guy's going to stay down and get in the felony prone position like we'd been ordering.

Once again, King let out a loud groan. Then, incredibly, he leaned to his right, braced himself on his right elbow, and began rising. The TASER hadn't stopped him. Two TASER blasts could put down two buffaloes, but Rodney King hadn't stopped. I yelled orders again for King to prone out on the ground. Again he ignored the command. King righted himself to a sitting position.

I kept shooting the TASER. This last burst of electricity seemed to work. Rodney King was now lying on the ground and I believed he might be willing to comply with our orders. Even so, I yelled to the officers present, "Does anybody have another TASER?" It seemed a prudent thing to do, even if King appeared finally to be complying.

The Videotape

None of the officers had another TASER. But somebody—not an officer—did have a videocamera. It was George Holliday, a resident at the apartment complex across the street. He had just purchased a new camcorder and hadn't yet had a chance to try it out. The scene being played out about fifty yards across the street was a perfect opportunity to see what the video-camera could do at night. He stepped out on his balcony and focused, then began taping.

All that had already taken place—the challenge to Officer Melanie Singer, the refusal to obey lawful commands, the bizarre behavior, the gibberish language, the incredible act of strength in throwing off four officers, and, finally, the survival of two fifty thousand-volt shots of nonlethal electricity—none of this was captured on the Holliday videotape. The next eighty-two seconds, shot out of context and edited as a complete account of the arrest, would determine public reaction to the Rodney King affair, as it quickly became known.[6]

And even this vastly shortened account of the incident, given the media's interpretation, was misleading, leaving the public with a completely skewed view of the entire episode.

More Force

But King was on the ground for only a second. After the second TASER blast, King continued to right himself. In an instant, he was on his feet. His arms outstretched, King rushed Officer Powell. If he had wanted to escape, there were plenty of avenues available. He could have fled across the street into the crowd of bystanders, or to his right into the park. But King didn't do that. He chose to collide into Officer Powell, and the two grappled for a split second. That's why all of the officers present interpreted it as an assault on a policeman instead of an attempt to escape. Powell was terrified; police officers get scared, too. He defended himself with his metal PR 24 baton, unleashing a furious series of power strokes. The first one hit King's collarbone. King was knocked to the ground, doing a one-point landing, face first, into the asphalt. This was the second time his face had been roughly introduced to the pavement, and most of us at the scene believe this is when the cheekbone was fractured.

But, incredibly again, Rodney King rebounded as if he hadn't

---

[6] After videotaping the incident, George Holliday approached the LAPD to learn what had happened and to offer a taped record of the incident. Rebuffed by the police—he apparently got a desk officer in a bad mood that day—Holliday went to KTLA Channel 5, which, after some negotiations, bought the tape for $500. Next to the purchase of Manhattan Island from the Indians for $24 in glass beads and trinkets, the $500 paid for the Holliday videotape must rank as one of the best bargains in American history. As soon as it was purchased by KTLA and shared with CNN, it became one of the most watched news videotapes in history, along with the explosion of the Challenger space shuttle and the funeral of President John F. Kennedy.

been touched. He was back up on his knees, trying to rise again, and Powell continued to strike him in the arms, hoping to take out King's support so he'd fall back to the ground.

The blows were coming perilously close to King's head, but I didn't want that. Powell was moving, King was moving, the baton was moving.

"DON'T HIT HIM IN THE HEAD!" I shouted to Powell. "DON'T HIT HIM IN THE HEAD!"

I believed that King, because of PCP intoxication, was an extraordinarily dangerous suspect. I wanted a managed, controlled use of force. I wanted LAPD policies and procedures followed. I did not want a group beat. I did not want officers injured by fellow officers, which is a frequent danger in a group beat.

So I decided to have only two officers, Powell and Wind, use force. As long as Rodney King failed to comply with the orders to get in a felony prone position, as long as he tried to get up and make another assault on an officer, Wind and Powell were to keep hitting him.

King was ordered again to get down. I told him to lie down, several times. He refused and began rising again. Powell and Wind unleashed a series of strokes to King's torso, arms, and legs. Powell and Wind performed exactly as they had been trained to do. Bursts of powerful blows were applied, three or four at a time. But King was still getting up.

At this time, I activated the second TASER cassette for the second time. Although its initial electrical discharge had been drained, the TASER, like a flashlight, retains a certain momentary, final burst of current that can be coaxed out. If you've ever turned on a flashlight with weak batteries, you know what this means. That's what the TASER did; it threw a new rush of voltage into Rodney King before the TASER expired. Officer Briseno stepped in to warn away Wind and Powell. He was doing so because training at the Police Academy with the TASER is hands on. During training, recruits are TASED, and others are in physical contact with them. The result is that whoever's getting TASED and whoever's touching him at the time get zapped. They don't become unconscious; that's one of the benefits of the TASER. They just go down. Briseno was trying to keep Wind and Powell from going down from absorbing the TASER charge being applied to King.[7]

Then the officers stepped back to evaluate the effect the blows were having on the suspect. That's strictly procedure, because it gives the officers an opportunity to determine whether the suspect intends to comply. More importantly, the pause gives the suspect an outlet to avoid any further blows by obeying the command to prone out, hands behind the back. These pauses are known as "pulsations" in police language. Yet they were interpreted by many viewers of the videotape as policemen simply taking turns beating an innocent suspect. That wasn't the case. They were following my orders and strict procedure: deliver the baton blows, then back off to see what effect they're having on the suspect. Are you beginning to get an idea about how your eyes can deceive you?

As long as King was lying still, making no effort to rise, he was not hit. He was commanded time and again, over and over and over, to lie down flat, to get down flat, to put his hands behind his back. An enhancement of the George Holliday videotape later would reveal that fourteen commands were issued in eighty-two seconds—an average of about one every six seconds.

But King would not lie still. He kept trying to rise. Once, in one of the more tense moments that is captured in stark clarity on the Holliday videotape, King began rolling toward Officer Wind. Wind backed quickly away. He knew what was happening.

Rodney King was doing the "Folsom Roll." To the casual viewer of the videotape, it appeared as though King were rolling away from the officers in an effort to avoid getting hit. But he wasn't being hit at the time.

King wasn't avoiding blows. He was rolling *toward* Officer Wind—he was doing the "Folsom Roll." Any LAPD cop who's

---

[7] Later, at the trial, Briseno claimed that he was trying to restrain Wind and Powell from beating King further. The jury didn't buy that argument anymore than I, Powell, or Wind did. Briseno wasn't trying to stop the violence; he was trying to prevent the TASER charge from hitting Powell and Wind.

dealt with ex-cons is familiar with the "Folsom Roll." Prisoners at California's Folsom Prison and correction units in other states have been photographed teaching it to one another in the prison yard. It's a technique for disarming an officer while proned out on the ground. The idea is to roll into an officer and tangle up his legs, then reach up and grab a gun belt and holster while the officer is off-balance. Then the officer is down and the suspect has the weapon. You can see where that leads. Although a probationer on the LAPD, Tim Wind had several years' experience under his belt as a police officer in Kansas. He recognized the Folsom Roll when he saw it. So he wisely backed out of King's reach, then moved forward to deliver a series of powerful strikes to King's arms and legs.

By now Rodney King had been subjected to a torrent of baton violence, at least twenty-five blows or more.[8] I had monitored the action of the officers and King's reactions. I was flabbergasted. Rodney King had demonstrated a complete lack of pain. It was as if his entire body had been anesthetized. My officers and I exchanged glances of amazement. We were astonished. We had never seen anything like it before. We had never encountered a suspect who could absorb the number of power strokes Rodney King had taken to his legs, arms, and torso and not show any pain. This was a nightmarish reality, completely contrary to our training.

I realized another plan of action had to be taken. I considered another swarm, but rejected it immediately. In the first place, the prior swarm hadn't worked. Rodney King was superstrong. There was no way I would risk the officers' safety by tying them up again with King. Besides, the officers were getting fatigued. And they probably would have told me to go to hell. I

---

[8] In his suit against the city of Los Angeles, Rodney King and his attorney claimed that fifty-six blows were struck and King sought compensation of $1 million for each hit, or $56 million in all. A count from the Holliday videotape indicates that thirty-three blows were struck, and twenty-three missed. The misses aren't a compliment to LAPD training with the baton. But the point is this: the numbers aren't really important, since King's claims of innocent injury were and are, at best, self-serving.

wasn't about to risk disobedience from my officers because of a stupid order.

In addition to being swarmed, King had been TASED and batoned. The next level of force was deadly—either a chokehold or pistol. I wasn't comfortable with either option. The chokehold had been classified as deadly force, equal to a pistol, because of pressure from Los Angeles's minority communities, who believed it was used too frequently on blacks and Hispanics. And I had already dismissed the use of a pistol. I wanted to avoid the possibility of unnecessarily escalating the incident. But something had to be done. Rodney King was on the rise again.

"What can we do?" I asked myself in that split second. We had gone through the entire use of permissible force, from officers' presence through verbal commands, the swarm, TASER, and baton. Nothing had worked. All the tools from the grab bag of tricks the LAPD had given me to subdue a resisting suspect had been used.

I was about to turn to deadly force and order a chokehold on King—an action that would have ended the entire affair in about fifteen seconds if it had been employed with the initial swarm—when another option occurred to me.

Maybe if the officers worked their batons on King's joints—his wrists, elbows, knees, and ankles—he would comply. I didn't like this option. I knew it would be even more painful than the prior blows. I knew it could cause serious injury, perhaps even cripple the suspect. But I was in a dilemma. Do I order the joint blows or move on to deadly force? I had to make an immediate decision. I opted to go with the risk of severe pain and potentially serious injury to the suspect. He might be crippled, but at least the guy wouldn't be dead. So I issued the order.

"HIT THE JOINTS!" I shouted. "HIT HIS WRISTS! HIT HIS ELBOWS! HIT HIS ANKLES! HIT HIS KNEES!"

Wind and Powell followed the orders and began power-stroking the suspect. I didn't see every blow that landed, but I do know that King was struck multiple times on his joints.

Larry Powell began to reach for his cuffs. Then Briseno noticed that King was reaching in his waistband, where weapons ordinarily are concealed. That's when he stepped forward to deliver a sharp kick to the upper middle of King's shoulders, right between the shoulder blades, to stop him from reaching into his trousers. Powell and Wind started hitting King again, as ordered. Also, Tim Wind was kicking King, trying to keep him down. It wasn't so much a kick as it was a shove, with his feet, to get Rodney King down on the ground. King went prone, but then again tried to rise.

After a few seconds, King got to his knees, raised his hands above his head, and said, "Please stop."

Those were the first intelligible words he had uttered. The strategy had worked. I directed the officers to stop hitting the suspect, and the blows ceased. But I wasn't happy with King's compliance. He was on his knees, still able to attack us or flee. He still had his hands free—and hands can kill. His feet were still free—and he could kick us. He could also still see the officers—and I didn't want him to be able to see us, to be able to form a plan to assault us or escape. What I wanted was for Rodney King to be prone on his stomach, face down on the ground, his heels flush against the pavement, his feet at 45-degree angles, and his hands behind his back, cuffed.

He wasn't doing what I wanted or what I had ordered. But at this point I was willing to take anything I could get from Rodney King. So I interpreted his action as compliance. I had been in charge of the officers, but Rodney King had been in control of the situation. Now, I chose to see his actions, unsatisfactory as they were, as an indication that he was turning control of the situation over to the officers he had been resisting.

Ted Briseno moved in to cuff him. King began to struggle and resist. But now more LAPD officers were on the scene, eight of them. I ordered the officers to swarm King. They did so, in one of the sloppiest swarms I'd ever seen. King was forced to the ground and his face once again smashed into the asphalt, for the third time. But Rodney King was finally double-cuffed, up behind his back.[9] I directed that we use a nylon rope to tie up his ankles, then connect that rope to his wrists in what is known as the "hog-tie" position.

At last Rodney King was controlled and in custody. He was no longer a danger to himself, to the officers, or to the community. I ordered King to be removed from the roadway, and had an officer request an ambulance for the suspect so he could be taken to a hospital for medical treatment. The treatment was necessary, not because we'd hurt him, but because it's mandated by LAPD procedure.

The officers present began to joke and laugh, a sign of relief. It wasn't the joviality of a party atmosphere. It was the release of the pressures of the incident. It was gallows humor. The officers had faced a very stressful situation and prevailed. They were on a high.

After the ambulance had come for King, we dealt with the two passengers in the car, Bryant Allen and Freddie Helms. We checked them for outstanding warrants. There were none. So there was no reason to hold them any longer. They were uncuffed and released.

Allen and Helms later filed a lawsuit against the city of Los Angeles, claiming they had been "traumatized" by witnessing the beating of Rodney King. On the Phil Donahue Show and other programs, appearing as instant celebrities following the King videotape, Allen and Helms insisted that they believed the incident was premeditated. They spoke of the psychological pain they'd felt from seeing their friend, Rodney King, beaten by the police.[10] If, indeed, they were "traumatized," neither gave a sign of it that night. Allen and Helms got "traumatized" only after they had become talk-show celebrities pursued by lawyers sniffing an opportunity to cash in on the

---

[9] This is standard operating procedure for a suspect believed to be on PCP. "Dusted" suspects have been known to break one pair of perfectly good handcuffs.

[10] Never mind that Allen and Helms were face down on the ground on the other side of King's vehicle, their hands cuffed behind them. The two were unable to see anything of the incident or hear anything other than our repeated commands for Rodney King to get on his belly and put his hands behind his back.

widespread publicity. "Trauma," it seems, is something that can sneak up on you when the scent of a lawsuit is in the air.[11]

A Bureaucratic Foul-Up

As soon as the scene was secured I returned to my black-and-white to inform the Foothill watch commander about what had happened. That's required whenever force is employed on a suspect. I used the vehicle's on-board computer and typed a message:

"U [meaning "You," the lieutenant] just had a big-time use of force.[12] TASED and beat the suspect of CHP pursuit. Big Time." It wasn't a complete report, because it wasn't intended to be one. I had filled in as a watch commander hundreds of times. An important part of the watch commander's job is to respond to the scene of unusual incidents, events that are out of the ordinary. This was such an incident. I was giving the watch commander a clue that he ought to leave the station and get over here to the scene.

The AM watch commander, Lt. Patrick Conmay, was new on the job. I knew he had spent most of his career on the inside in administrative jobs and had little experience as a street cop. So I didn't want to embarrass him in front of his subordinates at the station by pointedly requesting his presence on the scene. I assumed he could read between the lines of my message and be here in minutes. Lieutenant Conmay knew the department manual dictated that he respond to the scene, and he had an experienced sergeant as his assistant watch commander who could take over if necessary.

But the lieutenant didn't hotfoot it over the two miles from the station to the scene of King's arrest. Upon reflection while waiting, though, I wasn't surprised. The previous night I had been the ranking officer on the scene of a murder and asked for

---

[11] Freddie Helms was killed in an alcohol-related automobile accident shortly after March 3, 1991.

[12] "U" can also mean "unit," or my black-and-white. But in this case I clearly meant "You," the lieutenant.

Lieutenant Conmay to come to the scene and supervise. He'd declined. I had seen it many times in the past. This lieutenant, like so many others, was scared of the street. He wanted to control the ship from the safety of his watch commander's chair on the bridge, period.

This initial failure at the station to respond to my report for supervisory assistance at the scene was only the first in a series of bureaucratic mistakes that eventually led the Internal Affairs Division to conclude that a cover-up was in progress from almost the first baton blow that fell on Rodney King. Other mistakes would follow, making an almost laughable series of incidents into something deadly serious. We'll get to those later.

With the scene now secured, Allen and Helms released, and Rodney King on his way to the hospital, it was time for me as the supervising commander on the scene to follow up the arrest at the hospital. After what had happened earlier, I needed another TASER—who knew what the suspect might do while being treated! The Foothill Station was on the way to the hospital, and I decided to stop by and pick one up. I sent another message, asking that a TASER be readied for my arrival.

When I walked into the watch commander's office a few minutes later, the lieutenant and his assistant were seated at their desks. They both looked at me in eager anticipation. The desk officer immediately offered me a recharged TASER. Everybody obviously knew about the use of force and awaited my briefing.

Obligingly, I explained that it was a textbook use of controlled force. The suspect was obviously under the influence of PCP, in my view. I explained that we had swarmed the suspect, but that the four cops had been thrown off. I went on to tell how I had TASED the suspect, twice, and that it had had no visible effect. Then I told the lieutenant and his assistant that the officers had beaten the suspect with multiple baton blows to the legs, arms, and torso, again with no visible effect. And I reported that, finally, I had ordered power strokes to the joints, knees, elbows, wrists, and ankles, to avoid escalating to deadly force, and that the suspect was then taken into custody.

After the tree-top briefing, the assistant watch commander, Sgt. Richard Distefano, jokingly observed that it looked like I had a use-of-force report to complete. I corrected the sergeant. I reminded the watch commander that I could not do the use-of-force report because I had been an active participant in the incident by TASING the suspect. Reports were supposed to be more objective, which is why a cop who uses force on a suspect can't be the person who fills out the paperwork. After a brief discussion, the watch commander ordered Sergeant Distefano to complete the use-of-force report and pursuit summary, both of which were required by the bureaucracy. Not only could I not do the use-of-force report, it would be difficult for me to get the pursuit summary done because I would be off for the next two days. So Sergeant Distefano, the assistant watch commander, was directed to write up both reports.

This was the basis for the second bureaucratic foul-up that later convinced the IAD cops that a cover-up had been in progress from the beginning. You see, the pursuit summary wasn't filed the next day. That was because Sergeant Distefano had a flat tire on his way to work and never made it to the station. And neither he nor Lieutenant Conmay knew that both reports had to be filed within twenty-four hours. This failure to file timely reports was what later convinced the IAD that a conspiracy existed to conceal the incident. Not so. It was nothing more sinister than a flat tire and bureaucratic ignorance.

But we're getting ahead of the story again. After meeting with Lieutenant Conmay, filing a brief verbal report, and getting his orders on who'd do the paperwork, I took the new TASER and left for the hospital to check on the suspect's condition.

The Hospital

At Pacifica Hospital, where the ambulance had taken him, Rodney King was in leather restraints that bound his hands and feet securely, preventing any aggressive action. The restraints had been ordered by the Emergency Room physician, Dr. Antonio Mancia, because the hospital staffers considered King to be a dangerous patient. They didn't want him exploding into a drug-induced rage while being examined for injuries. The leather restraints were a safeguard in addition to the presence of several officers.

I asked Dr. Mancia for an assessment of King's injuries. The doctor's diagnosis confirmed my belief that King was dusted. He diagnosed King's condition as "(1) PCP overdose and (2) facial lacerations, superficial."[13]

The examination of King's injuries showed that he had a bloody mouth from an interior cut on his lip, and swelling and abrasions on his right cheek. King was mentally aware of where he was and what had happened. He didn't complain of any pain and didn't appear to be seriously injured. I had expected to find numerous broken bones and severe bruises and swelling, but the doctor's visual examination revealed only minor injuries.

I was in a state of disbelief. "PCP is some heavy duty stuff," I thought to myself.

Based on the doctor's assessment, my log entry stated that King's injuries were minor. After all, he'd been examined by a doctor. There was no need for me to speculate, not when I had a professional opinion for my log.

I stayed at the hospital about an hour, continuing to monitor King. It appeared that he had recovered from whatever drug he was using. He was going to have to be booked, because he was a felony evader. But the jail won't accept PCP suspects. So he had to go to the Los Angeles County-USC Medical Center (LA-CUSCMC). On the thirteenth floor is the hospital ward where jailed offenders requiring medical supervision are held. But it wasn't necessary for me personally to supervise his transfer to LACUSCMC. Officers Powell and Wind could handle the situation.

I gave Powell the TASER I had picked up at the station, and gave both him and Wind specific instructions. They were to

---

[13] Pacifica Hospital ER Record 579511, March 3, 1991, see Appendix C.

remove the back seat of their black-and-white and put it in the trunk. They were then to double-cuff King and put him in the back of the police car. The two sets of handcuffs supplied extra security in the event King went off again. But the handcuffs would be double-locked to avoid any tightening around the wrist, which could cut off the flow of blood to the suspect's arms. I told Powell and Wind that if King got crazy again they were to pull over immediately and request assistance. Under no circumstances were they to tie up with their prisoner. We'd already had enough use of force with Rodney King for one night. I didn't want any more.

That was the last I saw of Rodney King that night. He was taken to LACUSCMC by Officers Powell and Wind without incident, and examined by Dr. David Giannetto about 6:30 A.M. The exam indicated that King had bruises and soft-tissue swelling on the right side of his face. There were some facial lacerations on his right cheekbone area and right side of the chin; these had been sutured at the Pacifica Hospital emergency room. His jaw was intact. No teeth were loose. He had a good range of motion in his neck, and it was not tender. The lungs were fine, heart normal. He had bruises on his chest and back. There were no internal injuries. Dr. Giannetto said King was neurologically sound, mildly intoxicated but able to provide his name, date, time, and what was happening. The only injury requiring treatment wasn't discovered until almost twenty-four hours after the Foothill arrest. It took that long for X-rays to be examined. The X-rays disclosed a small, spiderweb-like fracture to his fibula, a small, non-weight bearing bone in the right leg. Rodney King was placed in a short leg cast and put on crutches. The X-rays also revealed a fractured right cheekbone, but no treatment was rendered. That is customary with this injury; it usually heals itself quickly.

A urinalysis test for PCP usage was negative. But, as Dr. Giannetto testified later at the trial, the results of that test were inconclusive. According to Dr. Giannetto, that was because a negative urine test could not reveal the presence of PCP if the urine had a high alkaline content, as Rodney King's did. Also, PCP apparently can be stored in fatty tissues of the body for years, then released when the body draws upon stored energy to support unusual physical activity—like resisting arrest. Medical authorities say it is possible for some users to have a PCP flashback years after taking the drug only once. So even if Rodney King hadn't popped some PCP that night, he still could have had a flashback if he'd ever taken the drug in his adult life.[14] And if he had such a flashback, it wouldn't have shown up in a blood or urine test, anyway.

It was remarkable that Rodney King hadn't been hurt worse than he was. Our use of force was unusually powerful. But he had come through it without serious injury. He hurt, but he was alive and in custody. Neither were any officers injured. And that's what a cop's use of force is supposed to accomplish.

At the station, while Rodney King was undergoing further examinations at LACUSCMC medical center, I completed my log entry on the incident. The entry related what had happened as you have just read it. I concluded the log entry on the Rodney King arrest with this notation:

"IMPORTANT NOTE FOR R/C [roll call] TRAINING— ALWAYS HAVE A B/U [back-up] WITH A USE OF FORCE. IT DOESN'T ALWAYS WORK THE WAY YOU'RE TRAINED. TASER DOESN'T ALWAYS IMMOBILIZE. PR 24 [baton] DOESN'T ALWAYS CRIPPLE, ETC. IF YOU DON'T HAVE A FRAME OF REFERENCE, OFFICERS TEND TO PANIC WHEN THINGS DON'T WORK THE WAY THEY'RE SUPPOSED TO. A B/U PLAN PREVENTS PANIC. AND IT DON'T [sic] HURT TO HAVE LOTS OF B/U—ESPECIALLY WITH PCP SUSPECTS."[15]

---

[14] A test using hair samples can determine whether PCP has ever been used, but that test was not administered at the hospital. Today, King's attorney will not permit the test to be taken. One would imagine that if such a test would prove King free of the substance, his attorney would be eager to have it substantiated.

[15] See Appendix C.

2

The LAPD's Flawed
System for Using Force

How LAPD Policies Made the Rodney King Affair Inevitable

Was Rodney King's arrest violent? Yes.

Was it brutal? Unquestionably.

The videotape of the Rodney King incident shocked both minorities and white citizens, but in different ways. Many blacks and Hispanics live in areas that are frequent scenes of police activity. This is especially true in large urban areas like Los Angeles. Minorities are accustomed to scenes of police violence in subduing suspects, although they rarely see it on prime-time television. In some neighborhoods, like the 77th Street Division where I worked for four years, they see it almost every day. Sometimes this violence seems unnecessary; that's a question for a court to decide (as it did with me and my fellow officers). More often, force is an absolute requirement in subduing a suspect who's trying to keep from going to jail.

Whatever the reason, blacks and Hispanics were less shocked by the George Holliday videotape of Rodney King's arrest than whites, many, by the way, police officers. White suburban dwellers aren't as exposed to crime and violence as those who live in inner cities. So when suburban dwellers saw the eighty-two seconds of edited videotape, they concluded that it was an aberration, an isolated incident of brutality by police being vented on an innocent citizen.

It wasn't isolated. While the use of such extraordinary levels of force is uncommon, the beating of Rodney King in order to subdue him wasn't a one-time phenomenon. Ask yourself this: Why do they issue police officers metal PR 24 batons? To direct traffic? Hardly. The reason is that sometimes a cop has to beat a reluctant suspect into submission in order to place that offender in custody. It's not something you like to do. It's something you're paid to do.

So the question isn't whether the Rodney King arrest was violent (it was), or brutal (yes again), or shocking (yes, depending on where you lived).

The question is this: Was it necessary? And again the answer is yes. But the answer is qualified.

The qualification is that it was necessarily brutal only under LAPD rules for using force. It wouldn't have been necessary if other tools had been available—tools the law enforcement community and other urban police departments have for subduing a suspect who doesn't want to be arrested. Unfortunately for Rodney King and everybody else who has suffered from this affair, the LAPD can't use those available tools.

Start with this unpleasant fact of life: police work is often violent, often brutal. It's not pretty, but that's the way it is. That's the way it has been throughout history.

You see, I am not just an unwilling practitioner of the use of force to command obedience to the law. Using force is not simply a matter of following the policies and procedures required by the Los Angeles Police Department. I learned this while I was delving into the philosophical basis for the work I did as a street cop. That was in 1978 while I was pursuing a masters' degree in criminal justice at Cal Sate University in Los Angeles, where I had received a bachelor's degree in that field four years earlier. (I got my master's degree in public administration in 1980 from USC.) The topic of my criminal justice master's thesis was a history of police organizations and how they have operated throughout the ages to enforce the rules that society imposes upon itself for structured, civilized interaction.

Police organizations have undergone many transformations throughout the centuries. In primitive societies, police functions were performed by hunters or priests. Then, as societies became more civilized and more complex, police work became more structured, with the society's military arm, the army or militia, usually assigned the task of civilian control. The modern era of police work, which you can date to about the late eighteenth century, saw the development of professional police organizations. Today, cops have an ever-widening array of sophisticated tools available to help them command civil order—tools such as vehicular on-board portable computers designed to speed communications, and advanced scientific techniques, like genetic analysis, to aid in the solution of crimes.

But throughout human history, one element of police work has remained relatively unchanged. It is this:

Force is sometimes needed to compel obedience to the law. In a perfect society, reason would replace force. But we are imperfect humans. So, occasionally, it is necessary to use force on somebody intent upon endangering or harming himself or other people.

Still, the use of force by police officers has become more civilized over the years. That's the way it should be. In the old days bad guys got shot because they were bad. But it's more complicated than that. Today good people can get screwed up on drugs, but that doesn't mean you have to kill them. It means you must try to keep them from hurting themselves or others. Quick-draw sheriffs might have been needed in the Old West, but in law enforcement on today's city streets an impulsive cop is almost as dangerous as a dusted felon.

For this reason, modern police departments have rigid policies on when to use force and how to use it. The policies have become tighter as minority groups have become more vocal, and justifiably so, in urging restraints to prevent abuse of police powers that so frequently characterized the use of official force in days past.

These are important concepts to understand in the context of Rodney King's arrest. This is because a decade ago the city of Los Angeles overreacted to minority demands on limiting force, and thereby restricted an officer's ability to subdue a suspect. Limitations on using force are fine, but they necessarily mean that cops must use other legal means when force is necessary.

Maybe the restrictions imposed by the Police Commission and endorsed by the mayor and the LA City Council were appropriate; that's a matter for politicians to decide.[1] But absent other tools, the limitations made it almost inevitable that the Rodney King affair, or something like it, would occur someday. Former Chief Daryl Gates made this clear in the early 1980s when he objected to the civilian Police Commission's outlawing of the chokehold as an acceptable, nonlethal use of force. (For the uninitiated, a chokehold involves using a wrestler-like armlock to apply pressure against a suspect's carotid artery in the neck, thus cutting off the flow of blood and oxygen to the brain for the few seconds necessary to render the suspect unconscious.)

Granted, the chokehold can be a dangerous tactic. If applied for too long, it can kill. But that level of force is below using a gun. And when Los Angeles officials outlawed the chokehold in the early 1980s, Chief Gates knew better than anyone else that it meant that either a brutal beating or an unnecessary shooting was just down the road.

That's what made it so surprising when he rushed to the front of the pack to condemn me and my officers for our handling of the Rodney King arrest. When the Police Commission began looking into restricting the use of the chokehold in

---

[1] All major policy and procedure questions must first be decided by the independent Police Commission, then approved by the mayor and City Council before implementation. Rather than confusing the reader with this long explanation every time we talk about such an action, we'll simply refer to it as an "official action."

1981, it was Gates who said the action created a "hole" in the LAPD's use-of-force policies. "The elimination of these [choke]holds would, in all likelihood, result in an even greater number of more serious injuries," Gates told the Police Commission, because otherwise batons or guns would be used to subdue suspects.[2] And when the City Council imposed a moratorium on the use of the chokehold in 1982, the *Los Angeles Times* described Gates's reaction to the Police Commission:

"In situations that are not life-threatening and where self-defense is needed by officers, 'A void has been created between the wristlock or karate kick and the deadly use of force,' Gates said in the report [to the Police Commission]. The wristlock and karate kick is [sic] near the bottom of the department's use of force scale. Deadly force is at the top."[3]

But even after the chokehold was banned as less than deadly force in May 1982, Gates wasn't ready to give up the fight, and he tried to get it reinstated. In a 1984 report to the City Council, he said that, since the moratorium on using the chokehold in situations that were not life-threatening, "there has been a steady increase" in violent confrontations between suspects and police officers. He noted that in the eighteen weeks before the May 12, 1982, ban on chokeholds, LAPD officers were involved in an average of 23.6 "altercations" a week with citizens, "resulting in injuries to approximately 1.4 officers and 3.1 suspects." But in the eighteen-week period that ended September 30, 1983, Gates said, these numbers had risen to an average of 75.6 violent confrontations per week resulting in an average of 8.7 officers and 23.6 suspects injured weekly. "Officers injured as a result of use-of-force incidents increased 181 percent," Gates told the City Council, "and the number of suspects injured during this period increased 395 percent. . . ." He urged that the chokehold moratorium at least be modified in non-lethal confrontations, if other means of subduing a suspect "have been exhausted or are unavailable."[4] But Gates's belief

---

[2] *Los Angeles Times*, October 7, 1981, p. II-8.

[3] Ibid., August 11, 1982, pp. 1, 10.

[4] Ibid., January 4, 1984.

that the chokehold prohibition had led to additional injuries to suspects and officers alike didn't convince the Police Commission, the mayor, and the City Council. The ban stayed in place.

So why was Gates surprised when he saw the Rodney King videotape? His almost immediate condemnation of my orders to subdue King—a condemnation issued publicly without any effort to learn the facts or the circumstances surrounding the incident—can be explained only as an effort to appease minority leaders and thus, hopefully, to avoid confrontation.

In doing so, Gates was merely following the lead set by his arch political rival, Mayor Tom Bradley, a former LAPD officer. A day after the videotape aired, Mayor Bradley made it clear that he had already tried and convicted me and my fellow officers without benefit of a trial. "This is something we cannot and will not tolerate," Bradley told the *Los Angeles Times*. "It's now a matter of identifying and finding witnesses. . . ."[5] Bradley merely sounded the clarion call for others to join the lynch mob. On March 12, the American Civil Liberties Union of Southern California ran a full-page advertisement in the *Los Angeles Times* under a headline that read, "WHO DO YOU CALL WHEN THE GANG WEARS BLUE UNIFORMS?"

The text went on to explain that "The brutal beating which shocked the nation did not, unfortunately, surprise the ACLU. Because this is not an isolated incident. The difference this time is that we have the proof . . . on tape." The ad contained a dramatic photograph of LAPD officers wielding their batons on a stopped motorist. An examination of one of the cars in the photograph bore a pre-1970 license plate, suggesting that the photo represented as the Rodney King incident was at least twenty-one years old. The ACLU ad ended with a demand that Chief Gates resign, and an appeal for donations. The appeasers were out in full pursuit now.

Well, we know where that appeasement—the political cowardice that made public officials fail to take responsibility for their own actions—led: It led directly to the riots.

If Gates and the Police Commission had made even a cur-

---

[5] Ibid., March 6, 1991, p. 1.

sory investigation of the Rodney King affair before judging the street cops guilty, they would have found, as the Simi Valley jurors found, no improper actions under existing LAPD policies and procedures. Which means, of course, that they would have had to take the heat for the department's use-of-force policies from the ACLU and other militant critics of the King incident. Heat's uncomfortable, but it's what politicians get paid for. Not only that, heat's better than a riot.

You see, the reason the politicians outlawed the chokehold that might have prevented Rodney King's beating was because minority leaders and their supporters—primary among whom was the ACLU—said it was being used too frequently with lethal results on minority suspects, more specifically, black people.[6] A leader of the anti-chokehold forces on the City Council was Robert Farrell, who represented a mostly black district. Farrell charged repeatedly that the chokehold was used chiefly against blacks, and that "most of those who die after their application are black and that other city leaders care little about the lives of black men."[7]

Farrell himself was partially setting the stage for the Rodney King incident, and it was clear that his concern wasn't just for the safety of black people. Another consideration, he said, was simply money. During the 1981 debate over using the chokehold, he observed that it would be more " 'cost effective' for the city to settle claims for broken bones of combative suspects who are hit with batons rather than to pay settlements to the families of individuals who die from application of the chokeholds."[8]

So, as you can see, another consideration was in the works here, too. Like so many other issues involving the LAPD, it was money.

---

[6] The number of deaths attributed to LAPD use of the chokehold is in dispute. According to the *Los Angeles Times* of May 13, 1982, "critics contend that since 1975 police chokeholds have claimed the lives of 15 or 16 people in Los Angeles. The Police Department says the number is considerably lower."

[7] *Los Angeles Times*, August 3, 1982, pp. 1, 3.

[8] Ibid., October 7, 1981.

Zev Yaroslavsky, another City Council leader crying to out-law the chokehold, said in 1982 that "financial effects" of using the chokehold "should be a persuasive factor" for people who "are not moved by considerations of conscience or public policy."[9] Yaroslavsky, now at the front of the mob decrying the Rodney King beating, went on to say that the chokehold was resulting in too many lawsuits against the city of Los Angeles, lawsuits with a potential cost of hundreds of millions of dol-lars a year. At the time, he noted that pending suits against the LAPD totaled about $200 million. The litigation costs saved by outlawing the chokehold, Yaroslavsky suggested, "could pay for an additional 40 police officers or firefighters . . . re-store almost half of the weekly street-sweeping programs that were eliminated last year, or increase the cultural arts budget by almost half." Yaroslavsky grew almost lyrical about the amount of money that could be saved by preventing cops from using a chokehold. "Imagine the consequences of several mil-lion dollars [in] judgments against the city in the next few years."[10]

Imagine, indeed. Yaroslavsky's argument fell apart after the chokehold was eliminated as a nondeadly use of force. For the fact is that the cost of use-of-force lawsuits against the city of Los Angeles and the LAPD soared after the chokehold was barred. In 1980, the cost of settling lawsuits (not to be con-fused with lawsuits pending, which Yaroslavsky earlier cited) against the city totaled $891,402. By 1990, this figure had risen to $9.1 million—and that didn't include the $2.2 million more the city was ordered to pay for attorney's fees.[11]

What makes all of this relevant to the Rodney King incident? If the chokehold had been approved as a nonlethal use of force—not associated with the death of black suspects, not approved as a cost-effective restraint on police—the Rodney King incident would have never occurred the way it did. All we would have had to do was to swarm him with a chokehold, and

---

[9] Ibid., December 28, 1982, Part II, p. 5.

[10] Ibid.

[11] *Los Angeles Times* graphic, March 29, 1991.

the entire episode would have been over in ten or fifteen seconds. Rodney King would have been cuffed and awaiting an ambulance for transport to the hospital. The videotape would have captured only a brief scuffle. There would have been no dramatic repetition on Cable News Network or thousands of local television outlets around the nation and the world of what was needed to subdue and cuff him. There would have been no public outrage, no riots. It would have been no more than a routine arrest of a dusted felony suspect—just another night on the LAPD, as Mary said. But it wasn't just another night, because politicians and some community leaders had put unrealistic restraints on police officers.

How to Use Force

You see, Rodney King forced us to dig as deeply into our bag of tricks as we could reach. We began with the first level of force: physical presence. You can't get much more physically present than four squad cars, lights flashing and sirens blaring, a police helicopter hovering directly overhead, its spotlight shining on the scene, and officers crouching behind their doors with guns drawn. That's industrial-strength physical presence. But it didn't have any effect on Rodney King.

So we escalated to the next use of force: verbalization. We verbalized Rodney King so much that he would have been bored if he hadn't been intoxicated. As noted earlier, in just eighty-two seconds of the videotape he got fourteen commands to get down in a felony prone position—on his belly, face in the dirt, hands behind his back. And this doesn't count the commands given before the videotape began, the orders to King by Officers Tim Singer and Melanie Singer and various LAPD patrolmen to get out of the car and down on his stomach.

Verbalization had no more impact on Rodney King than our physical presence. So I ratcheted the use of force up a notch. That's when I ordered the swarm. Ordinarily a swarm will end a confrontation and result in a suspect on the ground and cuffed up behind his back. But not Rodney King. He tossed four officers off his arms and legs like they were irritating insects, rather than armed, well-trained professional police officers. He was stronger than four street cops.

Now the use of force is getting serious. That's when I zap him with the TASER. Twice. A total of one hundred thousand volts in fifty thousand-volt increments. It put Rodney King to his knees, and eventually put him down. But he came right back up and charged Officer Powell.

The use-of-force cupboard is getting bare now. There's only the use of PR 24 metal batons between the TASER and deadly force—a gun or the chokehold. So we go to the baton. And here, too, we escalate and de-escalate the violence. Officers Wind and Powell used their batons in a measured way, moving in to strike the suspect two or three times, then stepping back to evaluate his response. If he's still, the beating is halted. It begins again only when Rodney King's on the rise and threatening another assault on the officers. Which Rodney King does, repeatedly.

The customary use of batons, striking the body mass, isn't working. So the decision must be made: Do we go to deadly force? A gun or a chokehold? Has the baton been exhausted? No. Not yet. I decide that a chokehold is especially ruled out, because chokeholds have been associated with the death of blacks. Rodney King is black. We'll be in a world of trouble if we use a chokehold, even if it's routine and doesn't cause any permanent damage. And we sure don't want to kill him. So let's ratchet the violence up only half a notch here, let's use the baton on his joints and see if the higher level of pain can force compliance. So we begin power-stroking the knees, the elbows, the ankles.

Finally, it works. Rodney King submits. The incident has been violent. It's been brutal. It's been ugly. But it's been necessary under LAPD rules.

None of this is intended as a brief arguing for the chokehold.

The point is, other devices and techniques are used by police in other large cities to avoid the type of violence employed on Rodney King, but the LAPD hasn't adopted them. Why? Because the Los Angeles Police Department believes its own propaganda. The LAPD believes it is the best in the world. The department is constantly told it is the best by its officials. LA coppers read about how great they are in newspapers, in books such as Joseph Wambaugh's *New Centurions*, in intradepartmental communications, and on such popular television shows as "Dragnet" and "One-Adam-12."[12] From the moment you enter the LAPD academy, you're taught that you are the elite of the law enforcement community. You're the best of the best.

And there's some truth to that. Due to the "pro-active" policies of LAPD chiefs that began with the legendary Chief Bill Parker in the 1950s, Los Angeles has been able to provide more cost-effective law enforcement than any other major city in the United States. What does "pro-active" mean? It means the LAPD tries to prevent crimes before starting to solve them. A black-and-white cruising an affluent neighborhood will stop somebody who looks out of place and suggest that they move on. The suggestion isn't subtle, either. It's "Leave. Right Now!"

The LAPD is extremely pro-active. For example, before the 1984 Olympics, I was on patrol in the Hollywood Division and our major efforts were directed at getting all the whores off the streets so visitors to LA wouldn't get an accurate impression of the city's vice activity. We spent so much time being pro-active in getting hookers out of town that other crime-fighting efforts suffered. Not surprisingly, a "pro-active" posture will result in some arrests that aren't altogether legitimate. That's one reason why the LAPD has a reputation for being too quick to take action. But it also helps explain why the city has a lower crime rate than New York City, which has four times as many uniformed officers per citizen as the LAPD, or Chicago, where the ratio of officers to citizens is more than twice that of Los Angeles.

When you think you're the best of the best, though, you can

---

[12] A bit of trivia here. The designation "Adam" is used for a black-and-white with two officers. "One" is the designation for the LAPD Central Division. "Twelve" is for the LA census reporting district covered by the cruiser. So "One-Adam-12" is a two-officer cruiser assigned to cover the 12th census reporting district of the LAPD Central Division.

become convinced that your ideas are the only ones that count. It's dangerous when you start to believe your own propaganda.

And that is one explanation why the LAPD has steadfastly refused to acquire other use-of-force appliances that would provide a cushion between using the baton to thump a suspect into submission or drawing your gun and pulling the trigger.

And what are some of the devices used in other modern police departments? Well, one goes back to antiquity. It's a net, a simple net that's thrown over a suspect so he or she can be pulled to the ground and cuffed without further injury to the suspect or danger to the arresting officers. The Romans used nets, but not the LAPD.

Another, more modern device is a Velcro blanket. It works somewhat like the net. Officers surround a suspect and wrap him in the blanket, securing it by merely pushing the Velcro outside panels together. The suspect is immobilized within the confining blanket. It's as simple as a straight jacket, and much easier to put on.

Then there's the "leg-grabber." Have you ever seen the device used in supermarkets and other retail stores to twist light bulbs out of ceiling sockets? It's basically a gripper on the end of a long pole. Some smart cops adapted this for use with struggling suspects. The leg-grabber is a vise-like attachment on the end of an extended rod that permits the officer to grip a suspect's leg and bring him or her to the ground from a distance without tying up in a physical confrontation. Once the suspect is on the ground, he or she can be swarmed and cuffed by other officers.

So, you see, using a metal baton to beat Rodney King into submission wasn't the only tactic available if we had been somewhere other than Los Angeles. Neither was the TASER, chokehold, or gun.

The Rodney King incident was more than a brutal beating. It was, in truth, a serious indictment of the Los Angeles Police Department and its ability to control violence on the streets. Because, you see, force is an everyday affair for street cops in Los Angeles. An LA street cop who doesn't learn to live with violence doesn't live very long.

3

The Education
of a Street Cop

The reason I like being a street cop is that somewhere along the line I decided that putting bad guys in jail was a good idea.

Ninety-five percent of the people in this world are wholesome, contributing members of society. Five percent need to be in jail, with the keys thrown away so they can't do harm to themselves or to the 95 percent who don't hurt others. And that's why I became a street cop instead of climbing a police career ladder through the administrative ranks, which is how most of the lieutenants, captains, commanders, deputy chiefs, and chiefs get to the top.

Police work wasn't my career of choice. In fact, it didn't even occur to me as a child growing up in Los Angeles and its suburbs.

My father and mother were natives of Kansas and Texas, respectively. They were married during World War II and, like so many other people at that time, found themselves in Southern California at the end of the war. My father guarded railroad bridges, and my mother was an operator at the telephone company. They liked Southern California so much that they decided to stay, my father working for the Southern Pacific

Railway after his military service and my mother for another large corporation. Both of my parents encouraged educational attainment, which explains a lot about why I have two masters' degrees.

At first, I wanted to be an economist. In fact, I began working at a bank before going in the Air Force in 1971. I worked the night shift in the trust department at a large Los Angeles bank, making clerical entries for stock transfers by large institutional and individual shareholders. I quickly saw that most of these transactions preceded press releases that influenced the market price of the shares being traded. So I started following the lead of such companies as Occidental Petroleum and its chairman, Armand Hammer, as well as Texaco, Coca-Cola, and other large-volume stock traders. There was nothing illegal in this. I wasn't trading on inside information (although others whose transactions I followed may have been tainted with violating insider-trading laws). In any event, I was able to run a $100 investment up to more than $2,000 the first year on the job. Making that much money in such a short period of time convinced me that economics, or banking, at least, was too easy. If anybody as uninformed as I could make $2,000 out of $100 in twelve months, then there was something wrong with the system.

So, upon entering the Air Force in 1971, I really didn't have a career plan. This isn't an autobiography, so we'll be brief with the personal stuff. Suffice it to say that my military experience didn't have anything to do with my becoming a police officer, either; my specialty was radar and electronics maintenance.

It was only after leaving the military in 1974 that I began drifting toward police work. I was studying economics at UCLA and didn't like it. Earlier, I had taken a police science course and enjoyed it. So, I settled on police work. The idea of being involved in government, and helping people, was appealing. But if I was going to be a police officer I wanted to be the best of the best. That meant the LAPD. And so, in August 1976, I entered the Los Angeles Police Department recruit academy, finishing five months later and graduating twelfth in a class of about sixty.

After the Police Academy, I was assigned to patrol duties in Van Nuys, the West Valley Division, and the Hollywood Division. Then I did a year as a supervisor at the Los Angeles jail after being promoted to sergeant. The promotion was what I hoped would be the first major step forward in a career that would lead to big-time command duties on the LAPD. But my real love was working the streets, especially during the morning watch from 11 P.M. to 7 A.M. That's when you find the bad guys on the street. That's when you get an opportunity to put bad guys in jail. And that's what I liked doing. So after a year on jail duty I eagerly accepted an assignment to the 77th Street Patrol Division. The 77th Street Division is the roughest in Los Angeles. Which means, of course, that it might be the roughest in the United States. That's where you get world-class work as a street cop.

The reason all of this is important to the Rodney King story is that fourteen and-a-half years as a cop—thirteen of them on the street (five months in the academy and a year in the jail)—provided the basis of knowledge that led to my handling of the arrest on March 3, 1991. I wasn't a rookie. I'd dealt with ex-cons, dusted felony offenders, and dangerous suspects before. Rodney King fit all of those categories, based upon what I had learned on the streets in thirteen years.

Let me give you some examples to give you an idea of my state of mind and where I was coming from shortly after midnight on March 3, 1991.

Be Ready for Surprises

It was August 1989. I was a field sergeant on morning watch at the 77th Street Police Division, the most violent in Los Angeles.

The call began like many others to the 77th Street station: shots had been fired into a home a mile or so west of the station. I left my coffee on the watch commander's desk and hurried to my black-and-white. I decided to head south on Broadway and then west on Manchester, a major east-west thoroughfare, hoping to pick up on the suspect vehicle. I wasn't disappointed.

The officers on the scene where the shots had been fired reported that the suspects were driving a white 1968 Chevrolet Impala with a spare-tire continental kit on the trunk. It would be an easy vehicle to spot. I saw it pass me going eastbound. There appeared to be only one person, the driver, in the car. I made a U-turn and began following, from a distance.

I radioed my location, advising the radio operator that I was following the suspect vehicle, requesting confirmation that it was a white '68 Chevy Impala with a continental kit.

The radio operator, who had been in contact with the officers at the scene of the shooting, quickly confirmed the auto's ID. He signed off.

Then, in a moment, he came back on the air. His tone and inflection had changed. He was worried. He said the weapon used in the drive-by shooting was an AK-47. An AK-47 is a Chinese-made automatic assault weapon that can fire thirty rounds from a banana clip in a matter of seconds. It was used by the Viet Cong and North Vietnamese with appalling results against U.S. troops in Vietnam. A steel-tipped AK-47 round can pierce the engine block of an automobile. Imagine what it can do to the body of a cop armed with a Smith & Wesson .38 caliber pistol. The radio operator advised caution. That was thoughtful of him, but unnecessary. I knew what an AK-47 could do. There is no protection against it, other than conceal-ment, prayer, and a steady hand with the .38. I was starting to get worried.

The back-up units monitoring my broadcasts must have sensed my fear. They knew that, like all sergeants, I drove alone. And they knew that nobody—repeat, nobody—faced an AK-47 alone. They radioed that they were speeding to the scene and were about three minutes away. It was a reassuring message. The suspect's car pulled into an all-night gasoline station. I coasted silently and came to a halt across the street, waiting for the backup. The suspect got out of the car. My attention went to his hands. Hands kill. There was nothing in his hands as he walked to the cashier's window.

I could hear the back-up unit's engine cut the silence of the early morning; at 2 A.M, few other vehicles are on the street. I got on my radio and broadcast the location. I moved my cruiser into the driveway of the gas station. I got out of the car and used the door and engine block for concealment. I drew my pistol. The backup unit pulled up next to my black-and-white. The officers deployed.

The officer in charge of executing the arrest (not me, because I was in tactical command) shouted a series of by-the-book orders:

"HANDS UP!

"GET ON YOUR KNEES!

"GET ON YOUR STOMACH!

"PUT YOUR ARMS OUT TO THE SIDE, LIKE AN AIRPLANE!

"SPREAD YOUR LEGS!

"PUT YOUR HEELS INTO THE GROUND. PUT YOUR RIGHT HAND IN THE SMALL OF YOUR BACK, PALM UP!

"PUT YOUR LEFT HAND IN THE SMALL OF YOUR BACK, PALM UP!

"PUT YOUR FACE INTO THE GROUND!

"NOW. DO IT NOW. FREEZE!"

Nobody could misunderstand what the patrolman was saying. He had his gun drawn, and that was a threat. But it was a contingent threat. He was using the second level of force, verbalization. The ultimate use of force, a gun, was clearly visible. That way, the suspect knows you're serious. The officer giving the commands approached the suspect's vehicle, his pistol at the ready. The officer checked the car; nobody else was in it. The suspect had obeyed the orders and was in a felony prone position. The officer holstered his gun and at the same time knee-dropped onto the suspect's upper shoulders from the rear. He grabbed the suspect's hands in a wrist-lock. In a moment, less than the blink of an eye, the suspect was cuffed. A systematic pat-down search was made for other weapons. The suspect had none. It was classic LAPD training.

Now we had the car. Now we had the suspect, who was

arrested for assault. But we didn't have the weapon. We didn't have an AK-47.

The victim whose house had been riddled with AK-47 rounds was brought to the scene. He immediately identified the suspect and, upon questioning, identified the missing suspect only as "Red," a light-skinned black man with red hair. He lived about two blocks away. It seems that Red and the victim had a serious disagreement over a gambling deal earlier in the evening, and Red decided to settle the matter by shooting up the victim's house.

I consulted with the other officers. They agreed that we should go after Red.

Our tactical plan was a by-the-book approach. The radio operator was advised of where we were going and what we were doing, told what the circumstances were, and given a description of Red. The radio operator was to tell the backup officers how to approach if something went wrong. Officers who weren't already wearing bulletproof vests—most street cops wear them as a matter of routine—put them on, even though we knew a vest was no protection against an AK-47. We drove to Red's neighborhood and parked about a block from his duplex.

Guns drawn, we approached the house. We hugged the front of the neighboring residences. Our portable radios had been turned off. Keys had been put away so they wouldn't jingle and signal our presence. A shotgun had been brought along. A tall hedge separated us from the suspect's duplex. The victim was with us. We stopped at the hedge. The victim was brought forward and asked to point out Red's residence specifically. He did so, and then moved back to a safer location.

Four other officers and I took up a position to the rear of the house. Approach from the rear was out of the question. No cover or concealment. An approach would be suicidal. We discussed the problem in hushed whispers. It was agreed that one officer would go back to the black-and-white and get a second shotgun. Two other officers would stay where they were. The other officer and I would move to the front of the house to assess the layout. We did so. It was the same as the rear. Just as bad. No cover, no concealment. My partner and I began whispering about tactics to solve the problem. Then, suddenly, a blast echoed through the still night air.

"KABOOM!"

In the quiet early morning it sounded as though a bomb had exploded. It seemed to come from the officers to the rear. I turned and saw an officer, shotgun in hand, being helped to his feet by his partner. The buildings had been recently stuccoed. A pile of rubble was at the corner of their position. It appeared as though the officer had tripped and accidentally fired the shotgun.

I whispered a hushed curse at the officers. "Why'd you have an accidental discharge?" I asked tersely but quietly.

One of the officers gave a muted yell. "We didn't have an accidental discharge! We got shot at!"

What had happened was that the two cops had set up shop at the corner of the duplex. The officer without the shotgun didn't like the location—too exposed. So, with a firm grip on the officer with the shotgun, he had pulled him behind the safety of the building. As he did so, the stucco—where the officer's head had been a split-second earlier—exploded. Red had fired his AK-47 assault rifle, the first of 15 rounds in the 30-round magazine. If the officer hadn't pulled his partner back at that exact moment, the AK-47 bullet would have taken off his head.

I turned on my radio and broadcast that an officer needed help, shots had been fired. I repeated it twice and gave my location. I wanted to be sure the radio operator picked it up. I spoke in hushed tones and tried to control my voice. It was useless. My voice had the bone-chilling quality officers never forget once they have heard it: officer needs help, shots have been fired.

The radio operator put the help call over the air. The first unit immediately acknowledged. The others kept quiet. It was training. The other units knew better than to clog the air with senseless, needless messages. That allowed me to advise the responding units how they were to approach, and give them the suspect's description.

We waited, my partner and I, again mulling over tactical options in hushed tones. I don't know why we kept our voices low. I guess it was because we had sneaked up on the location and deluded ourselves into thinking that if we kept quiet nobody would know we were there. You could have been deaf and still have heard the explosion from the AK-47. The suspect knew we were there. Hell, the whole block knew we were there.

I turned off my hand-held radio. There was silence. I began trying to collect my thoughts. My concentration was broken by a rapidly advancing slapping sound. It got closer. Something was moving quickly down the driveway. I was concealed by a large bush at the corner of the front duplex next to the driveway. I began to reposition myself. As I did, I heard a very distinct click—a click I had heard before. It was the safety being released on an AK-47. I peeked around the bush. I could feel the blood drain from my face. I saw the suspect. The porch light from a nearby house showed a light-skinned black man with red hair—armed with an AK-47. He adjusted the strap on the weapon. The strap! That had been the slapping sound. The suspect lifted the gun to his shoulder and began to take aim at my partner, who was out in the open, halfway between the duplex and the tree at the curbside. My partner couldn't see that he was a target.

I went on autopilot, reacting the way I had been trained. My .38 caliber service revolver was pointed at the suspect's torso, his body mass. I yelled:

"FREEZE! POLICE!"

The suspect was surprised. He switched his attention—and his AK-47—from my partner to me. All I could think to do was to put him down. I fired, twice.

"BAM! BAM!"

I saw the flash from the AK-47's muzzle before I heard the discharge.

"KABOOM!"

The sonofabitch was trying to kill me! I fired again, four times in rapid succession. "BAM! BAM! BAM! BAM!" Then: "CLICK! CLICK!" The hammer of my gun hit on empty cylinders. I was puzzled and scared. I knew I had hit the suspect with multiple rounds. But he still stood. There was no time to ponder why. I reached for my speedy loader. My eyes were focused on the suspect. He looked puzzled, too. I opened the chamber of my revolver and dumped the spent shell casings, then reloaded quickly, in a second or two.

The suspect looked at his weapon as though it were a curious object he'd never seen before. He began to stagger. He dropped the AK-47 and fell to his knees, then keeled over. He faced away from me when he fell. I yelled:

"LET ME SEE YOUR FUCKING HANDS!"

The suspect slowly began to raise his hands. I was scared. I was angry. I was frightened and mad because the suspect had tried to kill me. Now, for any reason, any reason at all, I would not hesitate to empty six rounds into the suspect's back and blow him away.

The suspect began to raise his hands. He had something in his hands. I began to pull back on my gun's trigger. Did he have a gun? The light was bad. I strained to see what was in his hands. I continued to pull back on the trigger. Then I saw. He didn't have a gun. It was a clump of grass in his hands. The lawn had been mowed earlier that day, and the suspect had instinctively grabbed his wound, so when he fell to the ground, the blood on his hands, acting like glue, adhered to a large clump of newly mown grass. He had complied, though. He had showed me his hands. I released the trigger on my gun.

Officers moved in and cuffed the suspect. I immediately radioed a Code 4—"Situation Under Control." I didn't want to alert the news media that monitored the police radio bands and in all likelihood would respond to a shooting call—especially if they knew an officer was involved. And I knew that when I requested an ambulance, the radio operator would need a justification, so I told the radio operator that we needed an ambulance because the suspect had fallen. It was true. It just wasn't the whole truth. The suspect had fallen as a result of being struck four times with .38-caliber bullets.

The investigation would later reveal that only one of my shots had missed Red. Four had hit him in the arms, a leg, and his torso. The last one, lodged near his heart, was the most life-threatening. But Red—whose real name was Robbins, with a record that included grand theft, carrying a loaded firearm in a public place, and possession of narcotics—survived the shooting and went to prison for trying to kill a police officer.[1] It was the third or fourth shot that saved me. The shot was aimed by somebody more powerful than me, probably God. One of my first rounds had struck the AK-47's magazine, causing the weapon to jam. It explained the suspect's puzzled look when he couldn't get the assault rifle to fire after the first shot. The shot that jammed his magazine saved my life and the lives of the other officers.

On the street, you've got to be ready for surprises.

Don't Be Too Quick to Pull the Trigger

After a few months on the streets in the Hollywood division, my partner and I knew all of the whores by sight. We even knew some of them by name.

One night in 1984, when we were cleaning up the streets so Hollywood would look good for the summer Olympic games, we ran across three unfamiliar faces. They were out-of-town prostitutes driving an old, decrepit Chrysler Imperial. They were new arrivals in Hollywood, hoping to get in on some of the big money action that accompanied visitors to the Olympics.

That was why we rousted them. We gave them our standard greeting speech.

"Welcome to Hollywood, ladies. Now leave."

---

[1] In a report on the incident to the Police Commission on March 8, 1990, Chief Daryl Gates said: "I have carefully examined this incident and I am very pleased with the tactics used by Sergeant Koon and his officers. . . . The success or failure of a police operation often rests on the qualifications of the supervisor. Sergeant Koon did an excellent job. . . ." For this action I was selected to receive the LAPD's second-highest medal for valor. But, because of the Rodney King incident, the medal has never been awarded.

The hookers promised faithfully that we would see them no more. But several hours later we came across them again, their vehicle parked on a side street known for prostitution activity.

I said to my partner, "Well, well, well. Lookie what we got here."

The whores saw us and gave us that "Uh-oh!" look. I said to them, "Ladies, ladies, ladies. What are you still doing in Hollywood?"

One of the women said, "We were just leaving."

I nodded. "Good, good, good."

As we talked, a fourth prostitute approached. She was obviously at least eight months pregnant, her belly bulging low and outward in that unmistakable way. But there was something in her walk, something about her look, something in her eyes that gave off danger signals. She had her hands in her jacket pockets as she approached.

I ordered her to stop, to turn around and get her hands out of her coat pockets. She ignored my commands. Something told me to unholster my gun. I repeated the instructions. She still ignored me, advancing. I raised my gun and extended it out at full arm's length. For the third time, I repeated the orders to stop, to show me her hands, to get them out of her jacket pockets. She kept coming.

As she neared, I saw the look.

She was not just intense; she had an intent. It was the look of a mental case. I had seen it many times before. Certain types of people are supposed to wear those peculiar white jackets with no arms, and she was one of them. She closed to within a few feet. My gun was pointed at her forehead. She removed her right hand from her jacket pocket. I began to squeeze the trigger. She rotated her arm and began to extend it in front of her. Then I saw it—the barrel of a small derringer. I pulled harder on my trigger.

Then, as she moved the derringer, I saw the barrel was plugged. I released the trigger on my gun. My partner, who had come up behind the whore, reached around and grabbed her right hand. He forced the gun from her grasp and handed it to me. It doesn't come any closer than that. She was an infinitesimal split second away from death, along with her unborn child.

What she had in her hand was a gun-shaped cigarette lighter. I became unglued. I looked at the whore, glaring, my face flushed. I shouted, "You stupid bitch! Don't you know I almost blew your fucking head off? What the fuck were you thinking of?"

I looked at her again. She hadn't heard a word. Her eyes were still glazed, glassy. I looked at the gun-shaped lighter in my hand. "Sonofabitch!" I screamed. I threw it as hard as I could at a darkened construction site across the street.

I knew it wouldn't do any good to continue ranting and raving about how close she'd come to dying, so I ordered her. "Get outta' here. Just get the fuck outta' here!" She turned and walked into the darkness. It was the last I ever saw of her.

I turned and looked at the three whores in the old Chrysler Imperial. I had momentarily forgotten about them. They looked at me in horror. One said, her eyes wide with terror, "That bitch was crazy!"

Now cold and back in control, I looked at the three of them. "I thought we told you ladies to leave." It was all I could do to keep from screaming at them, too.

They began to scurry and fumble around in the car, getting it started, one of them repeating, over and over, "We're going. We're going. You won't ever see us again." And you know something? They really did leave. And something else? I never did see them again.

It had been too close. It took me weeks to unwind from the incident. I played the encounter over and over again in my mind. At the time, the LAPD was under attack by the *Los Angeles Times* for an increase in police shootings.

I pondered how the *Times* would have portrayed the incident if I had shot the whore. I could see the headlines now: "White LAPD Officer Shoots Pregnant Black Woman."

If the *Times* and other police critics, including those with high-ranking police jobs, only knew how many times street cops exercise restraint. If they only had an idea how high an emotional price is paid in fear and in questioning your own judgment, both before and after an incident. If they only knew.

I certainly did.

PCP—A Cop's Nightmare

An LAPD training bulletin on angel-dusted suspects issued under Chief Daryl Gates's name in December 1983 showed a drawing of four officers trying to subdue somebody on PCP, as we believed Rodney King to be on March 3, 1991.

The suspect looked like the crazy old Tasmanian Devil of Bugs Bunny cartoons. The devil had mad, demented eyes, sharpened teeth, and was surrounded by a cloud of dust from the frenetic activity of an arrest in progress. Falling out of the cloud of dust were four LAPD officers. One was being choked. A second was being clubbed with a PR 24 baton the suspect had seized and was losing his teeth. A third was already dead, holding a lily in his hands. The fourth was shown lying prone, pistol in hand, urgently calling the station for help: "Hey, Sarge, Can You Send Us A Back-Up? I Think He's On PCP!"

The image isn't funny. It's real.

Several years after that bulletin was issued, in 1987, while working the 77th Street Division, some of my officers and I confronted a PCP suspect.

At the time, I decided to use the incident as a training exercise for less experienced officers and to try out management theory and its application to real-life situations. This thinking went against my belief in active participation and hands-on control of tactical situations, but I decided to take the risk. It was a mistake.

I gave my TASER to a less experienced officer. The suspect was a small man, only about five-feet, six-inches tall, and weighing only about 140 pounds. What harm could he do with six officers on the scene? Even though he was under the influence of PCP, and I knew what PCP could do, I calculated that little danger existed. With the other officers circling the suspect, we could control the situation.

The officer I had decided to train shot the TASER. It struck the suspect with a rule-book spread of the two darts. The officer then discharged the voltage, fifty thousand zappers. The suspect is supposed to go down, right?

Wrong. He didn't go down. Instead, he began running around the interior perimeter of the officers. The officers got wide-eyed. They were amazed and began to panic. The TASER hadn't done what it was supposed to do. The officers had been trained to believe that the TASER would put the suspect down. Obviously, the suspect wasn't down. The reality of the situation was true. The classroom theory was wrong.

So the officers got out their batons and began to pummel the suspect with power strokes. The blows had no effect. As the astonished officers looked on, the suspect broke through the perimeter of officers and ran toward a residence that had a large front-room picture window. As the shocked officers looked on, he jumped through the dome-shaped window. It shattered. The suspect landed in someone's living room. Almost immediately, the officers heard a hysterical scream. The cops illuminated the darkened room with their flashlights, creating a strobe-like effect in the darkened room. The flashlights revealed an elderly woman, still screaming. Then the flashlights hit the suspect. He was covered in blood. The suspect began crawling toward the screaming woman. She was in shock. The suspect was in shock. The officers were in shock. The neighbors, who had gathered on the sidewalk and lawn, stood by in horror and disbelief. The cops thought: this can't be happening! That's what their training told them. But it was happening.

My cops couldn't get in through the broken window. So they tried the front door. It was locked. The PCP suspect continued crawling toward the elderly lady, and she continued to scream. The officers tried to calm her with words. It didn't work. Frozen in fear, she couldn't move to open the front door.

I ordered the officers to kick in the front door. But they couldn't do it. The house was old, a Spanish-style bungalow built in the 1930s, as strong as a fortress. The door didn't budge.

Now the suspect was closing in on the elderly woman. The flashlight jumped back and forth from the suspect to the woman. The TASER clicked away. The arcs of electricity striking the suspect's body were reminiscent of an old Frankenstein movie. The pitch black interior illuminated by strobe-like flashes of light, the woman's screams, the officers' shouts, the pounding on the door, the bloodied suspect, the arcing electricity—it all added to the horror.

Finally, the door was forced open. A group of officers rushed inside, and one cop grabbed the elderly woman and led her to safety. He attempted to calm her down, but she appeared to be on the verge of a heart attack. An ambulance was called.

At the same time, another group of officers had pounced upon the suspect. After considerable difficulty, power-stroking him with their batons, they were able to cuff the suspect and take him into custody.

It had been a frightening incident. The suspect had taken control of the situation from the officers. As a result, the situation was out of control, out of my control. The suspect, not me or my officers, was in charge of what was going on.

It had been too dangerous. From now on, I told myself, a PCP suspect would have constant pressure applied. A PCP suspect would never again be allowed to wrest control from me and my officers. It was an important lesson, one that would have meaning on March 3, 1991.

What To Do When a TASER Doesn't Work

We could subtitle this story, "My First Appearance as a Film Star." Because that's what it was.

It was 1988, again in the 77th Street Division. The call had initially come in as a traffic accident with three people killed. I responded as the field sergeant on duty. Upon arrival, it seemed the entire Los Angles Fire Department had rolled in. Multiple engine companies were present, along with two ambulances. What they saw was this:

A van had run off the street, taken out a fire hydrant,

knocked down a power pole, and then plowed into the front of a store. The fire hydrant was spewing a geyser of water twenty feet into the air. Electrical wires from the light pole were sparking. A pond of water covered the entire area. Two bodies were spread out in the street, and the firemen were working frantically to give the victims first aid.

The first two officers on the scene had worked together only a short time but had gained a reputation as "shit magnets." This meant they attracted the best calls and arrests. This was no exception.

As I got out of my cruiser, a young Hispanic male—the driver of the van—was being chased by the officers. He was about the same size as the other PCP suspect I'd had to subdue—about five-feet, six-inches tall, perhaps 150 pounds soaking wet.

The suspect leaped on the rear of a fire truck and began trying to pull a large poker—a device the firefighters use to sift through wreckage, potentially a dangerous weapon—out of its restraining clamps. So the officers grabbed the suspect by his clothing and yanked him off the truck. The suspect then began to run frantically around the accident scene. It was obvious that he was dusted—high on PCP. I returned to my black-and-white and got my TASER.

A local freelance TV news team had arrived. They began to film the action. They turned their attention to the suspect and me. As they did so, I fired the TASER.

It struck the suspect in the torso. The film crew didn't know it at the time, but they had captured the first real-life TASING of a suspect. This wasn't a training exercise, like they have at the Police Academy. It was the use of a TASER on a dusted, dangerous driver already responsible for at least two deaths.

But the TASER didn't work. The suspect grabbed the wires with his hands, and sparks began flying out of his hands and out of the wires. He began running around in circles, his muscles rigid and anesthetized to pain. He stopped. Then he turned toward me. He yanked the hooked and sparking wires from his torso, held the ends of the wires in his hands, and began to reel in the wires as he walked towards me.

"Oh, shit!" I thought. I shouted at the suspect:

"GET DOWN! STOP! GET DOWN!"

He was oblivious to it all. He had a glazed look. He looked at me, but he was really looking through me. Then he began to speak in a language all his own. The words didn't make sense. They weren't Spanish or any other language I'd ever heard. He began moving closer to me.

I reacted. I kicked the suspect with all my strength. My boot came from the area of lower California and connected with the suspect's scrotum. He was lifted literally off the ground. He tried to speak, but he seemed to have something in his throat. It was probably his balls. He looked at me. His look had changed. He couldn't speak, but he conveyed this message: "I may be on PCP and can't feel pain, but I sure as hell felt THAT kick."

I was amazed. If that had been me who had been kicked that hard in that place, I would have curled up into a fetal position and died on the spot.

Other officers moved in with a modified swarm. We cuffed the suspect. He was controlled. It was over. And it had been captured on videotape.

The next night before going to work, I caught the ten o'clock news on Channel 5. The lead story was the videotape. There I was for all of Los Angeles to see. I TASED. I kicked. We took the suspect into custody. The news media loved it. The public loved it. The district attorney loved it.

Most of all, the Police Department loved it. The department couldn't show it enough. Everybody wanted a copy of the tape. Several days later, I ran into the film crew, and they were excited. They had made a small fortune, perhaps as much as $250,000, from selling the tape to every TV station in Los Angeles and hundreds of others across the nation. The tape was to become a legend in its own time.

Of course, the George Holliday tape of Rodney King's arrest also became a legend in its own time. But for different reasons.

You Can't Let a Suspect Go

The call said to meet the victim of an auto-theft on Sunset Boulevard. It was a busy Saturday night, the streets packed with pedestrians and vehicles. The way the call came out, it sounded more like a boy-girl dispute than a valid grand auto-theft.

As we waited in the lane for the victim to show, a Mercury Capri burned rubber at a stop sign a block ahead of us. The driver rapidly accelerated and pulled onto Sunset Boulevard. Our cruiser was in the turn lane. As the Capri turned left, he came right beside us. He stopped as quickly as he had started. He and his passenger looked at us. And we gave them THE LOOK!

The driver's body language immediately showed submission and apology. We could see that his eyes were bloodshot. He looked like a DUCE (pronounced "deuce," for DUI, or "Driving Under the Influence"), and he drove like a DUCE. We should have stopped and arrested him for drunk driving.

But we didn't. We had a higher priority call. We'd get reamed out by the watch commander if we sold back the call. So we let the DUCE go and waited for our victim to show. Minutes passed. The victim wasn't going to show. We got angry. We should have arrested the drunk driver.

Now the radio is blaring something about a traffic accident involving a possible fatality several blocks away. No units were available. Street cops like me cringe when it comes to traffic accidents. We're unfamiliar with the reports and hate to handle such calls. We don't mind going to the scene and observing the blood and gore and assisting the traffic units, but we hate to handle the call. The radio operator now tells us that a traffic unit has bought the call. We're saved. Also, the radio operator says there's nothing further on our auto-theft call. We're free. We can go to the traffic accident and catch sight of the blood and gore.

We got there only a few moments after the traffic unit. A head-on collision. One car, a Volkswagen Bug, had the front trunk area pushed into the rear seat. The two teenaged girls in the VW were both dead at the scene. The other car was a Mercury Capri, the car we had seen on Sunset Boulevard, our DUCE. Their car had crossed a double-yellow dividing line and crashed head-on into the innocent girls' VW. They had been aspiring actresses. Now they were dead.

We could have arrested him earlier. But we didn't. We had made an error in judgment. I wanted to go back and locate the alleged victim of the auto theft that had been reported. I wanted to drag her to the scene and show her the results of her insignificant spat with her boyfriend. I wanted her to see the bloodied bodies of two young girls. I wanted to do it, but there was no way I could locate her. That didn't help the rage.

A few days later the *Los Angeles Times* ran an article on the fatal traffic accident. The driver of the Mercury Capri had a high blood-alcohol content, far above legal intoxication. He and his passenger had survived.

On the night of March 3, 1991, I had flashes of thought about the two young girls killed by a drunken driver. Rodney King had been driving like a DUCE for almost eight miles before he finally stopped, stopped before killing himself or some other innocent person. We couldn't afford to let him go.

Things Aren't Always What They Seem

What you see isn't always what you see. That was true with the Rodney King videotape. It's been true for me in other ways, too. One incident stands out.

Once again, it happened in the 77th Street Division. It was about 8 P.M. A call came in, a burglary in progress. It was another typical 77th Street night—an abundance of hot-shot calls and no black-and-whites available. The helicopter unit was over 77th Street territory and answered the call, requesting backup. Nobody responded. I could see the helicopter circling in the distance and decided to answer the call myself. I punched numbers into my computer to call up the radio operator's notes on the complaint.

It seems two young men had been seen walking up the driveway toward an elderly lady's residence. The men didn't belong there, and the old woman was vulnerable. Whoever called in the complaint was worried about her safety.

I drove to the scene, parked my patrol car in front of a residence three houses away from the address where the complaint call had been made, and went to the house of the callers. They pointed out the house where the suspects were. I had parked right in front of that house. It was a lousy but unintentional tactical move. But there was no time now to correct the error, so I approached the house where the elderly woman lived.

The gate across the driveway seemed to have been forced open. I went to the front of the house and looked into the front windows. Several interior lights were on, and I could see the suspects—two black males—darting between rooms in the back part of the house. They didn't act like they lived there.

I used my hand-held radio to ask the air unit to put out a call for assistance. None was immediately available, but help would be rolling soon. So it was my solitary game to play until the cavalry arrived.

Through a window, I saw the suspects leave a bedroom. They were carrying what appeared to be a rolled Oriental rug, one on each end, holding it waist high. They dropped the rug along a dining room wall next to the kitchen. One suspect reentered the bedroom, while the other went into the kitchen, opened a drawer, and took out what looked like silverware. He then went to one end of the rug and, with his back to me, made several movements that led me to believe he was trying to stuff silverware into the end of the carpet.

Now help arrived. The first backup black-and-white unit arrived in front of the residence. Although the suspects didn't hear its arrival, they still appeared to be agitated. It seemed they were anxious to leave with their loot. I advised the air unit to keep a sharp eye on the rear of the house.

As the suspects left the back door, the helicopter used its

public address system to shout at the suspects to freeze. They were surprised. They hadn't heard the "whap-whap-whap" of the air unit's rotor blades overhead. They ran back inside the house. I directed two officers to go to the rear. Then a second backup unit arrived, and I sent one of the two officers to the rear and directed his partner to stay with me. The helicopter radioed that the two suspects had fled the house. One was running east, the other west.

I could see one of the suspects running across the backyard of the victim's house and I rushed to position myself at the corner of an adjacent house, shouting commands at my partner to back me up. I looked to my new partner, the cop who had arrived in the second assistance unit. She had recently been the subject of a nice human interest story in the *Los Angeles Times*. It seemed the officer had been fired, then rehired. To support her firing, the department had cited various incidents as explanation, among them that the officer, responding to a burglary call, had stopped to smell the roses in the garden of the victim's residence. This, mind you, was only one incident cited for firing the officer, but it was the one that captured the media's attention. Tonight, I noticed that she was adjacent to a large rose bush in full bloom. I thought to myself, if the officer smells the roses this time I'll shoot her.

The suspect ran right into our ambush. I stepped from my position and drew down on the suspect with my .38.

"FREEZE, ASSHOLE!" I shouted.

The suspect, who was about six feet tall and weighed more than two hundred pounds, was surprised. He looked at me. He looked at my partner. He was assessing the situation, trying to decide whether to risk an assault on us. I shouted again:

"FREEZE! GET DOWN! YOU COME TOWARD ME AND I'M GONNA' BLOW THE SHIT OUTTA' YOU."

The suspect sized me up. He sized up my partner. I could tell he was about to jump back and run. I yelled again:

"GET YOUR ASS DOWN OR I'LL BLOW YOU AWAY!"

The suspect thought about it for a moment and then got smart. He complied with the order. I love it when command presence works. Another set of officers arrived. They cuffed the suspect and then patted him down.

In the meantime, the other burglar had been captured. Both were in custody, and I could inspect the scene of the crime.

In the dining room next to the kitchen I saw the victim—the elderly lady who lived there. She had been brutally beaten. Her face, especially around the eyes, was severely swollen. A large blood puddle was next to her head and her neck had been deeply cut where the suspects had sliced her throat. She had almost been decapitated. She was wearing a multicolored mumu-style dress.

Then it hit me: The suspects hadn't been carrying an oriental carpet, they had been carrying the victim. I had mistaken the mumu for a carpet.

The suspect hadn't tried to stuff silverware into the end of the carpet. He had struggled to slit the victim's throat.

I had witnessed a murder and not even realized it. How could I have been so blind? Why hadn't I realized what I was seeing? If I had, maybe I could have prevented it. The question still haunts me.

Race Relations

Critics of our handling of the Rodney King incident have focused on the fact that he is a black man. The explicit charge has been made that the LAPD—my officers and I—singled Rodney King out for punishment only because he was black.

It shouldn't be necessary even to comment on something this ludicrous. For one thing, I had only a passing acquaintance with one of the officers, Larry Powell, and knew Ted Briseno only by reputation. Tim Wind and Rolando Solano I didn't know at all. Credibility is strained to the breaking point by the suggestion that we four got together and decided to go hunting a black man to beat that night. To do so we would have had to enlist the help of the CHIPs to initiate the Rodney King pursuit, about twelve other LAPD cops who eventually arrived on the scene, including a probationer just five days out of the

Police Academy, and the helicopter crew that hovered overhead providing lights. A conspiracy that broad would have
made Watergate look like child's play.

But beyond this, the charge that I orchestrated the Rodney
King incident because of racist beliefs is personally repulsive. I
was unaware of racial differences while growing up in Southern
California. My first memory of meeting a black person was in
the fifth grade, when my school was integrated. My teacher
came to me and asked if I would mind if a new student, Rochelle
King, shared my two-student desk. I recall thinking that the
question was curious. Of course I didn't care! It would be fun to
have a companion there. The teacher asked again if I would
mind, adding that the little girl was black. So what? I thought.
The only thing that bothered me was that it was a little girl. I
would have preferred a boy as a deskmate. I remembered the
incident after the Rodney King affair erupted; it struck me as
ironic that my first experience with a black person was wholesome, and that it, too, involved somebody named King.

Granted, I became painfully aware of cultural differences
between whites and blacks during my years on the street,
especially working the 77th Street Division. But these differences, I found, were based more upon economics than upon
any other factor. In fact, I am sympathetic to the economic
deprivation that has turned many people to drugs, alcohol, and
other intoxicants as a form of relief from the dreary urban
prisons in which they live. Unfortunately, crime usually be-
comes a means to support these vices.

While working at 77th Street, I often pondered why there
were so many liquor stores per capita in South Central Los
Angeles, with its predominantly black neighborhoods, compared with white enclaves. I wondered why every convenience
store in South Central Los Angeles hustled more beer and wine
than bread or milk. Could it be, I asked myself, that an economic conspiracy was at work here? A conspiracy intended to
keep minorities down and weak, so powerful white-owned
businesses would have a steady supply of dependent cus-
tomers and cheap labor? You don't have to be paranoid to
wonder if this could be the case.

But my belief in racial equality extended beyond these philosophical musings while patrolling the 77th Street Division in the early morning hours. On the street, my job was to protect, defend, and serve citizens. And most of those citizens in the 77th Street Division were black. Let me give you three examples.

It was 1988. I was working at the 77th Street Division. A black transvestite prostitute was brought in for disturbing the peace. While in the holding tank, he suddenly stopped breathing. Several officers looked on, taking no action. There was no way they were going to risk getting AIDS by giving this prisoner cardio-pulmonary resuscitation—mouth-to-mouth assistance in breathing. Why should they risk their health and lives on a black male whore?

I was disgusted by their reaction. So I entered the holding cell and, without hesitation, began giving the prisoner CPR. It didn't work. The prisoner was dead on arrival at the hospital where he was taken.[2]

The point is that this was a human being who needed help and my job was to provide that help. That he was black wasn't the issue. That he was a male prostitute wasn't important. That he almost certainly was infected with AIDS, or at least a high-risk potential carrier of the HIV virus, didn't enter the picture for me, either. The crucial factor was that he was a human being who needed police assistance to live, and I am a police officer. Ask yourself this: Would someone with racial bias deep enough to beat a prisoner simply for being black also go to the aid of another black who was a potential AIDS carrier, giving him mouth-to-mouth resuscitation? I think not. Draw your own conclusions.

The second example involved a young black cop and how I helped him with the LAPD bureaucracy, despite opposition from the department itself and the "what the hell" attitude of his superiors.

It seems this officer had been injured in an on-the-job traffic

---

[2] Later tests showed that the prisoner was a carrier of the HIV virus.

accident and was undergoing physical therapy. While driving one day for treatment, he was involved in a second accident that ruined almost a year's treatment. The medical liaison officer decided that the young cop was a malingerer trying to abuse the system, and the department cut off all financial assistance.

That was when I got involved. I was assigned to do a "revisit" to the young officer to determine whether he was really sick, or just malingering. I had worked with him earlier, and remembered him as a good cop. I went to see him at his home.

To begin with, he really was still sick. His injuries obviously hadn't healed, and he had trouble walking. It was clear that he couldn't continue as a police officer. Not only that, but his standard of living was lousy since the department had cut off financial support. His wife was pregnant with their second child, Christmas was nearing, and it would be hard for their two-year-old daughter. Debts had accumulated, and the couple's credit rating was shot—their savings had long been exhausted. Psychologically, the officer was a shell of the once-proud young copper I remembered.

I had seen many injustices on the LAPD, but this was one of the worst. I decided to take up the officer's cause.

First, I discussed the case with the captain, arguing forcefully, but he didn't believe me. He told me I had taken too personal an interest in the situation and that I should reconsider my stance, because it could hurt my career. That made me all the more determined to continue.

I contacted medical liaison and was told the young officer had "fallen through the cracks of the system." The way the term was used made me realize it was not an unusual event.

So I got to work with a medical file that was hundreds of pages long. I got it updated. I made arrangements and had the officer compensated for unpaid overtime and vacation time. That provided some quick cash. Then I went to the Police Memorial for financial assistance. That got the pregnancy and delivery of another baby daughter paid for. Finally, I helped the officer through the bureaucratic maze to a pension hearing. It had been about two years since his first injury, and almost a year since the department had provided financial assistance. After the hearing, he got a substantial tax-free pension.

All of this was something I didn't have to do, but wanted to because it was right. And I'm a racist? There's at least one ex-cop who won't buy that story.

The third example involved a cop using excessive force on two black suspects. It occurred only a few months before the Rodney King affair. The suspects in this case were transients, the type of people who don't carry a lot of weight with officialdom. Lance Braun was an LAPD officer who was working at the Foothill Division, and he had been the subject of a personnel complaint for using excessive force against the transients.

The District Attorney's office, meanwhile, had been dragging out its own investigation into the incident. It seems the DA's office couldn't find witnesses to support the complaint. But I went out and beat the bushes and found witnesses. I gathered physical evidence to support the victims' stories. I persuaded Braun's partner to break the so-called "code of silence" and come clean about the incident. Finally, I arranged for the victims to identify Braun in a line-up situation, an unusual procedure that generated hostility against me from some of my fellow officers.

The point here is that I went to bat for two black transients who had been improperly treated by the LAPD and the District Attorney's office. I do not condone or tolerate criminal misconduct, by either civilians or police officers. In the Braun case, I took the extra steps necessary to ensure that a diligent investigation was completed, going so far as to put my own reputation at risk to make sure criminal charges, if made, would stick. That incident alone should indicate that I was not about to condone or tolerate the same type of alleged misconduct on March 3, 1991.

Life on the Streets and the Rodney King Arrest

By now, it should be clear how all of this fits into the arrest of Rodney King on March 3, 1991.

King's driving patterns suggested serious intoxication—a suspicion that proved to be true. We couldn't let him go, because he might kill himself or other people. That had happened to me before. (As mentioned, it also happened, ironically and tragically, to Freddie Helms, one of the two passengers in King's car on March 3, 1991.)

After being stopped, his behavior indicated PCP usage. I had seen enough of that to be scared by it, to realize the danger it presented to officers trying to make the arrest, not to mention the suspect. The small PCP user who jumped through the window and terrorized the elderly lady indicated how much strength a PCP-intoxicated human being possesses. Rodney King wasn't little. He was big. He was much more dangerous.

The suspicion that Rodney King was on PCP was confirmed without any doubt in my mind after he overcame two blasts from my TASER. I'd seen it happen several times before, with suspects who were dusted on PCP. And I knew that when a TASER doesn't work, extraordinary physical measures have to be taken. That had been my experience with the kicking incident, and it was one of the reasons why multiple power strokes with the baton were ordered.

Finally we had to deal with appearances. My experiences had been that rarely does a speeding pursuit at night involve just traffic violations. Usually another felony is involved. Rodney King wasn't just speeding. He was committing multiple, big-time traffic violations and ignoring pursuing police cruisers that had their lights flashing and sirens howling. Was he fleeing because of a robbery or worse? Was he armed? Could this be another case where I might misinterpret the scene, as I had done with the elderly woman I had mistaken for a carpet? Would somebody die?

We didn't know. I didn't know. And I didn't want to find out in a way that might cost someone his life. Not even Rodney King's life, although his record before and after March 3, 1991, suggests that he's one of the 5 percent who need to be in jail so the other 95 percent of the population can live a bit more safely.

4

Cops vs. Cops

An Internal Affairs Investigation Tries to Prove Conspiracy

By midmorning on March 3, Rodney King was in the hospital jail ward, charged with felony evading.[1] But he wouldn't be there long. Anybody with even a primitive sense of public opinion could tell that he'd quickly be out, all charges probably dropped, as soon as the dramatic videotape shot by George Holliday began airing. By Monday, March 4, parts of the eighty-two-second tape were being shown on local LA television outlets several times a day. Cable News Network featured it at hourly news broadcasts. Local television outlets played it time and again, over and over.

Never mind that the tape had been conveniently edited, in most cases to cut the portions showing Rodney King rising from the ground to attack Officer Powell. Television had scored a beat. Newspapers, not to be outdone, were quick to pick up on the odor of a big story: cops had beaten a black motorist. No doubt about it. It was right there on a videotape for everybody to see. The videotape made it unmistakably

---

[1] He was not charged with the traffic violations, since these were misdemeanor offenses. The usual LAPD practice is to lodge only the most serious charges against a suspect. So the only charge filed was felony evading.

clear, or so it seemed, that racist police brutality was at work here. Rodney King was usually identified as either a "passing motorist" or somebody stopped for speeding. The high-speed 7.8 mile chase was ignored, as was his bizarre behavior, his attack on Officer Powell, and his repeated attempts to rise and avoid being handcuffed and taken into custody.

Over the next several days, the media-fed public outrage reached fantastic proportions. Politicians, sniffing votes if they joined in the hue-and-cry stepped all over themselves in their rush to condemn the LAPD generally and my officers and me specifically. Mayor Tom Bradley said, "The people of this city have been slapped in the face by the attitude and bigotry of these officers."[2] Not to be outdone, Chief Daryl Gates, at a graduation ceremony for a new class of officers from the Police Academy, stated that "A few thoughtless officers failed to have a reverence for the law . . . failed to understand their job to protect and to serve . . . failed the tradition and pride of the Los Angeles Police Department."[3] Former LAPD Chief Ed Davis, now a Republican state senator from Santa Clarita, predicted that I would soon be doing hard time in the slammer. In a signed article in the *Los Angeles Times*, Davis said:

"I have absolutely no doubt that justice will be done in this case. I am confident that the officers who beat Rodney G. King . . . will be charged and convicted by their own actions. While the accused are entitled to a full and fair trial, we all realize that the videotape of the incident is quite compelling enough to vault its stars into state prison. *The question is not . . . whether criminal acts have occurred or whether the actors will be punished*" (emphasis added).[4]

This gives you some idea of how one-sided the official reaction to the incident was from the outset. Mayor Bradley was in orbit. Chief Daryl Gates couldn't understand how his officers had reacted in such a brutal fashion. Heads were going to roll over this one. But the one head that wouldn't roll would be

---

[2] *Los Angeles Times*, March 20, 1991.

[3] Ibid., March 23, 1991.

[4] Ibid., March 17, 1991.

Rodney King's. He was an instant victim, an overnight celebrity. He was a poor defenseless black man, not an intoxicated ex-con with a burgeoning record of violence and dangerous public behavior who had assaulted an officer and resisted our efforts to get him in handcuffs. He'd get out of jail with all charges dropped, including an investigation into a complainant's report that Rodney King was a suspect in an armed robbery shooting committed the week before the Foothills incident. That investigation, which was backed up by an eyewitness and in-stop videotape, was stopped because of "insufficient evidence."

Given this tense public environment, the LAPD had to act— and quickly. And so, late on the afternoon of Monday, March 4, the Internal Affairs Division cops descended on the Foothill Station in an approximation of Desert Storm. General Norman Schwarzkopf would have appreciated their tactics, if not their techniques. Like the general, the IAD police had a mission. It was a mission of truth. And, like the general, the IAD had a driving force. But unlike Stormin' Norman, the IAD's driving force was not a moral imperative endorsed by the United Nations and White House. The IAD's compulsion was the ego force of the Los Angeles Police Department, the best of the best. The reputation of the LAPD had been tarnished. And so the palace guard from the Internal Affairs Division had been given their marching orders by Chief Gates: crush those cops responsible for this outrage and return the LAPD to its pedestal of pristine honor and public adoration.

The IAD cops had their marching orders. They wanted the Rodney King arrest report. They wanted the use-of-force report. They wanted the pursuit summary. They wanted the log of the sergeant in charge. They wanted the morning watch commander's log. They wanted all of the logs of officers from the mid-PM watch on March 2 through those on duty on the March 3 morning watch. They wanted these reams of papers, and they wanted them Now!

But what you want and what you get aren't always the same. The IAD detectives didn't get the crucial documents—the arrest report, the use-of-force report, or the pursuit summary. Why?

Simple. The arrest report had already been routed to the central record-keeping bureau in Van Nuys, as it was supposed to have been.

The pursuit summary and use-of-force reports hadn't been completed. Why? Again, a simple answer existed: the morning watch commander, Lt. Patrick Conmay, hadn't realized the reports were due within twenty-four hours of the incident. So he hadn't pushed the assistant watch commander, Sgt. Richard Distefano, to complete the reports within twenty-four hours, as required. And Sergeant Distefano, who had been directed to do them, had a flat tire and hadn't made it to work that day. Neither he nor Lieutenant Conmay followed the regulations.

Even so the IAD concluded: Aha! A cover-up. What we have here is a conspiracy to conceal wicked official conduct. The IAD's conclusion was erroneous. But, like most first impressions, it would become almost impossible to overcome. After all, the IAD troopers had seen the videotape. Insofar as the IAD was concerned, no explanation could possibly exist to justify the use of force captured on film by George Holliday. The cover-up theory would set the tone for the investigation. The Rodney King case would, moreover, be the plum of all IAD assignments, a career-making case for the IAD cops involved. They would almost certainly be knighted by Chief Gates.

And so, instead of an unbiased examination of the evidence and a conclusion supported by that evidence, the IAD cops sought to twist the evidence to fit their predetermined conclusion. Any evidence that did not fit that conclusion was conveniently ignored. Square pegs would be forcibly thrust into round holes.

I was concerned, but not from a sense of guilt. I knew the Rodney King arrest had been a managed use of force done strictly according to departmental procedure. But my warning sensors had started tingling. The IAD was not exactly a neutral organization. Neither was the Robbery-Homicide Division that assisted the IAD. They were not like what Rodney King got from the California attorney general concerning the charge of ADW on a police officer, a crime that King clearly had committed (and even the DA acknowledged), but that had been dropped by the state because of public pressure over the case.

Because IAD's mission is to seek the "truth," whatever it might be, the organization is granted much latitude. The IAD may err, may overstep its authority, may violate an officer's civil rights, may conduct illegal searches. But that's all OK, because the IAD is seeking the truth. The internal security division, however, does not have to be truthful itself; truth is immaterial when truth is your objective. In short, the Internal Affairs Division is a contradiction that does not wash with the troops. The IAD generates a great deal of hostility and resentment. Simply put, the Internal Affairs Division is not an officer's friend.

Like the city attorney and district attorney, the IAD has a win/lose ratio of accountability. It has to justify its existence and expenditure of resources. And that occurs through officer suspensions. This is not to say all officers are always innocent. They aren't.

Police Department employees tend to dislike the internal security cops. This is especially true with street cops. That's because IAD's role in life is to burn police officers. Only by doing a tap-dance on fellow officers' heads can an IAD cop demonstrate his loyalty to the department. An IAD assignment is coveted by cops who care more about their careers than about being coppers. Getting into IAD is a major step up the promotion ladder. Then, as they reach the rank of captain and above, different standards of discipline are imposed. Managers on the LAPD are almost above the law. In fact, evidence shows that they *are* above the law.

What this type of accountability does is to open the system to abuse. It creates a double standard of discipline—one for the managed, and it is harsh, and a second for the management, and it is lenient. This double standard of discipline has fostered a widespread attitude on the LAPD of them (management) versus us (street cops).

Let me give you some examples of how the system works.

In one instance, a high-ranking LAPD staff officer allegedly purchased stock in a company that had created a new, advanced, stolen car recovery system. His purchase came just before the LAPD announced that it was endorsing the company's system. The officer reportedly made a handsome profit, although his purchase would seem to be a clear violation of federal securities laws. Several other high-ranking LAPD officials reportedly did the same thing. No staff officer was disciplined.

Another staff officer reportedly gave favored treatment to one of his relatives in leasing undercover vehicles used by the department. The staff officer was not disciplined.

A third was alleged to have used information from departmental sources to undermine the political career of an opponent. This resulted in the politician winning a judgment of almost $4 million in damages from the city of Los Angeles. The officer was not disciplined.

I had personally seen the double standard at work. It happened in 1989 when I was working in the 77th Street Division. I had come in to work overtime and was typing at a desk in the detective unit. The desk officer hurried back to me. She was excited.

"Sarge," she stated, "the captain just shoved a female officer!"

"Yeah, sure," I said.

"No, really, he did," the desk officer insisted.

"Look," I answered, "nobody's that stupid. Not even a captain."

"I swear to God he did," she said. "The captain pushed her. She's out in the trailer crying."

I asked the officer, "You have any witnesses?"

"Yeah," she replied. "A whole bunch of people saw it."

I asked if she had informed the watch commander. She said she couldn't find him. How about the captain? "He left," she said.

I hunted down the watch commander in the workout room and told him what had happened. He left to investigate and I returned to my paperwork. About five minutes later the female officer who had been shoved by the captain showed up at my desk. She was a tiny officer, about five-feet tall and not more than a hundred pounds, barely big enough to meet the LAPD'S physical standards. The captain who had pushed her, on the other hand, was big, about six-feet, three-inches tall and 280 pounds. She was Hispanic. The captain was black.

She told me she had been assigned to the desk because of an injury received in an on-duty traffic accident. About a week before, her boyfriend had sent flowers to her at the station. The captain had intercepted the note attached to the flowers and read it at roll call that afternoon, embarrassing her. On this day, her boyfriend had sent more flowers, and the captain once again got hold of the note first.

The officer asked for the note. The captain refused. She begged. The captain continued to refuse. She tried to grab the note, but the captain held it chest high. The officer must have looked like a puppy trying to snap a treat from its master's hand. Then the captain reportedly made a pushing movement with his hand and arm, as someone would do while tracking through a jungle and moving bushes out of the way. The officer said she collided with the wall. It hurt her, physically and emotionally. The captain reportedly laughed, then walked out of the room.

After she told me the story I asked her what she wanted me to do.

"I don't know what to do. What he did was wrong. I shouldn't have to put up with it. No officer should." She was emphatic.

I took a deep breath and began to explain her options. For a moment I thought about the personal consequences. I asked myself, "Do I want to get involved? Do I want to jeopardize my career? What is right?" I decided to give the officer some advice.

I told her she had to understand something. She was in a very unique situation, and if she played the game properly she would come out a big-time winner.

The LAPD, I told her, was arrogant about sexual discrimination and harassment; it didn't treat it seriously. I advised her of her rights, as required of supervisors by the city mandate, and further told her that if she exercised those rights, she could win a personal triumph and strike a victory for other female officers.

But I advised her to be sure she had lots of witnesses present when she confronted the issue, to go to the watch commander and demand—not beg, ask, or plead, but demand—that a personal complaint be taken. Additionally, I pointed out that she had been battered, and that a criminal offense might have taken place. I further suggested that she have the captain arrested for battery and that she complete a crime report. Finally, I thought she should demand immediate medical attention and have the Scientific Investigation Division take official photos of the scene and her injuries.

She should also consult a lawyer from the Police Protective League and then explore the possibility of filing a sexual discrimination suit. In addition, she could go to the Equal Employment Opportunity Commission and file a complaint naming the captain and the LAPD.

But I also cautioned her. I said the lieutenant and the captain would try to con and intimidate her. They would attempt to play down the incident, shine her on, and sweep the incident under the carpet. And the captain would try to scare her. But, as long as she had witnesses, she was in the position of power.

Armed with knowledge of her legal rights, the small officer returned to the watch commander's office. She laid out her demands. It was a direct hit on the lieutenant. He called the captain on the telephone and said, "We've got a problem here." The captain said he'd be in immediately.

When he got to the station, the captain ordered the female cop into his private office. She refused unless she could have another officer present. The captain's anger erupted. He ordered her into his office again. She repeated that she wanted a witness, adding a nice touch: "I'm scared of you," she said. And it was true.

Then the captain exploded. He had a reputation for having a bad temper. I love predictability. The captain began to shout and threaten and intimidate. He told the officer if she pursued the complaint her life would be a living hell. He would fire her.

She responded by saying she didn't feel very good and

wanted to go to the hospital. She demanded that an ambulance be called.

The captain went nuts. He told her she wasn't going anywhere until she dropped the complaint, that if she didn't drop it she really would need a doctor and a hospital. But the officer stuck to the line I had given her. The captain got the bureau commanding officer on the phone. The commander had a forty-five-minute talk with the officer. It didn't work. The complaint stayed.

In the end, the captain went to a board of rights hearing. The street cops hoped justice would prevail, because it had been a serious allegation. And, indeed, the captain was found guilty. The penalty? A suspension of fifteen days. If it had been a street cop, he'd have been fired. I felt almost as though I had been responsible for betrayal, since I had urged the officer to play it strictly by the book, assuming that justice would be done.

That incident reveals something about how managers take care of one another on the LAPD. And that's why I was worried about the IAD investigation into the Rodney King arrest, even though I knew everything had been done strictly by the book. If I had embarrassed the department—and I had—then my neck was on the block regardless of the truth.

And I wasn't surprised. In other words, the IAD's investigation into the Rodney King incident began as a typical IAD job.

First, they would get the "truth" by rounding up all the involved probationary officers who were at the scene. It would be easy, IAD's finest moment. The internal security storm troopers would yank the young officers from roll call. They would tell the probationers who they (the IAD cops) were—an unnecessary charade, since everybody knew who they were, just as everybody in Germany in the 1930s knew it was the Gestapo when somebody came rap-tap-tapping on the front door at 2 A.M.

But the IAD troopers' practice of identifying themselves to young, inexperienced officers had a useful purpose; it bred fear and intimidation. They would then isolate the probationers, doing a double-team interview on each one. The IAD cops would not tell the probationers they had a right to a defense representative. They would not tell the probationers they were going to coerce statements from them. The IAD was not obligated to tell them any of these things. The probationers were supposed to know it. That's because officers' rights is a flash-in-the-pan course squeezed in during the six-month Police Academy curriculum. It is sandwiched in between a hodge-podge of other courses for overworked recruits.

Besides, the recruits reasoned, why worry about officers' rights? That was something only "bad" cops had to worry about. Nobody joined the LAPD to be a "bad" cop.

But now the recruits were probationers. Now they were viewed as "bad" officers. And now they were confused. Their minds raced. They hardly remembered the Police Academy course on officers' rights. At this point—while the probationers were in this state of fear and confusion—the IAD cops would tell them of possible criminal charges. The IAD police would read them their Miranda-warning rights, not because it was the proper thing to do or because it was required, but because it added to the probationers' fear.

This, then, was the way the Internal Affairs Division would start off getting at the truth. Although the more experienced officers would know about their rights and would exercise them, it wouldn't matter, because the IAD would be armed with the "truth" from the probationers. With this in hand, the IAD would go after the senior officers and the sergeant for the worst of all possible offenses—lying and denying. It's cause for immediate dismissal from the force.

And so, over the next several days, as public outrage grew from the media's constant repetition of the videotape, as public officials from the lowest LA City Council member to the highest levels of the White House joined the clamor for our heads, the IAD slowly, carefully interviewed all of the officers involved. They began with the most junior, working their way up the ladder. And I was at the top of the ladder, among the last to be interviewed, because I was the ranking officer at the scene when Rodney King was arrested.

Along the way, though, the IAD cops made a startling discovery. It related to their initial impression of the incident, the impression of guilt and conspiracy. The internal security police discovered there was a reasonable explanation why no use-of-force report or pursuit summary had been filed when they descended on the Foothill Station; that is, the assistant watch commander's flat tire and the watch commander's ignorance of the rules.

But did the bubble burst on the IAD?

Not at all. On the contrary, in fact. Something very strange was going on, and the IAD, in its paranoia, understood what was happening. Many officers had been interviewed and, oh so strangely, they all gave the same story about what happened on March 3—the story about Rodney King's dangerous, erratic behavior, about his attack on Powell, about his refusal to obey lawful orders, about his continued resistance, about his overcoming uses of force that had worked almost every time in the past.

From this consistency, the IAD concluded that their case was proved: A conspiracy indeed existed.

Because everyone agreed on a story so patently ridiculous (in the IAD's eyes), it had to be due to the infamous "code of silence." Police officers were protecting police officers, cops were lying for fellow cops. If one went, they'd all go. There was only one thing wrong with the IAD's conspiracy theory. To make such a conspiracy work, it would have to include three separate police agencies (LAPD, the CHIPs, and the LA school police) and almost thirty officers (if you count the two in the helicopter), most of whom didn't even know each other until the night of March 3, 1991.

With such clear "proof" that a conspiracy existed, the department began to apply psychological pressure on me to cooperate with the IAD investigation. Go along to get along. In short, I was to abandon my belief that I had acted properly and admit sins that hadn't been committed. It wasn't subtle pressure, either.

After learning from the initial radio report about the IAD investigation, I called my commanding officer, Capt. John Mutz, and told him that I had heard there would be an IAD investigation into the Rodney King incident. I assured him it was a by-the-book use of force and no misconduct had taken place, and I told him that I took full responsibility for every-thing that had happened, because it was all done at my direc-tion. His response was cordial, but noncommittal. After hanging up, something lingered in my mind. Mutz's tone was somber, almost ominous.

When I went to work the next night, Tuesday, March 5, I fully expected to be questioned by the IAD and I was eager to tell my side of the story. To my surprise, the IAD police weren't at the Foothill Station. But I didn't even make it to roll call before being told that the Foothill commander, Capt. Tim McBride, wanted to see me. I went to his office. We talked. I repeated what I had told Captain Mutz, that I took full respon-sibility for what had happened with Rodney King. I told him it was a legitimate use of force, one that followed policy, pro-cedure, and training. No misconduct existed.

The captain seemed surprised by my acceptance of respon-sibility. He explained that it might be best if I not go out into the field. Maybe I should work inside for a while.

Then the captain began to relate a story. He asked if I re-called an incident that had occurred several years ago, the Michael Burkholder incident. It involved a Rampart Division sergeant who shot a naked, unarmed man and killed him. The suspect was on PCP. Captain McBride said that in that incident the department had forgiven Sergeant Burkholder. Captain McBride asked me, "Do you know why?"

"No," I answered. "I don't. I didn't know there was a need to forgive him."

The captain continued. "The department forgave him be-cause the involved sergeant admitted he was wrong." The cap-tain paused, then asked, "Do you understand what I'm telling you?"

I was dumbfounded. I realized the captain was waiting for my response. He wanted repentance, a plea for forgiveness. Instead, I said, "Captain, I didn't do anything wrong. If any-thing, I did everything right. What's there to forgive?"

This obviously wasn't what the captain had hoped to hear.

His nonverbal body language, the tone and inflection of his voice, weren't lost on me. All he said was, "Well, just think about it." But what he meant was, "I'm sorry if you continue with this line of thinking. The department will have to take unpleasant action. I do not like it. I do not want to see this happen to you, but it is going to be necessary because you are being difficult."

We parted. I went back to work inside the watch commander's office. I was worried. This was serious stuff. I had just committed the most egregious and unforgivable offense possible: I had embarrassed the LAPD.

Although by now I had seen the George Holliday videotape, I still had no idea how shocking it seemed to ordinary viewers. To me, it was incomplete, and difficult to see what Rodney King was doing, the threat he posed to officers' safety and to himself. Taken alone, isolated, I thought the videotape was brutal. No question about it. But my memory was still fresh about the incident, and I could see things that weren't happening on the videotape. I simply assumed that people wouldn't overreact to an inconclusive and incomplete film account of the arrest. I was about to find out how wrong that assumption was.

After leaving Captain McBride's office, I returned to the desk where I had been assigned for the watch. The station had kept a list of irate callers. At first, I thought it was a joke. But the desk officer showed me a list of about fifty names. It seemed that every time the news came on, the tape was shown. And every time the tape was played, the phones went wild. I answered one such call. It was from a woman in Detroit, Michigan. She said she was a former police officer, and she was upset. The beating was uncalled for, she said. The officers were out of control. They should be arrested, put in jail, and the keys deep-sixed. She wanted an address where she could write the chief and register her displeasure. I was polite and put her on hold. But I was angry and upset. I composed myself, released the hold button, and in a calm, helpful, professional manner gave her the information she had requested. I thanked her for the call. After I hung up, I could literally feel my blood pressure rising. My head pounded. The assistant watch commander looked at me. He offered an early out for the day. I took it, and went home.

The next evening, March 6, I was due to return to work at 11 P.M. I was about to walk out the door of my home when the phone rang. It was the watch commander. I would not need to report for work. I had been assigned to my residence pending the outcome of the Internal Affairs investigation. The wolves were howling at the scent of fresh meat. And I was their main course.

Chief Daryl Gates Betrays His Troops

In his recent autobiography, *Chief*, Gates says he learned about the Rodney King incident on March 4, 1991, after returning from giving a lecture at Harvard and then attending a seminar in Washington, D.C.

His driver had seen the videotape, he explained. The driver, Gerry Sola, was quoted as saying that the videotape was "really bad." Then Chief Gates said he got home and his assistant chief called to report that an IAD investigation had already been ordered, whereupon Gates called his secretary, Mary Miller. Gates wrote:

"Mary was much more descriptive about the video... [She said] 'It was horrible, just horrible. They kept hitting him [Rodney King] and he went down on his knees and they still kept beating him for the longest time. He [King] was bleeding and not resisting at all. And then one of the officers went over and kicked him in the head. I almost threw up.' "[5]

Several things are wrong here. First, Chief Gates is being conditioned about what to see—being told what to expect by his secretary. Someone must ask: How did she know he was bleeding? Was that on the Holliday videotape? And how about not resisting? Had she been looking at Rodney King, observing what he had been doing? Or had she seen only

---

[5] Daryl F. Gates, *Chief—My Life in the LAPD*, with Diane K. Shah (New York City: Bantam Books, 1992), pp. 2, 3.

the police batons falling, which is what most viewers saw? And finally: What does the chief's secretary know about street-cop work, street-cop experience, about suspects resisting arrest?

For that matter, let's get back to Chief Daryl Gates himself. What does he know about street-cop work? Has he ever arrested more than one suspect on PCP? Has he arrested even one? His experience has been administrative. He's a bureaucrat, not a street cop. He knows how to work a budget through the Los Angeles City Council. That's an important job, to be sure. But it's hardly the same as arresting dangerous felony suspects. Which is why Gates may have been honest in his reaction. You see, he didn't know what was required on the street to subdue a suspect. He might have known academically, but he didn't know the reality of it. Or if he ever did know that reality, he'd forgotten it.

Consider his own words after watching the videotape:

"I stared at the screen in disbelief. I played the one-minute, fifty-second tape again. Then again and again, until I had viewed it twenty-five times. And still I could not believe what I was looking at. To see my officers engaged in what appeared to be excessive use of force, possibly criminally excessive, to see them beat a man with their batons *fifty-six* times, to see a sergeant on the scene who did nothing to seize control, was something I never dreamed I would witness. It was a very, very extreme use of force—extreme for any police department. But for the LAPD, considered by many to be perhaps the finest, most professional police department in the world, it was more than extreme. It was impossible. I sat there watching, terribly shocked. Feeling sick to my stomach, sick at heart" (his emphasis).[6]

Well, where had Daryl Gates been all his life on the police force? Had he been out on the streets? No. First he'd been a driver for Chief Parker, then gone up the ranks through administrative jobs. He wasn't a street cop. He had no realistic idea of

---

[6] Ibid., p. 4.

what was sometimes required to subdue violent, intoxicated suspects.

The fact is this: Chief Daryl Gates is, or was, at least, a good politician in his time. He knew how to work the system to protect Daryl Gates and his command staff. So when things went wrong, the street cops got screwed, as we knew we would be, while the big guys got protected. It was the LAPD double standard at work.

When the Rodney King incident got hot, Gates had to make a choice. He could stand up and back his officers, or he could waffle and protect himself from an increasingly hostile assault from his worst enemy, Mayor Tom Bradley. If Gates chose right, his street cops would follow him through the seven gates of hell. If he chose wrong, his officers would abandon him and he would lose his strongest base of support. Gates made the wrong choice. And the street cops turned their backs on him. That was when his departure from the LAPD was certain, not later, when he got in a silly dispute with the City Council and mayor over when he would retire. When the street cops denied Gates, when they no longer had confidence in his support, he was through.

He could have saved himself by supporting us. But he didn't. And he didn't do so in clear violation of the Fifth and Fourteenth Amendments to the U.S. Constitution, which guarantee that no person "shall be deprived of life, liberty or property without due process of law." Due process meant an accused person must be given a fair trial before a competent tribunal. Due process included the right to cross-examine witnesses.

Not only that, but Section 202 of the Los Angeles City Charter clearly defines a police officer's job as a property right. Implicit in this property right is salary. But the process used by Gates and the LAPD management was to accuse an officer, investigate, suspend the officer without pay, and then give the officer a board of rights administrative tribunal consisting of three staff officers, captains and above. It is hardly a jury of peers for a street cop. And it was only at the board of rights that the accused officer had an opportunity to cross-examine witnesses.

But, in the meantime, the officer is denied his or her salary (a property right) before the board of rights convenes (due process) and before being convicted of any wrongdoing.[7]

Chief Gates knowingly manipulated LAPD's disciplinary system to deny due process to me and three other officers involved in an alleged misconduct. As a result, he caused irreparable damage to officer protections, and grossly failed the men and women sent out into the streets to "protect and serve."

In the Rodney King affair, the chief denied due process to the involved officers by making judgmental statements when the investigation was in its infancy and prior to the due-process hearing. Gates said, in effect, that I was guilty, and my officers were guilty, of misconduct. And that all of us should be fired. The statements had to influence the IAD and RHD investigations, since the internal security cops' and detectives' future careers depended upon Gates's good will. Gates's influential control of promotions, pay increases, and assignments of subordinates who might sit on the trial board unduly tainted all potential members of the trial board and acted to undermine the due process requirements for a fair and impartial hearing.

Let's be specific here. On March 8, Gates made a videotape that was shown to all police officers and command staff at roll call. Attendance was mandatory. Everybody had to see it. Keep in mind, now, that the IAD investigation was not complete. I had not yet been interviewed by the internal security cops. This was before any facts about the matter had been determined. All that existed as evidence was the inconclusive and incomplete Holliday videotape.

Even so, Chief Gates videotaped this message to the troops.

---

[7] At this writing, August 1992, the trial board has still not convened. In the meantime, I and Officers Briseno and Powell remain on unpaid suspension, without salary since April 1991. As a probationer, Officer Wind was fired, but almost immediately reinstated on suspension without pay. And all of this despite the fact that the Simi Valley jury found Briseno, Wind, and me innocent of any wrongdoing, and was unable to agree on a not guilty verdict regarding one count against Officer Powell.

He condemned "those thoughtless officers who have destroyed our image." Again, image is more important than truth. Then Gates issued a clear warning:

"When I say that [my, Gates's, orders concerning force and the department's public image] is the way it is going to be, then that's the way it is going to be. I assure you that anyone who questions what I have to say—and questions it in any way—and demonstrates that in any manner, or chooses to disagree in some kind of action—that they will rue the day that they have disagreed with what I have to say."

With this message, Gates literally commanded the potential members of the board of rights to comply with his marching orders: find Sergeant Koon and his cops guilty, and get rid of them. As a result, Chief Daryl Gates, intentionally and not by accident, denied due process to the involved officers.

This is in sharp contrast to Chief Gates's own behavior when the Police Commission decided to suspend the chief—him. When Gates was assigned to his home with pay, the chief protested. He claimed a denial of due process and threatened to sue to restore his status—the same status he denied his own officers.

Yes, this is the same procedure, denial of property before due process, that Gates employed with his troops during his fourteen years as chief of police. If it was not fair for Gates, why was it fair for street cops? The answer is that it is not fair for either Gates or his officers. Something is inherently wrong with a system that favors management and denies due process to the managed. The Los Angeles Police Department is a fine organization, but it needs to be more even-handed in guaranteeing due process to all officers, regardless of rank.

Preparing to Do Battle

From the LAPD's viewpoint, the seriousness of the Rodney King affair was not King's alleged brutalization under the color of authority. That sort of thing had happened before. Neither was it alleged excessive force. Allegations of the use of too much force were commonplace. Even racism wasn't the problem for the department. The LAPD is accused of racism all the time. No, from an LAPD perspective, the problem was the George Holliday videotape, the one being played repeatedly on television. That videotape embarrassed the department. Which meant that I had embarrassed the LAPD.

And when I embarrassed the department, it unleashed a torrent of wrath. As the sergeant in charge, I was expected to fall upon my sword. What this meant was that I was supposed voluntarily to turn in my badge, gun, and identification card, thereby allowing the department to save face. I would be the scapegoat. When officers are wrong, they often try to save face. But officers are not always wrong. I was not wrong. I did not submit my badge, gun, and ID card. Rumors had me doing so, but it was wishful thinking on management's part.

Call it naive, but I thought I should give the department a chance to do the right thing. I thought that perhaps, given time, the department—if I did not back it into a corner—would allow a graceful exit. I needed to try this option. It called for a nonconfrontational defense representative to argue my case internally. I needed an intelligent, articulate cop who knew how the system worked and had a reputation for honesty and integrity. One person, and one person only, came to mind. I selected Thomas A. Dawson to be my defense representative.

Tom Dawson had been a cop for about eighteen years, most of it in the violent South Bureau. He had been assigned mostly to patrol duties, but somewhere along the line he became a defense representative for fellow coppers. A defense rep was chosen by an accused officer to be a quasi-attorney at administrative disciplinary proceedings. Being a defense rep was a full-time job. Consequently, somebody chosen for the duty was given a leave or placed on special assignment until the case was decided. Tom had been a patrol officer, had been promoted to detective, and then assigned to 77th Street. But he never filled the job because of the demands on his time as a defense rep.

The reason was that Tom was not only likable, he was reliable. Tom Dawson is a big man, bear-like in size, about six-feet, three-inches tall and weighing about 250 pounds. But he's a teddy bear. He's mild mannered and even tempered. He did things like baking cookies for the watch at the start of each new deployment period (a twenty-eight-day time-keeping method used by the LAPD). Tom is also a devout Catholic. He came across more as a parish priest than a street copper. He would sit in his patrol car, open a Bible, and pray before going out on the streets. Other officers carried an assortment of charms to help them get through a day—rabbit's feet, lucky tokens, other amulets intended to bring good fortune. Tom Dawson carried holy water and his rosary.

Another thing that distinguished Tom Dawson from the pack was his education; Tom had a doctorate in criminal justice/public administration. That was something else that brought us together. I had two master's degrees, one in each field. Our mutual educations, in related fields, created a bond.

I tracked Tom down at Employee Relations Division on Tuesday, March 5. Tom answered the phone in his customary fashion. "God Bless you. Thomas A. Dawson speaking. How may I help you!"

I asked Tom to be my defense rep. He said, "I'm free. I'm not doing anything. In fact, I was just sitting here awaiting your call."

How can you not respect somebody like that? Somebody who answers the phone with a "God Bless you," and then says he's just been waiting to hear how he could help you out of a jam?

Tom Dawson got to work on my case. He was the special individual I needed on the inside, a person with the unusual personality traits that were required to handle the board of rights hearing. He was intelligent, sensitive, firm, polite, respectful, and respected. He had unquestionable integrity. He was also devoted to his client and to the Los Angeles Police Department. The gamble I was taking was to show the department that it was wrong, which ran up against the department's inability to accept criticism. I realized this, which is why I selected Tom. If there was any single person who could advise the department that it was wrong, and do it in a diplomatic fashion, it was Tom Dawson. Tom would have to convince the department that the use of force on Rodney King had followed departmental policies, procedures, and training.

Tom Dawson did an outstanding job as my defense representative. He collected vital information proving that the use of force employed on Rodney King was within LAPD guidelines. And his institutional memory about the police department provided useful intelligence in determining which departmental witnesses would be good for our case, and which would be more loyal to the LAPD image-protection association encouraged by the chief and his senior commanders. In short, Tom Dawson was the ideal defense representative for so long as any approach was non-confrontational. But the LAPD's strategy required a different tactic. The Department wanted to push me to the wall. And I was not prepared to be shoved.

So later, I would have to replace Tom as my defense representative. The reason was that, as we prepared our case, a different strategy emerged. I had sought a nonconfrontational approach in hopes the department would allow everybody a graceful exit. But the department was unyielding in its determination to lynch me and my officers. Tom is more negotiator than street fighter, and so he agreed that I should get a different defense rep. I chose George Hofsteder, a tall, lanky man with reddish hair. He called himself a "BCMC"—Big City Motor Cop and had almost twenty-five years on the job and had been a defense rep for many of them. A departmental gadfly, he caused considerable consternation among LAPD management.

But all of this came later. By the end of the first week in March, events were catching up with me and Officers Powell, Briseno, and Wind. Public outrage over the videotape hadn't quieted. On the contrary, it continued to build daily. Television and newspapers were trying to outdo each other in carrying Rodney King stories. Culprits were necessary, and public opinion couldn't wait for a departmental board of rights hearing to try, convict, and punish the presumed guilty officers.

I could see the train coming down the track. And so, on

Wednesday, March 6, I contacted the Los Angeles Police Protective League (the equivalent of a union for officers ranking lieutenant and below) about legal representation.

At this time the union was in a state of organized agitation. But in short order, the union had done a damage assessment and had a good fix on where the train was headed—the political fallout, the impact on officers' morale, and so on. The league also did a fine job of organizing a group of defense representatives and attorneys to help me, Powell, Wind, and Briseno, the obvious targets of any action.

On March 8, a meeting was held at which union officials spoke to us of the rocky road ahead, of the IAD's methods and procedures, of officer rights, and of how to protect ourselves from a lynch mob.

After the meeting, a man, a civilian, I didn't know approached and introduced himself. He said his name was Darryl Mounger, and that he was an attorney. The league had invited him to the meeting and, with my approval, he would like to represent me in any criminal proceedings that might arise.

I asked him: "What are you in this case for, what do you want to get out of it?"

"Ego," he responded.

And he was being honest. It was true. Darryl is and was a certified egomaniac. He is also a brilliant lawyer. Almost as important, Darryl had been a sergeant on the LAPD. He knew how the department worked. He didn't need an education about policies, procedures, and training. He was also shrewd and canny, possessing an unusual blend of formal education, street smarts, and common sense. Innovative and not bound by conventional limits, he could not be intimidated—a gadfly in his own way with a tenacious, bulldog-like character.

One aspect to the case intrigued and appealed to Darryl. I told him that I realized it might not be in my best interest, but he had to understand that I accepted full responsibility for the incident. I would be accountable, not any other officer. It would get ugly and distasteful, and the possibility existed that one or more of the officers would cut a deal and betray me. In the end, it would be Darryl and I who faced the world. It was risky. If I had miscalculated, I could wind up in the joint as a sex toy for the prison population. I was risking the loss of my wife and family and everything we had worked for twenty years to acquire.

But if we prevailed, the reward was the deep pleasure of knowing I had fought for my principles and won. I had no problem with the decision. Darryl was in a similar situation. Losing would be an ego blow beyond belief for him. Winning, though, would provide ego gratification without parallel—righteously leading a battle to victory against an entrenched establishment and public opinion. And doing so in the full glare of national media attention.

I had no problem with the decision to take personal accountability for all that was done to arrest Rodney King. Darryl liked it, too. First, it was the truth. Second, I had strong faith in God and the American judicial system and its ability to sift through facts, evidence, and the law and arrive at a fair, judicious decision. Third, the evidence, facts, and law of the case supported us and worked against the one key piece of evidence—the George Holliday videotape of Rodney King's arrest. And, ironically, that videotape ultimately provided the strongest argument for our acquittal.

Victims Are Chosen

In 1990, California voters decided they were fed up with the state's court system. Justice was taking too long and, in the public's view, often wasn't effective. So they decided to streamline the system. The result was Proposition 115.

Prop 115 was intended to correct a multitude of perceived ills within the California criminal justice process. It removed long, drawn-out preliminary hearings and delays in getting cases to trail. Under Prop 115, preliminary hearings that indulged in such constitutional rights as the cross-examination of witnesses could be set aside; a district attorney could go directly to a grand jury for an indictment. The grand jury route also allowed the district attorney a greater degree of control.

With a grand jury, there were no pesky attorneys cross-examining witnesses and delaying justice. The DA put on his or her case, informed the grand jury about what the law was, and then interpreted the law. Finally the grand jury was advised how to vote. It was a system reminiscent of a method used in seventeenth-century England. Then, of course, it wasn't called a grand jury; it was called a Star Chamber. And anybody who's ever served on a grand jury knows this is precisely how they're conducted.

Once indicted, my officers and I would be guaranteed a speedy trial—another Prop 115 achievement—because it provided a time frame of sixty days from indictment to trial. But we also needed a jury. No problem. Prop 115 provided speedy juries for speedy trials. No need for troublesome attorneys to engage in time-consuming questioning of prospective jurors, the practice known as *voir dire*. Under 115, the judge could handle this all by himself. This is an important note to keep in mind, as we move toward the Simi Valley trial. For we were accused not only of unnecessarily beating Rodney King, but, along the way, it was suggested that the jury selection had been rigged to prevent blacks and other minorities from serving on the panel. So keep this in mind: under Prop 115, the judge was more actively involved in jury selection.

Given the benefits available to prosecutors under Prop 115, the Los Angeles DA, Ira Reiner, chose to go the grand jury route. It was not only more convenient, it was important to his political career. You see, Reiner was politically ambitious. He had already run for statewide office, attorney general, and lost. More importantly, he had failed to win some very high-profile cases. Remember the McMartin preschool molestation case? It was one of the longest and most costly prosecutions on record. Reiner had lost that. Even more significantly, he had lost three alleged police brutality cases that were highly publicized in Los Angeles, although they didn't receive national media attention. After these defeats, Reiner desperately needed a win, preferably a high-profile case. If the Los Angeles DA's office had been a National Football League franchise, Ira Reiner's losing record would have ensured a first-round draft choice.

Now he was presented with the mother of all cases—the Rodney King incident. This case was not just local news, or even state news. It was national news, world news, cosmic news. Most important of all, the Rodney King case was a 100 percent guaranteed win. Why? Because it had the best of all possible evidence—a videotape.

And so Ira Reiner decided to ramrod me and my officers through the justice system. He wanted to do it with the utmost speed. And he devised a brilliant plan. He utilized Proposition 115. Prop 115 would speed the case through a grand jury hearing he could control. Were he to go through the hearing process, he would expose his case to defense questioning, which meant there would be a strong probability all charges would be dropped. It was no contest. Reiner decided to use Prop 115 and regain his faltering political popularity.

The Los Angeles County Grand Jury convened for four consecutive days, on March 11, 12, 13, and 14, 1991. Deputy District Attorney Terry L. White represented Reiner. The intention from the outset was for the grand jury to return indictments against Officers Powell, Wind, Briseno, and me by presenting evidence that after Rodney King was stopped for a traffic violation and evading arrest, he was struck without cause and that excessive force was used. I was to be accused of aiding and abetting illegal acts. Powell and I were also charged with making false reports in an attempt to cover up the incident.

The grand jury heard a succession of witnesses. George Holliday told how he made the videotape. Josie Morales, a resident of the apartment area where Holliday lived, testified to witnessing the arrest and beating; she referred frequently to notes that she said were made starting Wednesday, March 6, three days after the incident. Ms. Morales said she couldn't remember without the notes. CHIP Officer Melanie Singer related the story of the pursuit. Carol Denise Edwards, a licensed vocational nurse, was on duty at Pacifica Hospital when Rodney King was brought in. She said King asked, "Do you think I'll be out of here by tomorrow morning?" According to Ms. Edwards, King said he wanted to go to the baseball game at Dodger

Stadium, where he worked as an usher. Nurse Edwards said she heard no derogatory or racist statements directed to King by the officers who were present.

Lawrence Davis was a registered nurse on duty at Pacifica Hospital when Rodney King was brought in. He testified that Rodney King was struggling on a hospital gurney when he was brought into the emergency room. Davis said he was with King for about ninety minutes and King was not in any pain. At one point, Davis said, an officer overheard Rodney King saying that he, King, worked at Dodger Stadium. According to Davis, the officer said, "Yeah, we had a pretty good hardball game ourselves tonight, didn't we?" Davis said King responded, "Yeah, you guys had a pretty good game. You played pretty good hardball tonight." Davis said the officer then stated, "Yeah, you know, we played a good game of hardball tonight and we hit quite a few home runs, didn't we?" King's response, Davis said, was, "I think so, yeah."

"Do you know who we were playing tonight, Rodney?" the officer asked. According to Davis, King's response was, "Yeah, me."

Davis said the unidentified officer then commented, "Yeah, and you lost the ball game, didn't you? We won it." King responded, "Yes," Davis said.

The assistant DA questioning Davis, Terry White, who would stay on the case through Simi Valley, then asked Davis: "Did they direct any other comments about the incident to anyone else?"

Davis answered: "No, I heard some racial slurs, but it was like low-key. I just heard a couple of words."

White asked: "What were those racial slurs that you heard?"

Davis: "It was something like, 'This nigger . . .' something or other."

This was an indication of a strategy the prosecution would follow. The DA would use radio transmissions and other testimony about statements we allegedly made that night to try to prove that the LAPD was rife with racism, and that Powell, Briseno, Wind, and I were leading practitioners of it, That would give a motive for beating King. But, as Davis's grand jury testimony suggested, the prosecution was never able to pin specific racial slurs on any officer involved that night. The reason is that there were none. Even King himself conceded this in his first news conference upon leaving the hospital. Asked specifically whether there were racial slurs, King said there were none. His memory changed after filing the $56 million federal civil rights lawsuit.[8]

The fact is, racism did not occur in the Rodney King incident, a supportable fact the grand jury did not directly hear.

After the grand jury hearings, when the civil lawsuits were in process, black leaders and the ACLU believed they had evidence for the first time that could prove their contention that racism was behind the arrest. The proof they first offered was that four white officers had beaten a black suspect. That was true. But it did not mean that this was a racial incident. Black officers would have done the same thing. The problem was that black officers deployed in the Foothill Division the morning of the Rodney King arrest consisted of only two cops; one was a male probationer who helped control King at the scene and agreed that the use of force appeared to be proper, and the other was a female sergeant who was back at the station.

The second piece of evidence the ACLU and its supporters sought was to have King himself attest that the incident was racial. Initially, King denied that racism was a factor. He failed to pick up his cue the first time. Later, of course, when it

---

[8] After the Rodney King incident, an independent commission headed by Warren Christopher, a U.S. deputy secretary of state under President Jimmy Carter and prominent Los Angeles attorney, was appointed to study LAPD policies and procedures regarding the use of force. More on this later, but one point is necessary here. An analysis by the Christopher Commission of 6 million individual LAPD radio transmissions revealed 1,400 were of a racial nature. And some of these were questionable. But even if all were offensively racist, that would represent less than two-tenths of 1 percent of all communications recorded by the department. Zero percent would be ideal, of course. But it is doubtful that many workplaces today can claim that routine communications among its personnel are as free of racial bias as the analysis of LAPD messages indicates.

became clear that a claim of racism would assist his lawsuit and contention of civil rights violations, King jogged his memory.

King's attorney, in a neatly orchestrated media move, portrayed King as a concerned citizen who had initially played down the racial issue to avoid throwing gasoline on a burning fire. But after due consideration, King could no longer remain silent. King now revealed that the officers who had used force upon him had called him "nigger."[9]

As proof of their claim, King's attorney offered up the videotape. The attorney or his investigator had gone to a large chain audio store, put the tape in a floor model, and listened to it. The sound track, the attorney claimed, verified that the officers had called King a "nigger."

What the attorney neglected to mention was that the FBI had examined the original tape by subjecting it to the most rigorous of all testing—cleaning up the tape's soundtrack and enhancing it by using state-of-the-art technical equipment—and that the FBI had pronounced the tape free of racial remarks.

But all of this came after the grand jury hearings. The grand jury spent four full days interviewing eighteen officers who were at the scene (not counting Wind, Powell, Briseno, and me), as well as bystanders and medical personnel. And, like the IAD investigation, the grand jurors began to hear the same story repeated: Rodney King was violent, he was out of control, he disobeyed repeated commands to get on the ground, to get his hands behind his back, to submit to lawful authority. Some bystanders testified that they thought the force used to subdue King was excessive. But all agreed on the basic facts of what happened, which were: Rodney King's behavior was bizarre, he

---

[9] As the civil rights suit began taking form, Rodney King began to claim that the police officers taunted him by calling him "nigger," repeatedly, and that one officer urged him to run because "I'm going to kill you." As *Vanity Fair* reported in July 1992: "That would have been especially useful testimony in the trial, except for the fact that King hadn't mentioned it earlier." *Vanity Fair*, op. cit., July 1992, p. 160.

deliberately assaulted an officer, he was uncooperative and wouldn't submit to lawful commands.

Even so, the videotape was too dramatic, still too fresh to be ignored by the panelists on the grand jury. And since neither my officers nor I could be present at the grand jury hearings, since we were not permitted to cross-examine witnesses or tell our side of the story in a thorough, convincing way, the outcome was a foregone conclusion, just as DA Reiner had hoped.

On March 14, 1991, only eleven days after the incident, sealed indictments for using excessive, illegal force were brought against Officers Theodore Briseno, Laurence Powell, and Timothy Wind. I was indicted for aiding and abetting their illegal acts, and for trying to conceal the incident from the department. That was a charge based upon allegations that my sergeant's log and Powell's arrest report were false and were intended to mislead about the extent of Rodney King's injuries. But the district attorney went all out to make sure every base was covered.

The specific charges were these:

Officer Laurence Powell:
1. Assault with a deadly weapon with great bodily injury enhancement[10]
2. Assault under color of authority with great bodily enhancement
3. Filing a false police report

Officer Timothy Wind:
1. Assault with a deadly weapon (ADW)
2. Assault under color of authority

---

[10] "Great bodily injury enhancement" is a serious matter. It means broken bones and the like, and the charge was intended to increase prison time and prevent probation. At first, the district attorney had sought a "GBI enhancement" charge against me, but later dropped it because, although I had overseen the use of force on Rodney King, I had only participated with the TASER. The use of the TASER was not grounds for assault with a deadly weapon or the GBI enhancement.

Officer Ted Briseno:
1. Assault with a deadly weapon (the baton)
2. Assault under color of authority

Sgt. Stacey Koon:
1. Assault with a deadly weapon
2. Assault under color of authority
3. Filing a false police report
4. Accessory after the fact to a felony

Ironically, I was indicted on the very day of my first interview with the Internal Affairs Division cops who were seeking to "get at the truth" of the Rodney King incident. In fact, I was indicted even before I was interviewed by the IAD. I had to cut short the IAD interview on March 14 because the next morning I had to make my appearance in court to enter a plea of not guilty and have bail set.[11] Frontier justice couldn't have been swifter. Never mind that the cowboy you're hanging might not be guilty. Guilt is presumed in frontier justice. My case was like that. And all because of an eighty-two-second videotape rarely shown in its complete form.

Thirteen days after the grand jury adjourned, DA Ira Reiner held a news conference to announce that the other police officers who were at the scene would not be indicted along with me, Powell, Briseno, and Wind. Reiner suggested that their "inaction" was "reprehensible," then conceded: "While many of the bystander officers were deeply disturbed by what occurred, I need to note that in the course of our investigation

---

[11] My statements at each of two separate IAD interrogations never wavered. I said the Rodney King arrest was a managed and controlled use of force, that it followed policies, procedures, and training, that there was no misconduct. The officers under my control did exactly as they were ordered, and performed exactly as they had been trained. The IAD investigators were shocked. They were caught dead in the water by a candid admission of the truth. "Look at the videotape," they urged. "Isn't that brutal? Isn't that excessive?" To each question, I repeated a stock answer—the truth. The IAD no doubt expected me to fall on my sword. Not only that, they were probably worried about how they were going to explain the truth to the chief of police.

we found that, to this very day, some of the officers present do not acknowledge that the incident should have been handled any differently than it was." The reason the officers didn't acknowledge this is because, having been at the scene, they knew it had been managed properly.

The black community was outraged by Reiner's failure to indict the other officers. Mayor Bradley called for a state law making it a criminal offense for police officers to stand by and do nothing when they witness excessive use of force. Bradley said: "Officers who are at a scene where they observe heinous crimes such as the Rodney King beating ought to be required to take some action to intervene and say, 'Hold it. Stop.' "[12] Presumed guilt? How much more evidence do you need.

Not surprisingly, the Los Angeles Unified School District, the California Highway Patrol, and the LAPD picked up on Ira Reiner's lead that while the bystander officers' conduct "is disgraceful, and perhaps cause for dismissal, it is not a criminal offense." And so, almost immediately, the LAPD fired probationary officer Timothy Wind and suspended me, Powell, and Briseno without pay. Powell, Briseno, and I attempted to have our pay reinstated, but the request fell on deaf ears. We demanded that our trial boards go forward, and that they be open to the public. The department wanted to wait until the criminal indictments were resolved. As a result, we were denied due process and had our salaries, our property rights, illegally taken away.

The Los Angeles Unified School District handled matters a bit differently. The school board convened and promptly fired both school police officers for getting involved in the incident.[13]

The California Highway Patrol in its turn investigated and suspended the CHIP sergeant who supervised Melanie and Tim Singer; the charge was that he had failed to understand the significance of the incident. The sergeant argued that there

---

[12] Ibid., *Los Angeles Times*.

[13] Eight months later, after the Rodney King hysteria had cooled, both officers were reinstated.

was no significance to it. The Rodney King pursuit was an everyday affair for the California Highway Patrol. No matter. This one had been captured on videotape. So he was suspended, his lieutenant was downgraded to sergeant, and the CHIP captain in the chain of command was given a stiff suspension. Melanie and Tim Singer were each given reprimands.

The LAPD didn't want to give the public the idea that it wasn't a tough disciplinarian. So the LAPD began handing out suspensions to the bystander officers. The suspensions—twenty-two days or less—were issued to the probationary and some senior officers. This was significant, because any suspension of more than twenty-two days would require a trial board hearing. This way, trial boards were avoided for most of the officers. Some senior officers were ordered to trial boards, and were suspended without pay pending those hearings. But, unlike my officers and myself, their appeals for reinstatement were quickly granted because of anticipated long delays in the tribunal process. In perhaps the most incredible disciplinary action, Officer Kenneth Phillippe, the observer in the helicopter, was handed a fifteen-day suspension.[14] The logic must have been that he ought to have ordered the helicopter pilot to land, alight from the aircraft, and pull officers away from Rodney King.

But here's the most disgraceful part, the ultimate revelation of a double standard:

The Los Angeles Police Department took no disciplinary action against any officer above the rank of sergeant. I was the ranking officer. And I was headed for trial.

I was also headed for another surprise. The battle of cops versus cops wasn't over yet. In fact, it had hardly begun. As Mounger and I suspected, one of my three co-defendants would have second thoughts about the incident and, accordingly, change his mind about what happened on the night of March 3, 1991.

Officer Ted Briseno was going to try and cut himself loose

---

[14] Phillippe later requested a trial board. His suspension was downgraded to a reprimand, the lowest of all disciplinary punishments.

from Powell, Wind, and me. Apparently, he hoped to save his own skin. He wouldn't win, but he wouldn't lose, either. In fact, he both won and lost. The jury decided that Wind and I had committed no crimes, and voted to acquit Powell on all but one charge—the jury voting not guilty by an 8–4 margin. These victories for the truth were a tribute to the imaginative, even brilliant defense that Darryl Mounger devised.

5

The Trial

Setting a Strategy

Exactly one year and two days passed between March 3, 1991, when an amateur cameraman's videotape made Rodney King an instant folk hero to many people, and March 5, 1992, when the trial of the LAPD four began in Simi Valley.

Many reasons accounted for the big delay of the sixty-day deadline required for trial by Proposition 115. One was a bout of pneumonia that took me out for a couple of weeks. Another was the trial judge's insistence on examining individually each of the endless, repetitive motions that accompany any criminal trial. It would have been more efficient to consider them in batches. But the original trial judge, Bernard Kamins, wanted to do it differently. Kamins, to be generous, was a different kind of judge.

The delays were useful to the defense, though. That was because it was essential to get the venue changed from Los Angeles proper to an outlying suburb, where our attorneys believed and polls suggested passions did not run so high. Only one week after the incident, the *Los Angeles Times* reported that 86 percent of the people surveyed in a poll of LA County residents had seen the videotape, and 92 percent of those respondents believed excessive force had been used on Rodney

King. An LA *Times* poll almost two weeks later indicated that more than 70 percent believed the use of force on Rodney King was racially motivated. Not only was public opinion almost unanimous in its hostility towards my officers and me, the court had been getting anonymous threats of violence, perhaps even of rioting, if the case was moved out of the city of Los Angeles. In ordering a change of venue, the California Court of Appeals took note of these pretrial threats. The court opinion said:

"The threat of violence here does not yet arise from the ultimate determination of guilt or innocence but from this pretrial procedural matter dealing with venue. If the mere possibility of an order ... gives rise to such threats, we must draw the inevitable inference about the possibility of threats which could surface during the trial itself."[1]

And people were surprised when rioting erupted within hours after the verdict? By the time of the trial, of course, the media had conditioned public opinion to expect our guilt. That expectation was fed throughout the reporting on the trial, and it led most people to anticipate, almost as a foregone conclusion, guilty verdicts when the matter eventually went to a jury.

Pretrial publicity wasn't the only reason a change of venue was necessary, though. It was also clear that Judge Kamins was prejudiced against the defense. More important than his sometimes balmy courtroom behavior,[2] Kamins at first refused to consider our request for a change of venue. Not only that, he assured the prosecutors of his political reliability on the change of venue motion. In a private communication with prosecutors, he told them to "trust me" on the motion to move the trial—a clear violation of procedure and clear evidence of

---

[1] In the Court of Appeals of the State of California, Second Appellate District, Division Three, 2d Civil No. B058842 (Super. Ct. No. BA 035498), July 23, 1991, p. 24.

[2] Which included such actions as bringing into court Dame Justice's scales to demonstrate his impartiality. And then explaining to all present why he had the scales with him.

bias. Our attorneys filed a motion to have Judge Kamins dismissed from the case, and we won. As the appellate court noted, Kamin's "actions have contributed to the publicity surrounding this case and have resulted in no small amount of public confusion about the venue issue."[3]

The new judge assigned by the Superior Court to our trial was Stanley Weisberg. Judge Weisberg had a reputation for being smart, fair, and tough. Of all the available choices, he was the best possible judge for the defense, and the worst for the prosecution. That was because, by being fair, Judge Weisberg would not be predisposed to favor the prosecution over the defense. He would not be swayed by the politics surrounding the trial, or by the intense, media-fed emotionalism over the case. Before becoming a judge, Weisberg had been a prosecutor for several years. As a judge, he had presided over some high-profile cases, most notably the McMartin preschool retrial and the Leisure trial, the second of which involved an LAPD officer charged with murder. In both cases, Judge Weisberg ran a tight court. He was the consummate jurist. We didn't always agree with his rulings, but he was fair.

One of Judge Weisberg's first actions was to meet with prosecuting and defense attorneys to determine where the trial should be held. The state judicial agency had provided three possible locations. Judge Weisberg announced that they were Orange County, Alameda County, and Ventura County.[4]

It had been rumored, early on, that if a venue change were ordered it would be to Alameda County. That was obviously where the prosecution wanted the case tried. Outwardly, it seemed not too bad. Census data showed a population breakdown of 60 percent white, 18 percent black, 14 percent Hispanic, and the remaining 8 percent other ethnic minorities—Asians and Pacific Islanders, primarily. The problem for the defense came when one considered where in Alameda County the case had the highest probability of going. That

---

[3] Op. cit., Court of Appeals, p. 5.

[4] Orange County later was removed from the list by the state because of its heavy caseload. It was replaced with Riverside County.

was Oakland, an overwhelmingly black, liberal community. Oakland wouldn't be good for the defense.

We preferred Orange County. It was the opposite of Oakland. Orange County was John Wayne territory, Green Beret country. Orange County was overwhelmingly white and conservative to an extreme. Alameda County versus Orange County: neither would have been fair.

Then there was Ventura County—seemingly a compromise between Orange and Alameda, and a neutral venue.

Several days later, Judge Weisberg addressed the issue. He heard arguments both for and against Orange County and Alameda County, and threw in Riverside County as another possibility. After hearing all of the arguments, Judge Weisberg ruled that the trial would be held in Ventura County. Ventura County officials made the decision that the trial would be held in Simi Valley. The reason for this short course in the judicial venue selection process is to make the point that Simi Valley, which has been severely criticized as a site for the trial, was selected in an appropriate fashion after consideration by at least three separate judicial arms—the state Justice Department, Judge Weisberg's court, and the Simi Valley court.

All of these legal proceedings took time. Days, weeks, and months were required to settle the matters of changing the trial site, reassigning judges, and other procedural motions. The Proposition 115 clock requiring a trial within sixty days had long since run out. So you'd think, given all this time, that a coordinated defense strategy for me and my officers would have been well established.

Not so. About three weeks before our case was to begin in Simi Valley, Mounger arranged a luncheon meeting to discuss strategies with me and the attorneys for Powell, Wind, and Briseno, all of whom had been retained by the police union. They were Michael Stone, Paul Depasquel, and John Barnett. Briseno's attorney, Barnett, declined—an early indication that solidarity might be in jeopardy—but Stone and Depasquel agreed to meet with us.

As we sat down to lunch, Mounger opened the conversation.

"We want to talk about our plans and how the case fits together," he said to Stone.

Stone replied, "What plans?"

Mounger, surprised, said, "The plan of the case. The plan of how we're going to present the case."

Stone remarked, not sarcastically but in genuine astonishment, "You don't have a plan, do you?"

Mounger looked at me, shooting Stone a glance of contempt. I knew what Mounger was thinking. Mounger and Stone had known each other for years. Stone, as a Los Angeles Police Protective League attorney, had represented Mounger years before when he was Sgt. Darryl Mounger of the LAPD. Simply put, Stone and Mounger despised each other. In fact, it was Mounger's contempt for Stone that stoked the fires within Mounger to become an attorney. If Stone could get through law school and pass the bar, Mounger reasoned, then he certainly could, too. And he did. Now, they were colleagues attempting to forge a team defense effort on one of the biggest police cases ever.

Mounger was firm with Stone. "Well, I know where I'm going to be at the end of the case. I may take different routes, but I'm starting at 'A' and going to 'Z.' "

Stone, wiping his mouth with a napkin, said he had a different tactic. "I was going to wait until we see what the DA does, and then respond to the case they put on." He seemed unconcerned.

Mounger was getting angry. "Let's talk about what they're not going to put on," he said. "They won't want to talk about PCP, they won't want to talk about use of force [policies]." What they'd want to talk about, Mounger suggested, was race and police brutality. The prosecution would talk about an innocent black man beaten with pitiless malice by four of Los Angeles's finest, Mounger theorized.

Mounger's point was this: the district attorney usually had the burden of proving guilt. But not in this case. If there ever was a case where the defendants were presumed guilty, where they had to prove their innocence, this was it. And that meant we needed an aggressive defense. We couldn't just sit back and wait to respond to the district attorney.

After lunch, Darryl and I returned to the parking lot. We discussed the rude awakening we had just experienced: Stone and Depasquel were not on board. They had no plan. They were not prepared. Could it be that they thought we were guilty and merely going through the motions of putting on a case? The obvious answer was disturbing.

Mounger ranted about his colleagues, excluding Barnett, for whom he had the highest respect. He said Stone and Depasquel were ill prepared. He then reminded me of something he had been saying since taking my case, something he always said when he got angry at Stone and feared that Stone would draw me into a guilty verdict. "We should have severed," Mounger said, again urging that I have my case tried separately from the other officers' cases.

I responded with my stock answer. "Maybe we should have, but we didn't. It was my call and I made it knowing full well the consequences." I wanted to stand trial with my officers. It was the right thing to do. And it was my belief that it was the only way a jury would find all of us not guilty. So the question was: How do we get the other attorneys on board?

Mounger and I had been working on our defense strategy for almost a year. We knew the use of force had been proper, that it had been managed and controlled, that it followed the policies, procedures, and training of the LAPD. But how were we to convince the jury of that?

About a month before our lunch with Stone and Depasquel, Mounger hit upon what would become the centerpiece of the defense strategy: the use of force could best be explained to the jury by showing Rodney King continually trying to get to his feet after assaulting Officer Powell. King's own actions made it clear that he was not an innocent victim, that he was a dangerous felony suspect intending to harm police officers engaged in a lawful arrest.

It was brilliant. Better yet, it was the truth. We then applied the theory to the George Holliday videotape, over and over and over again. It worked. We had taken the enhanced FBI version of the tape to a photographic business that could play it frame-by-frame and take a photograph of any particular frame we wished to isolate. Our case got stronger. Viewed continuously, you couldn't make out precisely what Rodney King was doing all the time. But when you isolated each frame, he could clearly be seen trying to rise to his feet. When he did so, he was struck. The enhanced videotape also revealed that when King wasn't moving, he wasn't being hit. We had the evidence to prove our innocence. And, ironically, it was the very same evidence that the district attorney intended to use to send us to jail.

After an analysis of the entire videotape, we knew that we definitely wanted the first few frames. This was the portion seldom seen by the public, the crucial first two seconds usually edited out by the media.

This portion of the tape presumably isn't dramatic enough for viewer interest in commercial television, because it shows no batons swinging on Rodney King. What it does show is Rodney King rising from a fully prone position to launch a full-charge attack on Officer Powell.

We knew that action had been fast, so fast that it was hardly discernible on the tape. But we didn't know how fast until the videotape frames were isolated. It took only six frames to reflect the two seconds—a blink of an eye—that it took for Rodney King to rise from the ground and charge into Officer Powell. We took them to a second photo shop and had the photos blown up, cropped, and backed with a foam board. We also had several other items enlarged so the jury could inspect them easily. These included LAPD training bulletins on the use of force and PCP, my sergeant's log, the Pacifica Hospital emergency room report showing that Rodney King's injuries were minor, and several other documents. But the blown-up photos of the first few frames of the George Holliday videotape were the core of our exhibit.

So Darryl and I had done our homework. We were ready. We were going to put on a dynamite case. It would be Mounger's finest hour. It was to be big-time, Olympic-class ego gratification for Darryl Mounger. He would be brilliant. He would win the case. And, in the process, he would humiliate Michael Stone.

Realizing this, it required great sacrifice for Mounger, the ultimate professional, to share this evidence with Stone, an attorney he loathed. But he did just that. Arrangements were made to have Stone, Depasquel, and Barnett, review the evidence we had put together. Again, Barnett did not attend. By now it was becoming clear that Briseno intended to cut himself loose from me, Wind, and Powell. Depasquel was impressed with what we had done, but Stone's reaction was the most gratifying. He was stunned when he saw the photographs of Rodney King's assault on Officer Powell. He was in a complete state of shock. He had seen the videotape countless times, but he had never noted the attack on Powell, his own client.

Mounger then put clear plastic overlays on the blown-up photos. With a white grease marker, I had outlined Rodney King's body in a series of photos. The blurred frames leaped to life, almost like an animated cartoon. It was finally and fully clear that Rodney King was constantly rising, constantly on the move, constantly threatening the officers.

It was as if Stone had witnessed a miracle. He looked through the other exhibits like a kid in a candy store. He couldn't get enough of them. Mounger then walked through our defense strategy. By the end of his presentation, it was obvious that Stone and Depasquel, probably for the first time, realized that a defense existed. Not only was it a valid, truthful, sustainable defense, but it was one that in all likelihood would lead to verdicts of not guilty. The presentation had done what we had hoped. It had dashed ice-cold water on Stone and Depasquel and aroused them from a defeatist attitude to a belief that we could win, that we would win. That evening was a turning point.

As the days passed, more meetings took place. A division of labor was set. It was agreed that Mounger, due to his LAPD background, would handle the use of force. This meant he would have the task of explaining the LAPD's use-of-force policies, and then have experts analyze it. To do so, he enlisted the help of two men, Sgt. Charlie Duke and retired Capt.

Robert Michael, both experts on why, when, and how force is used by the LAPD. Mounger also discovered that the DA's use-of-force experts had records on using force that were hardly unblemished. One of those experts, in fact, had been involved in a use of force that mirrored the Rodney King incident. The other had similar vulnerabilities. Their credibility wouldn't be a problem. We could destroy them on the witness stand, if that became necessary. As matters turned out, it wouldn't be, because the prosecution use-of-force witnesses never were called.

Stone was given the responsibility of handling the medical aspects of the case. This included a review of the medical reports from the two hospitals where King was treated, the rescue ambulance report, and post-treatment medical reports by private doctors.

This was a huge task, for four reasons. First, Rodney King's civil attorney, Steven Lerman, had constantly fed the media reports about how serious King's injuries were. We knew the reports weren't true, and could provide convincing evidence to sustain the point. But would the jury believe it?

Second, the taped beating appeared to be extraordinarily brutal. In fact, it was brutal. But if there's one thing the LAPD teaches its officers, it is how to beat a suspect without inflicting serious injuries. This is done by striking the legs, torso, and arms. Rodney King was not seriously injured. Still, the tape showed violence. Could we persuade a jury that it was not unnecessary?

A third crucial issue was whether Rodney King had been deliberately hit on the head with a baton. I knew I had not seen any head shots, but some of the other officers present indicated they believed they had. What did the evidence show? And, if head shots were made, were they deliberate or unintentional? If deliberate, it was deadly force and excessive. If not, it was perfectly within LAPD policy. Accidental head blows were a common occurrence, because you have situations where the officer is moving, the suspect is moving, and the baton is moving.

Here again, we encountered a problem posed by King's attorney. Steven Lerman kept feeding the media reports that the baton had struck King on the head, causing serious injuries, and the media kept parroting that assertion. We had examined the tape and knew that it did not reveal any head shot, deliberate or unintentional.

And something else we knew that everyone else had overlooked: the videotape provided evidence of how Rodney King had gotten his head injuries—by slamming face first into the asphalt three times. Stone lined up two doctors who would support our contention that King's cheekbone was fractured when he did a one-point landing on the pavement. The problem, as with all experts, was whether the judge would allow their testimony.

The fourth and final important factor delegated to Stone was an analysis of how King's injuries were reported in my sergeant's log and Powell's arrest summary. These were key to the DA's efforts to prove the allegations of false reporting. Although we were not charged with conspiracy, we knew it would be an underlying unstated theme that the prosecution would try to develop. We knew it was easy to disprove. But, again, would the jury buy the truth?

Depasquel was handed the relatively easy chore of Rodney King. That was a piece of cake. Rodney King's biography wasn't happy-face reading. Not only did he have a troublesome criminal record before March 3, 1991, his conduct afterwards had been less than exemplary. It included an arrest for picking up a transvestite prostitute and then trying to run over two LAPD vice squad cops.[5]

Everyone assumed that Rodney King would take the stand to

---

[5] These charges also were dropped, as have been all other complaints lodged against King for alleged transgressions after March 3, 1991. One of these was a complaint filed by his wife for physical assault. To arrest King, the LAPD sent a deputy chief—on a domestic-disturbance call, a call routinely handled by ordinary patrol officers. Rodney King clearly enjoys a status of special favor with the Los Angeles Police Department; he can indulge in certain types of behavior denied to all other citizens. Only when Rodney King gets out of Los Angeles and the domain of the LAPD is he at risk. This explains his most recent arrest, a July 1992 charge for driving under the influence. That arrest was made by the CHIPs in Orange County. This charge was dropped, too.

testify. District Attorney Ira Reiner made a lot of mistakes, but putting King on the stand wasn't one of them. To have put King on the stand would have been a disastrous decision, and Reiner knew it.[6]

You see, Reiner knew that King's attorney had developed a cloud of misconceptions about Rodney King. Reiner knew these misconceptions played well in the media, but wouldn't hold up in court. Reiner knew that King had not been seriously injured, and Reiner knew we could prove it. Reiner knew Rodney King hadn't suffered brain damage, and Reiner knew we could prove that too. Reiner knew King had made post-March 3 statements that were false, and Reiner knew we could impeach King's testimony based upon King's own words. Reiner knew race wasn't an issue, that Lerman had only raised the issue for his federal civil rights suit, and Reiner knew that we could prove that as well.

Also, Reiner most likely had heard several rumors we too had heard, and may have verified some or all of them. These included the rumor of the existence of a taped interview with King following his arrest for the robbery charge for which he was sent to prison. An examination of that interview and King's speech patterns before and after March 3, 1991, reportedly revealed no difference, indicating no brain damage.

A second rumor was that King's erratic speech patterns were well documented in his school records because he had been in special-education programs, again suggesting that he suffered no brain injury from the March 3, 1991, incident.

Finally, there was the rumor that Attorney Lerman was keeping Rodney King in seclusion for King's own protection, a

---

[6] The media have landed hard on Reiner for not calling King as a witness. *Time* magazine, for example, called it "the prosecution's biggest blunder" in its May 11, 1992, postmortem on the acquittal. Acknowledging that King's record would have been introduced as evidence had he testified, *Time* said that liability would be offset by compelling the jurors "to come face to face with the obscure figure in the videotape. . . ." That was the last thing Ira Reiner wanted, because he knew King would come across as precisely the type of person he is, and that his claims of serious injuries would either be watered down or pursued as perjured testimony.

rumor later reported by *Vanity Fair*, among other publications. From Rodney King's occasional interviews on television, it seemed clear to even an untrained eye that he was under the influence of medication. We strongly suspected, due to his robot-like movements and speech patterns, that he was being medicated with Librium, Thorazine, or a similar heavy-duty, behavior-modifying psychiatric drug. Rumor had it that King was being given this medication not because of injuries suffered at the hands of the LAPD, but to control his behavior because Lerman wanted to prevent Rodney King from screwing up the $56 million federal civil rights suit.

In short, the district attorney knew that Rodney King was the worst of all possible witnesses, and that the defense would rip him to bite-sized shreds on the witness stand.[7]

All of this is important because Mounger had been on record several times as stating that Rodney King's character would be an issue in the trial. Both Mounger and Depasquel were eager to put Rodney King's character on trial, because that meant the prosecution could attack my character and Officer Wind's background. And we were more than willing to compare our respective biographies with King's.

My life is on the record—Air Force veteran, working student, a bachelor's and two master's degrees, almost fifteen years on the LAPD with 94 commendations, one for personal heroism, and only three minor disciplinary actions, active member of the Catholic church, married, and a father of five children.

Tim Wind's background makes him stand out like a saint compared with Rodney King. Wind was a classic case of the goodness of the simplicity of country life versus the not-so-good complexity of modern urban society. Tim Wind is a mature and wholesome man with strong Midwestern values. Before joining the LAPD, he had several years of prior police experience, but all in small departments. He wasn't exactly

---

[7] In the pending federal civil suit, it is unlikely that King's attorney, Steven Lerman, will permit his client to take the stand for the same reasons.

Andy Griffith and Mayberry, USA, but it was close. Wind yearned for the excitement of the big city. He wanted to be the best, and was told the best was the LAPD. So he left the country and came to the big city. He had been out of the Police Academy only three months on March 3, 1991.[8]

Yet our eagerness to compare life histories and lifestyles with Rodney King before a jury posed a knotty legal problem. All four defendants were being tried together. But we were also separated; each defendant had his own defense. If Wind and I elected to attack Rodney King's character, then we placed our own characters up for inspection. No problem there. But it did pose a problem for Ted Briseno and Larry Powell. Briseno had a previous sixty-six–day suspension for excessive force because he had kicked a handcuffed suspect. And there were reports of Briseno's alleged abusive behavior in a prior marriage. Powell, too, was vulnerable. He had been accused of excessive force several times. Although no disciplinary action had been taken, the suspicion of bad behavior could be planted in the jurors' minds. We'd have to wait and see how the judge would rule on this. Would he allow character evidence to benefit all defendants and limit prosecution attacks to only those defendants who raised the character issue? Or would he allow character evidence to benefit all defendants only if all defendants' characters were opened to prosecution probing?

Rodney King's character and other matters involving procedural issues would have to await the trial, though. The important point was that we had a strategy set and we were ready to be heard. The next step was to try to get as impartial a jury as could possibly be found in Simi Valley. Ventura County might not be as bad as Alameda County and Oakland, or as good as Orange County. But it was an acceptable compromise, and we were ready to begin.

---

[8] The impact of the incident has been more harmful to Tim Wind than to any other officer involved, I believe. It is disgraceful that such a potentially valuable, committed police officer should lose a career to deceit, political cynicism, misrepresentation of the truth, and betrayal by his superiors.

Choosing a Jury

As Darryl Mounger and I neared the Simi Valley Courthouse for the first day of jury selection, we were surprised by the army of news reporters, photographers, and videocams that had descended on the scene. The dirt parking lot next to the courthouse had been transformed into a media staging area. Cars, vans, trailers, and trucks bearing microwave satellite transmission dishes had been pulled into the parking lot. You could have provided central communications for a world war from Simi Valley that day.

As we pulled into the paved parking area next to the media lot, we were spied by reporters. A microphone- and camera-wielding throng rushed to the car. It was the American version of the Italian paparazzi. The crowd was so thick Mounger and I had a difficult time opening our car doors. Reporters were banging their bodies and camera equipment into his car. Mounger got angry. He shouted, "You hit my car again and we're going to have another Rodney King beating." I sympathized with Mounger, but thought his analogy extremely inappropriate.

The camera shutters were going crazy. All of the reporters were shouting questions simultaneously. It was a zoo. We slowly inched our way to the courthouse. The media mob was so intent on doing their jobs that they cast safety aside. Cameramen tripped and fell to the ground, and their colleagues stampeded all over them. Appeals for reason and safety fell on deaf ears.

After the first day, Judge Weisberg intervened. He limited the media to an area outside the courthouse doors we entered each day. From then on, we daily ran a gauntlet of reporters when arriving at court. But the limitation effectively allowed the reporters to do their job, and it eliminated the media feeding frenzy whenever an interviewable warm body appeared.

Ventura County officials had sent out two thousand subpoenas for jury duty on this trial. To accommodate the hundreds of jurors reporting, Judge Weisberg moved his court to a large upstairs room. In all, about five hundred potential jurors were available for the trial. Judge Weisberg exhibited exceptional management ability in culling through the names. Over the course of the next several days, he demonstrated remarkable patience and compassion in balancing the needs of potential jurors and our right to a fair trial. He discharged about half of the roughly five hundred jurors due to their requests for a hardship exemption. To the remaining 250, he handed out a thirty-page, two hundred-item questionnaire to determine their beliefs about the issues involved in the trial, their personal biases, and their exposure to pretrial publicity. The questionnaire had been written by the prosecution, the defense attorneys, and the judge. The responses, Judge Weisberg's personal *voir dire*, and scrutiny by the prosecution and defense would act as the filters to determine the twelve jurors and six alternates.

It was at this time that the media began to make a major issue of a supposed rift between Briseno and Powell, Wind, and me. Jokingly, but not altogether so, Briseno's attorney, Barnett, was referred to by us as the third prosecutor. If so, he was a far better prosecutor than the primary assistant DAs assigned to the case, Terry White and Alan Yochelson, combined. While it was true that each defendant had his own defense attorney, it was also obvious from pretrial pleadings and other signals that Briseno had not aligned himself with either me or the other defendants. Rumors persisted that Briseno had made some kind of deal early on with the DA. The rumors were stoked by the media's so-called "legal experts," who reasoned that the only reason Briseno had been charged at all was as a tactic by the DA to ensure a conviction of the rest of us.

Maybe all of this was true. As the trial progressed, it certainly seemed so. Still, John Barnett had a good working relationship with—and, I suspect, a healthy respect for—Darryl Mounger, although he might have had difficulties with Stone and Depasquel. Despite the differences, all of us actually cooperated on many issues of mutual interest. This was most evident in the jury selection process.

Barnett took the initiative in selecting a jury. He recom-
mended a grading system for jurors. It was a 0–5 point system,
based primarily upon the questionnaires. Among other things,
potential jurors were asked about their experiences with the
Los Angeles Police Department, how much they knew about
the Rodney King incident, their personal and educational
backgrounds, their professions, and other information that
could provide insights into their individual characters and
beliefs. From our grading system, the best juror was a zero; the
worst, a five. Each defendant and attorney reviewed the juror
questionnaires and rated the potential panelist.

We were willing to take any juror between zero and three.
About 65 to 70 percent of the 250 jurors fell into this category.
We definitely had more "good" jurors than "bad" ones. Also,
given the random jury listing developed by Judge Weisberg,
which will be explained in a moment, we had large pockets of
"good" jurors before encountering a pocket of "bad" jurors.
Altogether, the average rating of jurors was about a two. Needless to say, we were very pleased with the potential panel.

In my case, Mounger and I were generally looking for an
older individual, preferably fifty years of age or older, who had
a stable life and an investment in the community. But it was
not an exact process, and we did allow personal biases to enter
into the decision. For example, Mounger insisted that we exclude all Libras; he believed they were fickle and could be
easily swayed by more forceful jurors. He also insisted that we
get a particular female Hispanic on the jury; she seemed like
the salt-of-the-earth type of person we wanted, even if she
didn't fit all of the profile. I agreed.[9] Once the ratings from
juror profiles were made, Barnett put the information into his
computer.

In the meantime, Judge Weisberg had developed a random

---

[9] She was selected as a juror, although Larry Powell probably will never forgive
us. That's because she wound up being the juror who hung on Powell's one
count and convinced three of her colleagues to her point of view. This led to the
jury's inability to reach a unanimous decision on one count and thus resulted
in a mistrial for Officer Powell.

list of jurors, from one through 250. That is how they would be culled, starting with number one and going through number 250. This is important in regard to the charge that racial bias permeated the jury-selection process. Race was not a factor. Even if all of the peremptory challenges allowed by the defense, prosecution, and Judge Weisberg had been exercised, there still wouldn't have been any blacks on the jury. That's because the random selection put most of the qualified blacks so near the end of the random list of 250 that they couldn't have been chosen.

The media and the black community have made a big issue about the absence of black representation on the jury, and how, consequently, there could be no fair trial for Rodney King. This was sheer nonsense, an example of the twisted logic some minority leaders and their political allies were able to impose upon the public through an eagerly receptive media. Why was it misguided?

For openers, Rodney King, a black man, wasn't on trial. Four police officers, all white, were on trial. The Constitution requires a jury of peers, and the Simi Valley panelists were largely our peers, not King's peers. This is not to say that blacks were not included as our peers. The inclusion or exclusion of blacks on the jury was not part of our criteria for a fair trial. Our basic criterion was the juror ranking system, not race.

Of the approximately five hundred jurors who responded to subpoenas, only about fifteen to twenty were black. Statistics reported in the media indicated that blacks represented about 2 percent of Ventura County's population. What this means is that the number of potential black jurors was about 4 percent of all jurors, or twice the ratio of blacks in the Ventura County population as a whole.[10]

So the question occurs: Why were there no blacks on the jury? One reason was that most of the blacks excluded themselves due to hardship pleadings; many jurors could not serve

---

[10] Although 2,000 subpoenas had been mailed, about 250 potential jurors showed up each day. Judge Weisberg used only the first 500, and never got to the remaining 1,500.

during a long trial without hardship to family and work. Another reason was the admitted bias of other prospective black jurors. They honestly stated that they were prejudiced against the police officers and could not live up to their obligation to impartiality. This spoke highly of the integrity of these potential jurors.

These weren't the only reasons, though. Early on in the case, black activists made it quite clear that they intended to monitor the trial closely to ensure that "justice" was done. "Justice," of course, meant a guilty verdict, not a fair trial; it was a lynch-mob mentality. Several minority organizations, such as the NAACP, and influential black leaders, such as John Mack, head of the Los Angeles Urban League, made frequent pilgrimages to the Simi Valley Courthouse to make their presence known. It was their right, and they freely exercised it.

But by design or overzealous commitment, one individual (not a potential juror) contacted several blacks on the jury list and spoke with them. Whether these were innocent chats or something more sinister was never revealed, and the issues of motive and affiliation were never fully resolved. But the black potential jurors that had been contacted told the district attorney, who in turn advised the defense and Judge Weisberg. Judge Weisberg considered potential jury tampering a very serious breach, and he conducted a hearing in open court in an effort to get to the bottom of the matter. The potential jurors and the person involved took the stand and testified. No wrongdoing was uncovered, but Judge Weisberg ordered the individual to have no further contact with the panelists. The district attorney sought to exclude the entire panel, but Judge Weisberg refused.

After this incident, several blacks remained in the jury pool, but only two were within range of being potential jurors, according to our ranking system. One was an elderly female. All of the defendants had rated her as average to low, without knowledge of her race. She had been one of the potential jurors approached by the individual. We were not pleased with her responses to those contacts, and so we excluded her. The only other black within our acceptable range was a young man. The answers on his questionnaire put him in the midrange, again without knowledge of his race. We seriously considered him as a possibility. But after his responses to Judge Weisberg's questions, we elected to exclude him, a decision we made with many other jurors, regardless of race.

All in all, the rating system served us well. And it contained some intriguing data. I computed, for example, some quick statistics on media influence on potential jurors. Approximately 25 percent of the 250 juror questionnaires indicated that they had made up their minds on the basis of media coverage, were predisposed to find us guilty, and did not believe anything could be brought to their attention that could change their minds. That's a disturbing statistic—25 percent. It says something about the power of the media and the concept of trial by media. It causes one to wonder how many innocent defendants the media have helped send to prison by inaccurate or biased reporting.[11]

Before the trial, District Attorney Ira Reiner and his assistant, Terry White, said they had no problem with the change of trial location. They said they could try the case anywhere in California and were confident that a jury would find us guilty. But this didn't seem to be the case when Assistant DAs White and Yochelson got into jury selection. Curiously, they kept rejecting certain jurors we found unacceptable, and allowing jurors we wanted. We couldn't figure out the DA's logic.

After several such incidences, it started to become embarrassing to the prosecution. Even the media began to rumble. But all that aside, the district attorney finally accepted a jury of twelve panelists and six alternates.

Remember: if the prosecution hadn't been pleased with the jury composition, it had plenty of exclusions left to use; the

---

[11] Almost every one of the eighteen people chosen as jurors and alternates revealed the same preconceived notion of our guilt. But there was an important distinction: each person chosen as a juror or alternate expressed a belief that he or she could set aside his media-imposed bias and decide the case on the facts, law, and evidence as presented in court, not on what he or she had been conditioned to believe by the media.

district attorney had used only about half of the prosecution's approximately thirty-five allowed exclusions. Assistant DA White later complained that he didn't get a single person he wanted on the jury. Well, if he didn't like it, why did he accept it? The question would become even more important as the case progressed and the prosecution got weaker. The complaints about the jury were, and are, nothing more than a feeble attempt to explain how the DA office blew a case that it and the media considered a walk in the park. After all, the Rodney King incident was captured on videotape, there for everybody to see. And doesn't everybody know that your eyes can't lie? But, then, how about that old country song, "Don't Believe Your Lyin' Eyes"?

And so, in the trial's second week Judge Weisberg swore in the twelve jurors and six alternates who had been selected after the time-consuming process of questionnaire completion and *voir dire*. Our jury consisted of six men and six women. The panel included one Filipino, one Hispanic, a printer, a retired teacher, a maintenance worker, and a retired real estate broker. Three had worked as security guards or served in the U.S. military. Three others were members of the National Rifle Association. One was the brother of a retired LAPD sergeant.[12]

The judge admonished the jurors about reading, watching, or listening to media coverage about the case. He told them they would not be sequestered—legal language for being confined to a hotel room, away from newspapers, TV, and radios—during the trial, but that they would be sequestered once deliberations began.

At last, an appropriate forum—the court, not the media, would hear our case. We had been beaten badly by the media for more than a year; we had taken a tremendous pummeling. It was now our turn to fight back.

---

[12] It may be unbecoming to offer this thought, but why the prosecution allowed the relative of a former Los Angeles police officer on the jury is baffling. The defense, of course, was delighted, but was the prosecution asleep at the switch during jury selection? The question begs an answer.

Arguing a Case—and Winning

DAY ONE

A criminal trial in the United States is a stylized ritual, much like Japanese Kabuki theater or Italian opera. Minor variations in trial procedures may be found from state to state, but the basic format is generally the same. After jury selection, the court convenes, the indictments are read, and the defendants' formal pleas are read to the court. The prosecution then makes an opening statement, telling the jury what it's going to hear, what heinous villains the defendants are, and why they should be isolated from society. The defense responds with its opening statement, pointing out the erroneous, unfair judgments the prosecution has made and why decency and common sense require a finding that the accused parties are innocent. After the opening arguments, the prosecution puts on its case, following which the defense presents its side of the story. Closing arguments by both sides summarize everything that's gone before. Then it's up to the jury.

The opening statements are posturing, of course, but they serve a useful purpose in advising the prosecution, the defense, and the jury what to expect.

What we didn't expect was the opening statement made by the prosecution. It could almost have been made by the defense. Assistant DA Terry White began by telling the jury how Officers Melanie and Tim Singer ran across Rodney King on March 3, 1991. (Or, perhaps more accurately, how Rodney King ran across the Singers.)

Then White began making our case for us. He told the jury that the evidence would show that Rodney King was driving at a speed of about 115 miles per hour, that he ignored police sirens and flashing lights, that he committed multiple traffic violations, including running stop signs and red lights. White conceded that King and his companions had been drinking earlier in the evening and readily admitted that King was intoxicated at the time of the incident.

After being stopped, Rodney King didn't cooperate with the

police, White stated. White further conceded that King could not be controlled by the officers. Finally, White did not dispute that, although flat on the ground for a time, Rodney King rose and either attacked Officer Powell or sought to run away.

As to the charges of excessive force, White was dry and almost deadly dull. He said the evidence would show that Rodney King was not aggressive, not resisting arrest, and that the beating continued for no justifiable reason. White went on to say that the evidence would show that Rodney King was TASED, but that the TASER darts didn't work, that they didn't deliver the intended fifty thousand volts of electricity. (We would counter that argument.) White also said that CHIP Officer Melanie Singer would testify that Powell repeatedly struck Rodney King in the head (which we also would dispute).

White then played the dramatic George Holliday videotape. It was precisely what we wanted. The videotape was now in evidence, and we could dissect it with devastating precision when our turn came.

After playing the eighty-two-second tape, White said the evidence would show that the other officers and I tried to cover up the incident by falsifying the arrest report and sergeant's log, and that there were contradictions in how we officially described the incident. The assistant DA said my log was "an absurdity" when compared to the Holliday videotape. White specifically noted my reference to Rodney King's injuries as relatively minor, and that his facial cuts were a result of his hitting the asphalt.

White's opening statement took about forty-five minutes. After he had finished, our attorneys were pleased. From our perspective, it was the best possible opening. It was dry, apologetic, and almost somnambulant. More importantly, White had conceded several key issues—especially concerning Rodney King's behavior and actions—that we did not think the prosecution would easily grant.

After White had finished, it was our turn. Since it was a four-defendant case, it was agreed that Mounger would lead the opening argument, even though he was the least experienced of the defense-team lawyers. (He had been an attorney for only

two years, and had only one prior jury trial under his belt.)
Mounger would be followed by Stone for Officer Powell, Depasquel for Officer Wind, and Barnett for Officer Briseno.

Speaking for twenty minutes without notes, Mounger told
the jury how our evidence would be presented. We would be
using witnesses, physical evidence, rulings by the court, and
common sense. He told the jury the evidence would show the
force seen on the Holliday videotape was reasonable and necessary.

Mounger told the jury about my background, a veteran officer with fourteen and-a-half years on the LAPD and thirteen
on the streets of Los Angeles. He told the jury that I was *not* in
charge of the situation on March 3, 1991, but that Rodney King
was in charge of the situation. He told the panelists that I *was*
in charge of the officers, because that's what a sergeant does—
he oversees officers.

Then Mounger presented a different view of how the Rodney
King arrest unfolded. He gave a police officer's view. It was
after midnight. The California Highway Patrol chased a speeding car that refused to stop, and asked for help. Three suspects
were in the car, and there were only two CHIP officers.
Mounger posed the question all officers ask when they are
involved in a pursuit, especially at night: Why weren't the
suspects pulling over? What had they done that they did not
want the police to learn?[13]

---

[13] Mounger would have loved to have told the jury the reason: Rodney King had
just gotten out of prison on parole and he was in violation of his parole. If
stopped and captured, Rodney King would have been sent back to prison for
parole violations. He was also under the influence of alcohol, had marijuana
in his system, and was in association with other ex-cons. It meant 365 more
days in the slammer. No time off for good behavior, no early out, just one year
in prison. Simply put, King did not like prison, and Rodney King didn't want
to go back. But Mounger couldn't tell the jury all of this because my officers
and I didn't know it when the incident occurred. We were bound by facts
known to us at the time.

Another point. Even the prosecution conceded facts that proved parole
violation by drinking, associating with ex-cons, and felony evading. Yet King
is a charmed character. His parole has not been revoked. And charges of felony
evading conceded by the DA were dropped.

The jury was told that King and his companions had to be regarded as desperate felony evaders, willing to risk injury to themselves, the officers, and the public. The experience of the officers, Mounger said, rarely included somebody who evaded police because of misdemeanors or minor infractions, like trying to escape a traffic ticket.

Mounger then outlined what happened after King stopped, the tactical plan I formed. He began laying the groundwork for a key element in our defense—the proper use of force under LAPD policies, procedures, and training. He displayed a use-of-force chart showing the options available for LAPD officers in subduing an uneager suspect. There were only six:

1. Physical presence.
2. Verbalization—commands.
3. Physical contact—the swarm.
4. The TASER.
5. Striking the suspect with batons, kick.
6. Deadly force: the chokehold or a gun.

Mounger explained to the jury that physical presence had no effect on Rodney King. Verbal orders had been ignored. The swarm too had failed. The TASER was used twice without success, two and a-half times if you count the extra surge of power applied after the second TASER cartridge had been used. Finally, the metal PR 24 baton was employed extensively to beat the suspect. Mounger concluded by stating that the only remaining option was deadly force. It was the one option that I and my officers wanted to avoid.

Mounger was followed by Stone, who specifically addressed the issue of whether Officer Powell had struck Rodney King in the head. He told the jury that medical evidence would refute Officer Melanie Singer's testimony that she saw King hit in the head. Stone also began getting the jury accustomed to our interpretation of the George Holliday videotape. He put up photographic exhibits of the videotape frames, and then added outline overlays clearly demonstrating that Rodney King was repeatedly on the rise. This was important, because it was the centerpiece of our argument—that Rodney King was in control of the situation, not the officers. The photos showed that, at any time, he could have complied with our legal orders and been handcuffed without incident, as his two passengers were.

Then, suspecting but not yet sure that Officer Ted Briseno was going to make his own deal with the prosecution, Stone split the sheets between Briseno and the rest of us. Trying to neutralize Briseno's suspected defection, he told the jury that Briseno never stopped to intervene in the beating. He explained that the only time Briseno said, "Stop," was when Wind and Powell were in danger of getting zapped by the final surge of electricity I was applying through the TASER. Moreover, Stone said, if Briseno was intent upon stopping the violence, why did he step forward and stomp Rodney King between the shoulder blades when King appeared to be reaching into his waistband, possibly for a weapon? Stone let the jury ponder the question.

Depasquel was next in line, on behalf of Tim Wind. He was more brief than Mounger and Stone. He merely related Wind's background, and reminded the jury that Wind was a probationer, only a few months out of the Police Academy. Depasquel noted that, at the time of the incident, Officer Wind was under the supervision of both Officer Powell, who was his training officer, and me, the supervising field sergeant. Wind's use of the baton and other measures of force—the stomp, or shove with a foot, for example—were strictly within LAPD training and guidelines. In short, when Officer Wind used his batons and kicks, he was doing as he had been taught and as he was ordered.

Finally, Barnett delivered the last opening statement. His client was Ted Briseno. If Stone split the sheets between Briseno and the rest of us, Barnett broke the bed.

Aggressively, in a tone of controlled rage, Barnett said the evidence would show that Rodney King charged Powell. For emphasis, Barnett picked up Powell's metal baton and began slapping it against the palm of his hand. Then, raising his voice, Barnett said Powell hit King in the face with the baton. Powell continued to strike King with a torrent of blows, many of them to the face, Barnett stated.

Then Barnett explained the role he said Briseno had played. He claimed that Briseno had tried to stop Powell, that he pushed Powell back because he feared for Rodney King's safety. Briseno took this action at great risk to himself, Barnett argued, because Powell almost struck Briseno in the head. Barnett said Officer Briseno yelled at King to stay down—not as an order to be cuffed, but because Powell wouldn't stop hitting King and Briseno reasoned that perhaps this tactic would "stop the relentless beating." Barnett had a curious explanation for Briseno's foot-stomp on Rodney King's back. It was done, Barnett told the jury, in an effort to keep Rodney King down and thus stop the baton blows.

According to Barnett, Briseno believed the incident was out of control—all he was trying to do was to protect Rodney King without endangering his own safety. Briseno wanted only to cuff Rodney King and get him in custody so King would not be hit any more with batons. So said Barnett, ending the defense's opening statements.

Most of the trial's first day was devoted to these opening arguments. But three prosecution witnesses were also heard.

The first was star cameraman George Holliday, who testified that yes, he had shot the tape, and yes, it appeared to be a true illustration of what he had seen happen across the street from his apartment on March 3, 1991. Holliday testified that he had heard shouts, like officers yelling commands, but could not make out any particular words.

Next up for the prosecution on Day One was Bryant Allen, one of the two passengers riding with Rodney King that night.[14]

Allen said he and King had known each other since they were kids. He said Rodney King picked him up at his house about five or six o'clock on the evening of March 2. About two

---

[14] The reader will recall that by this time Freddy Helms, King's other passenger that night, was dead as a result of a traffic accident.

hours later, they picked up Freddy Helms, then went to a liquor store where each purchased a 40-oz. bottle of beer. Over the course of the evening they drank the beer, Allen testified.

Allen said he recalled the police lights once the chase started, but didn't hear a siren. When he did become aware of the pursuit, Allen said, he asked Rodney King to stop. King didn't do so, but continued to drive in a go-stop-go-stop fashion. Allen said he repeatedly yelled at King to stop, and King finally did so.

Once out of the car in response to police commands, Bryant Allen said, because of the helicopter overhead he couldn't hear, nor could he see Rodney King. But he could hear hollering and screaming. He said he and Helms were cuffed and taken to a police car, then released. He said he didn't see King again that evening.

Upon cross-examination, Allen was emphatic that only three 40-oz. bottles of beer were consumed, and this was done by 8 P.M. They were feeling "comfortable," he said, but none felt the effects of alcohol.

A key point Barnett brought out in cross-examination was that Allen believed Rodney King's behavior was "strange" that evening. He said it was as if King were in a trance and not responding. He had known King since they were youths, he said, and he had never seen King act this way. He testified that King was acting so strangely that he, Bryant Allen, was worried and seriously considered jumping out of the car, but King was driving too fast. Allen said he yelled and pleaded with King to stop, but it did no good.

Depasquel's line of questioning addressed Bryant Allen's past, his credibility as a witness. Under cross-examination, Allen admitted he was an ex-convict, sent to prison for robbery. Depasquel sought to have Allen admit that he had also been convicted of burglary, but Allen said he didn't know what burglary was. At this point, the assistant DA sought damage control to avoid embarrassing Allen. The prosecution stipulated to the court that Bryant Allen had, indeed, also been convicted for burglary.

The final witness on the first day was Sgt. Robert Ontiveros, a longtime Foothill Division cop who knew all of the LAPD players. His only role was to identify the defendant officers on the Holliday videotape.

DAY TWO

CHIP Officer Melanie Singer was a cornerstone of the prosecution case. That was because she had testified earlier, at the grand jury proceedings, that I had taken over the arrest without cause, that Powell had repeatedly struck Rodney King with head shots, and that it appeared to her that the level of force used to subdue King was excessive.

Assistant DA Terry White conducted the examination and tried to portray her as a veteran officer, familiar with using force and arresting suspects in the proper manner. But as Officer Melanie Singer testified, it became obvious that she was inexperienced. First, she was stiff and nervous. It could have been the publicity. After all, she was now on local, national, and international television. Whatever the reason, she came across as well rehearsed. Perhaps too well rehearsed, almost a RoboCop witness.

She told about how they had encountered Rodney King and what happened afterwards. She said she reached a speed of 115 miles per hours and believed King was still pulling away from her. She was emphatic about that point.[15]

But during her testimony, Assistant DA White unwittingly helped the defense by undermining her experience. For example, she said she wanted to pull King over, but her partner/ husband advised against doing so. She was traveling about

---

[15] The media made much over whether King's Hyundai Excel could go this fast. Two points are important here. First, why was Melanie Singer so insistent on the 115 miles per hour figure? It was because the speedometer on the cruiser she was driving that night tops out at 115 miles per hour, and she had the accelerator to the floor and was unable to catch up with Rodney King until he slowed to about 80 miles per hour because of increasing traffic. The second point is that the speedometer on King's Hyundai was pegged at 120 miles per hour top speed, indicating that the manufacturer, at least, believed 115 was an attainable velocity.

eighty miles per hour, but was within only a few car lengths of King's vehicle. This was clearly unsafe. She wanted to stop King before checking on whether the auto was stolen or wanted on outstanding warrants, another sign of an inexperienced officer. Her more experienced husband had issued a call for LAPD assistance. All this testimony suggested that she was not in control when the incident occurred.

Melanie Singer testified that her partner advised the school district police that the suspects were wanted for speeding only. This was an important point, because it revealed the mindset of CHIPs. They were trained to think only in terms of vehicle-code violations, their primary responsibility. Also, she testified that she had planned to issue Rodney King a ticket for not wearing a seat belt—testimony that directly contradicted an earlier assertion by Bryant Allen that King had a seat belt fastened.

At this juncture, White tried to make the point that the CHIP officers had begun the pursuit and asked for help, but had not turned the arrest over to the LAPD. He was trying to demonstrate overeagerness on our part and that the CHIPs should have been permitted to handle the arrest without LAPD interference. He insinuated that the LAPD cops conspired to cover up a planned felonious act, clearly a silly argument since it would have required enormous cooperation among a score of officers from three different police agencies. White's arguments were useless and without foundation, and the jury knew it. The jurors knew the LAPD got involved because Melanie Singer couldn't control what was happening.

Officer Melanie Singer then testified that after a delay, Rodney King kicked open the driver's door and made a rocking motion to get out of the car. (At some point the two other passengers got out, but she said she couldn't recall when this happened.) She said Rodney King faced the officers and began smiling, acting as though he were in a jovial mood. He ignored orders to prone himself out on the ground. He pointed to the helicopter and waved. He then turned his butt to Melanie Singer and shook it. She said she took this as indicating that something was wrong, so she drew her weapon, pointed it at

King, and commanded him to get down on the ground. King continued to dance around, she continued, but then finally got down on his hands and knees, almost in a push-up position.

At this point, Melanie Singer said she made her move. She approached King, pistol drawn as dictated by CHIP policy and training, and when she was within about five feet of Rodney King, she said, a sergeant, whom she later identified as me, ordered her to get back and told her the LAPD would handle it. She testified that I did not give an explanation, but appeared to have a diversionary tactic and a plan to put into motion. She said she still believed it was a CHIP matter, but complied with the order because it came from a sergeant.

As she withdrew, she said she saw two LAPD officers approach Rodney King—Officer Powell grabbed King's left wrist, and an officer unknown to her grabbed the right wrist. Rodney King was rigid, she said, and he pulled away, rolling left and right, and then jumped up. She said that a cluster of "six or so" LAPD officers "came out of nowhere," and without being given any commands, attempted to get King under control, but were unable to do so. King flung his arms about, she continued, trying to throw off the officers, and with a back-hand motion struck one officer in the chest. She stated that the sergeant (me) repeatedly commanded King to stop resisting, but King ignored the orders. Then, she said, the officers were ordered by the sergeant to back away.

At this point, she testified, after King ignored more commands to prone out, the sergeant fired a TASER and it hit King in the back, on the right side. She heard King scream and moan, but he was still standing. Again the sergeant ordered King to the ground, to get down, she said. King refused, and instead moved toward the sergeant. Then a second TASER was fired, striking King in the upper chest area. King was like a monster, Melanie Singer testified. He staggered. He fell to his knees. Then Powell came in from the right side and delivered a power blow with his baton to the right side of Rodney King's face. According to her testimony, the impact split his face from the right ear to the jaw, and blood poured out. She said that King screamed, reached up, and covered his face with his hands. King was then hit a second time across the knuckles by Powell, then a third, fourth, and fifth time on the left side of his head, she testified.

White made sure that Melanie Singer emphasized that these blows were to Rodney King's head, power strokes delivered with all the strength Powell could muster.

After Powell had hit King in the left temple, she testified, the sergeant intervened, saying something like, "Stop, stop, that's enough!" Then, she said, Officer Briseno reached up and grabbed Powell's palm. It was her perception that the sergeant and Officer Briseno had stopped the beating, that the incident was over, the situation under control, and King would be taken into custody. At this point, she said, she went to the other side of King's vehicle to help take the other two suspects into custody.

She went on to say that afterwards, she saw King before he was taken to the hospital. She said he was cuffed and bound, his face covered in blood. Although King was quiet, he mumbled and garbled his words but he wasn't hostile. The sergeant, she stated, told her the LAPD would handle the arrest due to the extent of the injuries to the suspect. There was never any mention of PCP, she said.

White wound down his examination of Officer Melanie Singer by asking how many drunk drivers she had arrested. She said between three hundred and four hundred. After stopping Rodney King, White asked what charge she planned to lodge against him. She responded: DUI (driving under the influence).

White concluded with this, his key witness, by having Officer Melanie Singer demonstrate with a PR 24 metal baton the strikes she said she saw Powell deliver to King's head and hands as King covered his face.

It was late in the day, and the defense attorneys were eager to cross-examine Melanie Singer. They wanted to run the clock until the end of the day, then begin a fresh assault the next morning. Once again, we would use our strategy of turning the prosecution witnesses into defense witnesses once they were on the stand. Officer Melanie Singer had made some serious allegations against Officer Powell. It fell to Powell's attorney, Stone, to use his talents. It was a task he relished.

Stone started off very low key. He had Officer Melanie Singer confirm that she had her baton with her, but never took it out of the ring on her belt. He verified it was CHIP policy to approach a suspect with gun in hand—a tactic avoided by the LAPD. He also spoke of her excitement during the pursuit, and she admitted that her adrenalin was pumping. But she said she was in control. She had used her baton before, and was proficient in its use, but she admitted that she had never seen full power strokes to an individual's head prior to March 3, 1991.

After this initial banter, Stone got tough. He moved, spider-like, to lure Melanie Singer into his web. He got her to increase the number of head blows from five to seven. The significance of this was lost on Melanie Singer, but any cop who's ever been involved in a use-of-force inquiry knows it is very significant. That's because if the evidence were to show a lack of injuries—which was the case with Rodney King, although Melanie Singer didn't know it at the time—the credibility of the witness is sharply diminished; a contradiction exists between what the witness perceived and what the facts and evidence prove. The bigger the discrepancy, the more unbelievable the witness. Melanie Singer was about to become a totally worthless prosecution witness.

Stone emphasized the number of blows—seven; she confirmed it.

He asked if they had been delivered with a metal PR 24 baton; yes, she answered.

Did the blows strike the head, Stone asked, and were they full power strokes? Yes, Officer Melanie Singer responded.

Afterwards, did King have any difficulty carrying on a conversation, was he coherent? Melanie Singer got more entangled in the web Stone was weaving. No, he had no difficulty talking, and yes, he was coherent, she answered.

Stone paused for a long moment to let the jury absorb what she had said. You don't have to be a rocket scientist to realize that somebody struck in the head seven times with a metal PR 24 baton—the equivalent of being hit seven times with a piece of galvanized steel pipe one inch in diameter—is going to have trouble carrying on a conversation. That's because somebody so struck will probably be either comatose or dead. Yet Melanie Singer had testified that Rodney King was not physically impaired.

Stone then showed Melanie Singer the prosecution's photo display of Rodney King, pictures taken within days of the incident. He had her admit that she had previously seen the distinctive marks left by a PR 24 baton when it makes contact with an individual's body. And she verified that no such marks existed on Rodney King's hands, where she said Powell's baton had fallen with full power. Stone pressed the point. She insisted that "I saw what I saw." It was a weak statement.[16]

By this time, Melanie Singer no doubt wished the examination were over. But it wasn't. Stone was an advocate possessed. He was intent on destroying every point of Melanie Singer's testimony.

He asked her about the George Holliday videotape. She acknowledged seeing it at the CHIP station on March 5, 1991. But when asked about the portions showing Rodney King's attack on Powell, as well as the absence of anything showing that Powell had delivered head shots to Rodney King, she backed away. After being shown the unedited videotape, she acknowledged: "I didn't see any of that."

Melanie Singer was frustrated and confused. She was unable to explain the paradox between what she recalled and what was on the video. So she gave what she believed to be the only logical answer—the blows were struck before the video started.

This was the response Stone had sought. She was trapped. Now he moved in for the kill. He had her verify that the blows

---

[16] Although not shown to the jury, Stone was ready to play a videotape of Rodney King's initial interview upon release from jail. In the interview King gave a completely contradictory description of the events as testified to by even the prosecution witnesses. More importantly, the videotape shows King adroitly moving his hands and fingers. There was no indication that the fingers, which are easily broken, had suffered any trauma, much less been power-stroked with a metal baton.

she had seen were struck before the George Holliday videotape began. Stone knew very well that the evidence, and her own testimony, would refute this argument.

Stone played the enhanced FBI version of the videotape. He then had Melanie Singer do a version of "Where's Waldo?" except in this case it was "Where's Melanie?" in the Holliday videotape.

She identified herself and her partner/husband on the right side of the TV screen. She said she had no memory of seeing King attack Powell at the scene. But on the video, before her very eyes, she saw herself and she saw King rise to his feet and rush Powell. It was extremely damaging testimony for the prosecution. She wasn't a credible witness.

Day Two was almost over. Mounger had a few more questions for Melanie Singer, but nothing dramatic. Stone, though, wasn't through. He'd be back on Day Three to shred the remaining credibility of Officer Melanie Singer's testimony.

DAYS THREE AND FOUR

When Judge Weisberg began the proceedings the next day, Michael Stone swung toward the witness stand and Melanie Singer. He produced a large photo of Rodney King's face. The picture had been taken a day or two after the incident. The photo showed no visible sign of injury. Stone reviewed her testimony—that Powell had struck Rodney King at least seven times, once on the right side of the head, once on the fingers, and five times to the left side of the head.

These were the blows Stone wanted Melanie Singer to identify. He provided red sticky-tabs for Melanie Singer to mark on the photo where each of Powell's alleged blows had landed. She took the tabs. She examined the photograph for any signs of injury. Finding none, she began placing the tabs. One went to the nose. Another was placed on the end of the eyebrow. A third was on the temple.

Then she realized the absurdity of what she was doing. She was putting tabs on places where no injuries were evident. The

jury realized it before she did. So she began again. She put
the next two tabs on parts of King's head that were covered by
hair. She must have reasoned that the hair might conceal the
injuries. Stone didn't even need to comment on what the jury
had just seen.

Stone then moved to his next topic. Actually, it was a continuation of where he'd left off on Day Two—with the George
Holliday videotape. He began playing the tape, then stopped it
at the frame where Powell first struck Rodney King with his
baton after being assaulted. This was the blow that Melanie
Singer said had opened up Rodney King's face from ear to chin.

That was bad enough for the prosecution by itself, because
Melanie Singer had testified the previous day that all of the
blows were struck before the videotape began. But worse,
Stone then showed Melanie Singer and the jury photos taken of
Rodney King immediately after the incident. They showed
that he had baton marks on his arms, but none was visible on
his hands. And his face wasn't split open from ear to chin.

Stone then produced a blow-up of Powell's seven-page arrest
report. Five pages had been written by Powell, and two by
Officer Tim Singer. The significance of this was lost on the
jury at this time, but Stone later pointed it out: if Powell had
lied on his report, as the prosecution claimed, then did it make
any sense for Powell to attach Tim Singer's report to his own
summary of the incident?

With this, Stone began a line-by-line reading of the arrest
report. As he did so, he had Melanie Singer identify the observed traffic violations—speeding, unsafe lane changes, two
unsafe turning movements, failure to yield, failure to stop at
a posted stop sign, failure to stop for a red light. The list
went on and on and on, serious traffic violations numbering
in the high teens to low twenties. Even the news media, who
had often portrayed Rodney King as a "motorist," were hard
pressed not to admit that Rodney King was a menace to public
safety that night.

Slowly, methodically, Stone chipped away at Officer Melanie
Singer, a cornerstone of the prosecution case. By the time he

was done, all that remained was rubble. There was little left for the other defense attorneys to contribute. The district attorney's case had suffered major structural damage, and the trial had barely begun. Assistant DA Terry White tried some damage control on his redirect examination of Melanie Singer, but it was too late and nobody on the jury seemed to care.

All was not victory on Day Two, though. In fact, we suffered a defeat that came back to haunt us in the continuing media coverage of the trial. Until this point, daily news conferences had been conducted for the media by defense and prosecution attorneys at the lunch hour and again at the completion of each day in court.

Essentially, the attorneys would try the case in court, and then try it to the news media. The lawyers used the news conferences to reinforce the salient points of their arguments. Mounger tended to avoid the media. Depasquel and Barnett enjoyed the media sessions, as did Assistant DAs White and Yochelson. But none was better than Stone. He relished media attention and handled the press superbly.

Probably too superbly, because following Stone's news conference after cross-examining Melanie Singer, and just as we felt we were on the verge of turning the media around to our case, Judge Weisberg asked all parties to put a halt to the news conferences. Getting in a dog-fight with your judge in the middle of a trial isn't a good idea, so all parties agreed to stop the practice.

The media complained for a day or so, then reluctantly accepted the ruling. But it hurt the defense, because these news conferences served as a major source of sound bites for television and radio, and as the best way to clarify points for the print media. In my opinion, halting the news conferences severely hurt the defense, and may have contributed to the media's subsequent inaccurate and incomplete reporting of the trial. The fact is, we had made mincemeat out of the prosecution from the moment the trial began, and any casual observer could tell that the verdict was moving easily toward a finding of innocence. But you'd never know it from reading newspaper accounts or watching commercial television reports about the trial while it was in progress.[17] While the media faithfully reported Melanie Singer's testimony, for example, they never explained the inconsistencies developed under cross-examination.

After Melanie Singer, the prosecution called her husband/partner, Officer Tim Singer. His testimony was unremarkable, with the prosecution attempting to show that Officer Powell had lied in his report of the incident. Powell's attorney, Stone, easily demolished that argument in cross-examination by showing that Officer Tim Singer's own report contained certain inaccuracies.

One intriguing mystery flowed from Tim Singer's testimony, though. The prosecution voluntarily brought up the topic of PCP intoxication while questioning Tim Singer. Assistant DA Yochelson established through questioning that Officer Tim Singer had been a police officer for thirteen years and had extensive training and experience in dealing with PCP suspects. He testified that he personally had made eighty to one hundred arrests of PCP suspects. This tidbit of information, voluntarily given, captured our attention.

Why was it brought up? Was Tim Singer ready to testify that Rodney King didn't exhibit the characteristics of someone intoxicated with PCP? And, if so, how, we asked ourselves, could an officer with so many PCP arrests not arrive at the same conclusion reached by every other officer who had contact with Rodney King that night? We wanted to know the answers to these questions. But at the same time, lights, bells, sirens, and red danger signals flashed. Something wasn't right here. After some analysis, it was agreed that Tim Singer's PCP comments were a juicy morsel, but a bit too glib. We decided not to bite when the time came for cross-examination.

---

[17] An exception, of course, was the Courtroom Television Network, which carried most of the trial proceedings live, without editing. Steven Brill of American Lawyer Media, a part owner of CTN, said after the trial that his "strong sense" from viewer response "is that those who watched the trial were not nearly as surprised at the [innocent] verdicts as those who had only seen the much-broadcasted portion of the [Holliday] video." *Legal Times*, June 8, 1992, p. 26.

Barnett, Briseno's counsel, conducted the most useful part of Tim Singer's cross-examination.

First, he had Tim Singer describe his own height (six-feet, three-inches tall) and weight (two hundred pounds). He then asked Tim Singer to compare himself with Rodney King. Tim Singer said King was substantially bigger, in both height and weight. This was important because we were still debating whether to call Rodney King to the stand as a hostile defense witness. If we didn't call him, we wanted the jury to have a picture, a comparison, of just how big King was. Barnett brought the picture into focus. Rodney King is BIG.

Just how big was Rodney King? Barnett asked. Tim Singer described him as a "monster." He went on to compare King with the monster in a monster movie—the creature who just keeps coming after being shot. In this case, Tim Singer testified, Rodney King hadn't been shot, but he had been TASED and struck repeatedly with batons. And yet he just kept coming.

Then Barnett got into the drunken-driving issue. It was a clever approach. He got Tim Singer to testify that he had made hundreds of DUI arrests, that anybody with a blood-alcohol level of .08 or higher was unsafe as a driver, and that any driver with a blood-alcohol level of .19, like Rodney King had when the incident occurred, was dangerous to himself, his passengers, the public, and the police.

Stone followed Barnett, and the questioning was routine. Then, almost as an afterthought, Stone asked Tim Singer whether Rodney King got out of his car on asphalt, and if the entire use of force occurred on the asphalt pavement, not the dirt shoulder. Singer confirmed that everything occurred on the paved roadway. The jury was puzzled, because the question appeared to be unrelated to anything else that had been said. But Stone had laid the groundwork—no pun intended—for our defense against the charge that Rodney King was subjected to multiple head blows that had fractured his cheekbone. In fact, where the incident took place—on asphalt or dirt—was essential to explaining Rodney King's facial injuries.

On balance, once again one of the prosecution's premier witnesses was dead in the water. The defense attorneys, primarily Barnett, had turned Tim Singer around on the stand. As White had done with Melanie Singer, Yochelson tried on redirect examination to salvage what he could. But it was a lost cause. The DA closed out Day Four with two inconsequential witnesses who neither added to nor subtracted from the jury's growing knowledge about what happened on March 3, 1991.

DAYS FIVE AND SIX

For the next two days, the prosecution concentrated on medical testimony. The prosecution intended to show that Rodney King was seriously injured by my officers, and that our reports of the incident sought to cover up the seriousness of the physical harm he suffered. The prosecution also tried to establish that Rodney King was merely drunk on beer and not intoxicated with PCP.

The first medical witness called to the stand by the prosecution was Dr. Antonio Mancia, the attending emergency room physician at Pacifica Hospital where Rodney King was first taken. To even the casual observer, it was obvious that Dr. Mancia would rather undergo root canal surgery than be involved in this case. He was decidedly unfriendly to everybody, and difficult to understand because of a thick Spanish accent.

Dr. Mancia said King had five superficial facial lacerations that required suturing. The first was on the right side of the scalp: two stitches. The second was on the right cheek: three stitches. The third was on the right side of the chin: five stitches. The fourth was on the lip: two stitches. The final laceration was inside the mouth, on the right side: four or five stitches.[18]

After this short course in cosmetic surgery, Assistant DA Yochelson walked Dr. Mancia through other observations on Rodney King's emergency room chart: bruises on the scalp, a nose bleed, bruises on the chest, back, and legs.

---

[18] By my count this totaled at most seventeen stitches. But Assistant DA Yochelson used some creative mathematics and upped it to a round twenty, the number he consistently used in further discussion of Rodney King's injuries.

Yochelson then asked about Dr. Mancia's order transferring Rodney King to the thirteenth floor, the jail ward, of the Los Angeles County/USC Medical Center (LACUSCMC) or, as we called it on the police force, "County Generous." Dr. Mancia said it was due to Rodney King's need of medical treatment; according to Dr. Mancia, King was bleeding and had bruises, and tests not available at Pacifica were required.

This was simply not true.

Rodney King was taken to "County Generous" because he was an intoxicated felony-evader suspect. And he was suspected of being on PCP. The LAPD jail will not take a prisoner dusted on PCP. Therefore, he had to be transported to County Generous, which has the LA County Jail Ward on the thirteenth floor. It's the only place a PCP suspect can be jailed. Rodney King would either be taken to LACUSCMC or turned loose, which obviously was not an option.

This issue—taking Rodney King to a second hospital, his injuries, and his medical treatment—was another "lie" the defense had to address. We were disgusted that we had to address the issue at all, since it was so slanted and skewed. But this is the kind of thing the DA had presented to the grand jury, where we could not defend ourselves. If the DA had had the integrity to present even the semblance of a balanced case to the grand jury, we believe no indictments would ever have been handed down. So far, we had been treated badly by the judicial system, but now it was different; we would no longer just sit back and take it quietly. This time, instead of sulking, we'd come out fighting. We got our motivation from playing bump-and-run with the prosecution every day in court, and from beating them every time.

My attorney, Mounger, got the bump-and-run play started with a simple question to Dr. Mancia: Had he signed off on the Pacific Hospital emergency room report?

Yes, Dr. Mancia testified. He had. Enough said. That report showed minor injuries to Rodney King, *and* PCP intoxication.

Then our resident medical expert, Stone, began to dissect Dr. Mancia's testimony as if it were a lifeless medical school cadaver. He got Dr. Mancia to admit that he was a pediatrician by practice and only moonlighted at Pacifica Hospital, that he had no special education or training in the treatment of injuries like Rodney King's.

Then Stone tied Dr. Mancia into Tim Singer's earlier testimony that the use-of-force incident had occurred on asphalt pavement, not the dirt shoulder of a roadway. Stone got Dr. Mancia to admit that Rodney King's facial injuries were more consistent with blunt force, such as the head striking asphalt, than with sharp force—a baton. The connection was made with the jury.

Stone asked Dr. Mancia about "PERL." Dr. Mancia said it was a medical acronym for "Pupils Equal and Reactive to Light." Then Stone got Dr. Mancia to admit that Rodney King's PERL test was normal. This was important because it proved that Rodney King had suffered no serious head injuries.

Stone concluded by asking Dr. Mancia whether Rodney King was considered combative when brought to the hospital and had to have his hands and legs bound with leather restraints. Dr. Mancia conceded that he had ordered the restraints.

If Dr. Mancia's mood was sour when he approached the stand to be examined by the prosecution, it got worse as the defense proceeded. Depasquel took over for Stone, zeroing in on why Rodney King was transferred to the County Generous hospital.

What was Rodney King's problem, Depasquel asked. Did Dr. Mancia suspect that King's injuries were worse than they appeared? The obvious answer was a firm no—because of Dr. Mancia's own diagnostic impressions, recorded on the Rodney King emergency room record. This record had been deliberately ignored by the district attorney. According to the Pacifica emergency room record signed by Dr. Mancia, Rodney King's diagnosed condition was "(1) PCP overdose/ (2) facial lacerations, superficial."

Depasquel continued to bludgeon Dr. Mancia with the emergency room record. There were no X-rays. Yet earlier Yochelson had implied, and Dr. Mancia had seemed to confirm, that Rodney King was transferred to County Generous because of the possibility of serious head injuries.

That couldn't be the case, Depasquel argued, because the

emergency room chart signed by Dr. Mancia himself showed that Rodney King's head injuries were not serious, not critical. Depasquel finished up his cross-examination by noting that the box labeled "Walked" had been checked as the means by which Rodney King left Pacifica Hospital. It was a significant point, because it meant that as King left the emergency room, he complained of no pain—he walked out.

Before breaking for lunch on Day Five, Depasquel brought out one final point. He had Dr. Mancia testify about the opinion that Rodney King was not under the influence of alcohol. Even the prosecution had admitted that Rodney King had a blood alcohol level of .19 at the time of the incident. The point was not lost on the jury.

We returned from lunch in a good mood. The question of the day was this: Are we having fun yet? The answer was an emphatic yes! But the fun wasn't over yet.

Barnett took up the cross-examination where Depasquel left off. He got Dr. Mancia to admit that any individual with a .19 blood alcohol level would be intoxicated. Barnett then reeled off a series of PCP characteristics and Dr. Mancia confirmed them: a person on PCP has superstrength, fails to respond to commands, and his friends cannot get his attention. Barnett then had Dr. Mancia admit that if these characteristics were exhibited by a suspect it would be reasonable to conclude that the person was under the influence of PCP.

Once again the DA's office was left with the bones of a witness. After the defense attorneys had picked Dr. Mancia's carcass clean, Yochelson tried to breathe some life into the testimony. It didn't work, because after Yochelson asked a couple of minor questions about procedure, Stone and then Depasquel were permitted to take their parting shots at Dr. Mancia.

First, they brought out that if Rodney King was so critically injured, as Yochelson alleged, wouldn't Dr. Mancia have ordered him transferred to LACUSCMC in an ambulance instead of a black-and-white? And, second, if Rodney King's injuries were as bad as Yochelson contended, wouldn't safety dictate that he be admitted immediately to Pacifica Hospital?

In fact, Depasquel pointed out, wasn't it true that a patient cannot be transferred to another hospital unless he's in a stable condition?

These questions must have ruined Dr. Mancia's day, which hadn't been too bright to begin with. Everything the defense attorneys were saying was true. Antonio Mancia was a thoroughly discredited prosecution witness.

As Day Five ended, the defense team was euphoric. We had been beaten up daily in the media for more than a year. For more than a year, we had been unable to fight back. Finally, now in court, we were able to answer the charges that we were thugs, or worse. And we were soundly drubbing the prosecution. We knew it, the jurors knew it, the prosecution knew it. The only frustration was that the media continued to concentrate on the prosecution's case, not on our defense. The public continued to get inaccurate reporting. Never mind. We were within a few days of getting our time to shine.

The first witness called by Yochelson on Day Six was Dr. David Giannetto from County Generous hospital. He was a young man who had just completed medical school and was in residency at LACUSCMC emergency room, the busiest in all of California. He appeared to be smart. He was handsome, clean-cut, and after testifying probably got hundreds of letters from admiring mothers who wanted him to meet and marry their daughters. I had a good feeling about Dr. Giannetto from the beginning.

Yochelson led Dr. Giannetto through Rodney King's medical records upon examination after arriving at LACUSCMC. Rodney King was alert, his pulse slightly elevated, blood pressure normal, respiration slightly elevated, and temperature above normal at 99.8 degrees. Dr. Giannetto said King had sutured lacerations, not extensive in length, on the right cheek and right forehead. The patient had soft tissue swelling, but no bruising, on the right eye. Lacerations over the right forehead and right corner of the lip were also noted. Yochelson asked about X-rays. Dr. Giannetto said these tests were ordered, but he left before receiving the results.

Yochelson then asked Dr. Giannetto about results as noted in the medical reports. The physician said Rodney King apparently had a fracture of the zygomatic arch—cheekbone, to a layman—below and to the side of the right eye. It seemed to be broken in two spots. There appeared to be fluid in the right sinus cavity. Facial trauma was evident and might indicate a fracture; Dr. Giannetto said the night of examination that more evaluation was needed. Multiple bruising was evident on the upper and lower back, chest, and arm areas. King's legs were normal, but a later X-ray of the right leg and ankle area showed a hairline fracture to one bone. Dr. Giannetto noted that Rodney King's right eye, where it is normally white, was filled with blood. The doctor explained that it looked bad but was only a minor injury, nothing more than a bruise. Finally, Dr. Giannetto testified that Rodney King appeared to be mildly intoxicated. He said it could have been from alcohol or a number of any other sources.

Medical expert Stone cross-examined. He asked Dr. Giannetto if Dr. Mancia had phoned to ask if King could be transferred to LACUSCMC. Dr. Giannetto said yes, Dr. Mancia had called and said the patient was stable for transfer, that he possibly was under the influence of PCP, that he had been involved in a problem with the police and received several superficial lacerations. The transfer, he was told by Dr. Mancia, was only so Rodney King could be observed for PCP.

Stone then asked a series of questions that laid the foundation for refuting the charges that Powell and I had lied in our reports when we said that Rodney King's injuries weren't serious. It was noted first that King had not been taken to LACUSCMC for a CAT scan to determine brain damage, because if King had required a CAT scan he would not have been stable and thus could not have been transferred from Pacifica. More importantly, Dr. Giannetto testified that County Generous doesn't have CAT scan equipment.

It was then brought out that King arrived at LACUSCMC at 5:30 A.M., a nursing assessment was conducted by 5:45 A.M., Dr. Giannetto saw the patient at 6:15 A.M. and left about 7:30 to 8:30 A.M. To emphasize the point to the jury, Stone had Dr. Giannetto reconfirm that the X-rays had not been completed by the doctor's end of the shift—which meant, of course, that Powell's report and my log had long since been completed. And the significance of this was that we could not possibly have known about any injuries revealed by the X-rays. Our reports were based on what we knew at the time—the Pacifica Hospital emergency room report indicating that Rodney King's injuries were only minor and superficial, and Dr. Giannetto's confirmation of that diagnosis later at LACUSCMC.

Following the X-rays, which weren't studied until almost twenty-four hours after the incident, Dr. Giannetto said Rodney King had his right leg placed in a cast and was discharged, receiving no other treatment and no surgery. Even the cheekbone fracture required no treatment.

Stone pressed for a more detailed description of King's fractured bones. Dr. Giannetto said the leg fracture was actually a minor, spiderweb-like break and not the type of fracture where a bone is broken in two parts. The purpose of placing the leg in a cast was merely to immobilize it so no lingering disability could occur. The cheekbone injury, Dr. Giannetto testified, was a very common fracture. It was a bone easily broken because it is so thin, he said.

Stone asked, with studied amazement, if those were the extent of Rodney King's injuries. Yes, Dr. Giannetto said. Then Stone asked if the facial wounds were consistent with falls, contact with pavement, or a traffic accident. Yes, Dr. Giannetto testified.

Depasquel had no important questions to ask Dr. Giannetto, but Barnett did. Barnett expanded on a response Dr. Giannetto had given to the grand jury and started to elaborate when he was cut off by the district attorney. It had to do with the validity of a urine test for disclosure of alcohol and drugs.

The test, Dr. Giannetto explained, could be inaccurate due to the acidity of Rodney King's urine. Therefore, a substance such as PCP might not be revealed by a study of Rodney King's urine. Instead, Dr. Giannetto said, PCP could be stored in fatty tissue. This was of major importance, because the prosecution had made a big deal out of the failure to detect PCP in Rodney King's urine test. Now evidence was on the record—evidence that had existed from the beginning—that the urine test was invalid.

Once again the defense had turned a prosecution witness to our advantage. With the testimony of Drs. Mancia and Giannetto, we had offered evidence to the jury and the public that Rodney King was not seriously injured as a result of what the media referred to as a "brutal" beating of a black man by four white LAPD officers.

We knew that King's attorney, Lerman, was the major source of inaccurate information about the injuries, and we knew why this misinformation was being fed to the media: it helped Lerman in his demands for $56 million in damages. We also knew that the district attorney had no desire to correct the misinformation about King's medical condition, because the inaccuracy helped the prosecution's case.[19]

Day Six of the trial ended with Sgt. Richard Distefano of the LAPD, who was the assistant watch commander at the Foothill Division on March 3, 1991. Distefano's testimony was routine, noting that at roll call training Officer Timothy Wind had been selected to demonstrate the use of the PR 24 baton because he was "exceptionally proficient" in its use. Powell, Distefano said, was weak and needed to use more power.

Distefano then got into use-of-force policies. He said officers were trained to use as much force as possible if it became necessary to wield the baton. He explained that officers were taught to hit with the upper third to upper fourth of the baton. If the baton were used, officers were taught to strike such areas as the shoulder, elbow, and wrist. Then he dropped the bombshell. Officers were taught to strike with an intent to immo-

---

[19] An interesting side note here is that Briseno's attorney, Barnett, was doing a superb job of cooperating and assisting with the defense, a fact the media ignored. I began to suspect Barnett was playing both sides against each other, and in so doing he was representing his client to the best of his ability. I was impressed. Not only was Barnett smart, he was sly. I suspected that my attorney, Mounger, envied Barnett's skills and talent. But Mounger was no dummy. While respecting Barnett, he fully realized Barnett's abilities were a double-edged sword: they could help the defense, but they could also be used to destroy the defense.

bilize a suspect; they were taught to try to break the bones of a suspect, Distefano testified.

Mounger got Distefano to testify that he was directed to complete the pursuit summary and use-of-force report, but failed to do so within the required time frame. The reason was that neither he nor Lieutenant Conmay, the watch commander, knew the bureaucratic deadlines imposed, and Sergeant Distefano had not made it to work the day he was going to complete the reports because he had a flat tire. So much for the cover-up.

DAYS SEVEN THROUGH NINE

This would be the time when you'd think the prosecution would put its clean-up hitters in the batting order—the witnesses who could hit home runs and drive us out of the ball game.

But it was not to be. Instead, as it wound down its case, the prosecution continued to show its ineptitude. Witnesses for the final three days of prosecution arguments were all over the field. There was a computer expert who tried to explain communication messages, a nurse who wasn't a nurse, and cops whose testimony was intended to show something about medical evidence. Our defense team was encouraged. If the prosecution had any more goodies in their piñata, they sure weren't breaking them out into the open.

The first witness on Day Seven was the computer expert. It isn't necessary to go into great detail about what he said, because his only purpose on the stand was to get him to testify in support of computer messages transmitted that night which the prosecution believed would show racial bias on the part of the officers.

Even so, the testimony here provided some comic relief, not because of what the witness said but because of the assistant DA's logic. What the prosecution did was raise the curious argument of "adoptive admission." That means, according to the prosecution, that by being silent, I was a party to racism.

It seems that after sending my "big-time use of force"

message, a computer communications operator had answered and referred to the suspect, Rodney King, as a "lizard."[20] In the first place, I did not receive the message. In the second, even if I had it would have been unnecessary to respond because a response was not required.

But the prosecution said my silence demonstrated racial bias. Assistant DA White argued that my silence, or non-response, to the "lizard" message meant that I considered Rodney King a low-life kind of person. It was "adoptive admission," the prosecution said.

I thought White was joking. Did not responding to a remark that I didn't see or read make me a racist? And was I a racist because I considered Rodney King a "lizard"? Because I said nothing in response to a word I hadn't seen on my computer that wasn't racist to begin with?

White wasn't joking, though. He was deadly serious. I thought at the time: the district attorney must really be hurting if this is the best he can come up with. It wasn't bad enough that we had to defend ourselves against our own words and actions. Now we had to defend ouselves against our silence. Well, the media apparently thought so too; they made a big deal out of the "lizard" communication.

Mounger and I consulted about how to counter the testimony. I told him that I never received the "lizard" message in readable form, that it came out totally babbled on the screen of my on-board computer because it was sent just as I was starting the engine on my black-and-white. To explain why starting the engine would screw up the computer transmission would have taken hours, perhaps days. So Mounger and I decided to let it pass. If the jury was going to send me to prison for not responding to an objectionable message I hadn't read when a

---

[20] The operator was Leslie Wylie. The term "lizard" is used in the LAPD verbal judo course—which is intended to teach officers how to subdue suspects verbally rather than using force—to describe suspects. It applies to all suspects of all races and gender. Ms. Wylie thought after taking the course it was standard operating language. That's why she used it.

response wasn't even necessary, then I probably deserved to be behind bars.[21]

After this charade, the prosecution called Larry Davis and Denise Edwards. They were nursing personnel from Pacifica Hospital and assisted Dr. Mancia in examining Rodney King. But the reason White wanted their testimony was to prove to the jury that Officer Powell was a racist and big-time suspect-beater. These witnesses alleged that it was Powell, not any of the other officers present, who taunted Rodney King about playing "hardball."

But Powell's attorney, Stone, did a good job of seriously damaging the credibility of these witnesses. In fact, we actually used them to our benefit—as we had done with every one of the other witnesses called by the prosecution.

For example, Davis testified that he had removed the TASER darts from King's clothing, a fact which helped us prove that the TASER had made contact with Rodney King.[22] But, beyond this, we were able to play these witnesses to the jury to our advantage.

We sought to appeal to one juror in particular. She was a registered nurse. We specifically raised three issues for her benefit. We reasoned that this juror would prevail upon her peers and convince them to discredit the testimony of Edwards and Davis.

First, we raised the issue of Davis completing his supplemental nursing notes on the incident two days after it had occurred. We knew our juror would think this was wrong. Second, we reminded the jury that Rodney King was placed in leather restraints at the hospital. We knew that our nurse juror would know that leather restraints required a doctor's order

---

[21] Judge Weisberg later ruled that such testimony was admissible, but that it would be for the jury to decide if my silence represented an admission of wrongdoing.

[22] It is a common misconception that unless the TASER darts strike the skin they won't work. That's not true. For the TASER to zap a suspect, all that's necessary is for the darts to hang up in the clothing.

and were used only on combative, noncooperative patients who were feared to be violent. Finally, prosecution witness Denise Edwards had testified that she was a "nurse."

This might seem like a small point, and technically it was correct. But we had watched our nurse juror, and she listened intently as she evaluated the testimony of her colleague.

Mounger passed a written note to Depasquel, which said: "Ask her if she's an RN [registered nurse] or an LVN [licensed vocational nurse]."

Depasquel asked the question. We watched the juror for her reaction. Edwards, looking slightly embarrassed, answered that she was an LVN—a professional designation below the RN category. I'll never forget our nurse juror's reaction. Her right eyebrow looked like a caterpillar on the move as it rose up a good inch or so toward her hairline. She was then seen to mark on her notepad what appeared to be the bold letters, "LVN." Mounger and I were silent as we exchanged glances. We were guilty of "adoptive admission" by simply being silent. We'd taken care of Edwards and her testimony.

The prosecution was winding up its case by Day Eight. Over the next two days, the DA's office would call several LAPD officers to the stand as prosecution witnesses. The first was Lieutenant Conmay, the morning-shift watch commander at the Foothill Division on March 3, 1991.

Conmay's testimony offered nothing new. He merely recounted my briefing after the incident, but he did testify that he had never received my abbreviated computer message about "big-time force." Initially, Mounger and I had expected Lieutenant Conmay to try to flay me. When he did not, we were surprised. It's a good thing he didn't. We were prepared to do a number on the lieutenant. We had evidence that would cast him as a new and incompetent watch commander. But after his testimony, which had not been damaging, it was agreed there was no reason to make him look foolish.

After Lieutenant Conmay came Sgt. Robert Troutt, the Valley Traffic watch commander on the morning of March 3, 1991. Troutt was the officer who approved booking Rodney King for felony evasion. Assistant DA White made a point from Troutt's testimony that Powell and Wind had made no mention of drunken driving or possible PCP intoxication when arranging for King's booking. This posed no problem for the defense; on cross-examination, Stone and Depasquel got Troutt to admit that DUI and PCP were not relevant elements of felony evasion, so there was no reason for Powell and Wind to mention them.

White also struck out with his next police witness, Sgt. John Amott. This officer approved Powell's arrest report following the incident. Using Amott's testimony, White stressed that Powell's arrest report made no mention of blood or urine samples being taken from Rodney King. The insinuation was that the officers knew King wasn't under the influence of PCP, and also knew that if they took blood and urine samples the lab would verify that King wasn't under the influence of PCP. Consequently, the conspiracy and cover-up would be exposed.

But White's overactive imagination got punctured on cross-examination. Under questioning by Stone, Amott conceded that LAPD booking policy dictated that someone who was arrested should be booked for the highest level of offense charged. Lesser charges could be included, but didn't have to be included. Had King been charged with DUI, it would have been necessary to provide these test results. But King was charged with felony evading, which did not require that blood and urine samples be taken. So much for this argument. White appeared frustrated by the logic. It seemed to make no sense to him. In fact, it probably didn't, because White possessed no understanding of police work generally and LAPD policies and procedures specifically. He hadn't done his homework.

Thus did the prosecution case limp to a conclusion after nine days of testimony. In a way, we were disappointed. We had expected and prepared for a far more aggressive case than the one presented by the prosecution.

We had two theories about why the DA's office came on so weakly. First, we theorized that the prosecution put on an abbreviated case in hopes that we would do the same. If we were to do so, it was almost certain that the advantage would fall to the prosecution and might result in guilty verdicts. The second theory was that if we responded with a full-blown case, then the prosecution would have a full-blown rebuttal case in its hip pocket to spring a trap on us after we'd revealed our hand. This is what we expected to happen. Because starting on Day Ten of the trial, we planned to provide the jury with a dog-and-pony show that could only lead them to one conclusion: Not guilty.

DAYS TEN AND ELEVEN

Our first witness was Catherine Bosak. She was a paramedic with the Los Angeles Fire Department and the first medical professional to provide treatment to Rodney King. She testified that King's injuries were minor. If the damage had been serious, she testified, he would have been taken to a designated trauma center, which Pacifica Hospital was not. She said King appeared coherent, alert, and oriented, and did not seem to be in any pain or distress.[23]

Further questioning revealed that Bosak regarded King as combative and uncooperative. She said he was continually cursing, spitting blood at officers and medical personnel, and fighting his restraints.

White cross-examined. He asked about King's head injuries. Bosak testified that she believed the head injuries resulted from contact with the ground, because dirt was intermixed with blood on King's face and head.

Then White asked his final question. It was apparently intended to blow the witness out of the water and destroy her credibility. He asked if she considered a broken bone, a broken cheekbone, to be a minor injury. Without hesitating, Bosak gave an emphatic, "Yes." White went into orbit. He had failed

---

[23] Remember that Rodney King had just undergone the beating seen on the Holliday videotape. We now had verified evidence of what we had been saying all along: Rodney King was feeling no pain from the PR 24 metal baton. There is no dispute that he got beaten. The dispute is: how seriously was he injured, and how much of it resulted from his being beaten and how much from his slamming into the ground three times.

to understand police work, and it was now evident that he also had no knowledge of medicine. Broken cheekbones are a very common injury, and, when compared with other bone fractures, minor in nature.[24]

Our next witness was Police Officer Susan Clemmer. She identified herself as the secondary LAPD unit involved in the Rodney King pursuit. This was important. Powell and Wind had identified themselves as the primary unit, and this information had been broadcast over the police radio. It led me and others to assume that the CHIPs had turned the pursuit over to the LAPD once inside the Los Angeles city limits.

Officer Clemmer testified that she saw Powell at the scene immediately after King had been handcuffed. She described Powell as scared and breathing hard, out of breath and gulping air. She said Powell took a quick walk to calm down, and recalled hearing Powell say that he had feared he was going to have to shoot King. During this time, King was laughing, she said, and in a deep voice repeatedly shouting "Fuck you" to any and all.

I had ordered Officer Clemmer and Officer Wind to ride with King in the rescue ambulance to the hospital. She testified that on the ride to Pacifica Hospital, King kept spitting blood on her shoes and uniform trousers. He was asked to stop, but didn't. At the hospital, she said, King appeared to be alert but had a blank stare. She then recalled a bizarre statement King made to me at the hospital, although I have no recollection of it. She said King looked at me and said, "I love you." Then he smiled and laughed. Officer Clemmer said that Wind and Powell did not taunt King either on route to the hospital or when they got there.

Next for the defense came Officer David Love, the only black policeman present at the scene. Judge Weisberg initially had Love testify with the jury absent, because he wanted to rule on whether an officer who was at the scene could offer as

---

[24] White wasn't the only person who was astonished by Bosak's response. King's attorney, Lerman, and King's aunt, who attended nearly every day of the trial, acted as if they were possessed.

evidence any details not personally witnessed but later seen on the Holliday videotape.

With the jury absent, Love said that he had been at the station when the pursuit began and responded right away. He said that when he got to the scene he was within fifteen feet of Rodney King and saw the TASER wires attached to King's body. He said King approached an officer, who delivered a power stroke with the PR 24 metal baton to King's upper torso. He said the blow was consistent with LAPD training.

Then Love said he turned his attention momentarily to the other two suspects. They were securely cuffed, so he turned back to King. Now, Love testified, Rodney King was on the ground but rising. He said he saw two to four blows delivered to King's legs, and the blows were appropriate. He continually heard shouts, "Hit the legs," and "Lie down, get down." He said King was not passive on the ground, but constantly moving and trying to get up. Love also testified that LAPD training taught an officer not to tie up with a suspect, and that the baton was the appropriate tool to use in controlling a resisting suspect. He saw no head shots, Love stated.

Finally, Officer Love testified that he saw certain incidents on the video that he had not witnessed at the scene. After having viewed the Holliday videotape, Love said, it was his opinion that the force used was excessive and unnecessary.

That could have been damaging testimony. But it wasn't, because the jury never heard it. Judge Weisberg ruled that a witness who was on the scene couldn't testify about incidents not observed until viewed on the Holliday videotape. So all the jury heard when it returned was testimony confirming that the force used on Rodney King was within LAPD guidelines and training.

White cross-examined Love. Because Love was the only black police officer present at the scene of the incident, it was vitally important that the prosecution either turn Love around or impeach his testimony. White, who also is a black man, was unable to do either. He began by asking Love to state where he, Love, had eaten lunch this day. Love said he had eaten a roast-beef sandwich in the defense offices. White was not-so-subtly accusing Love of fraternizing with the defense, implying a "boy's-club" camaraderie among police officers—one for all, and all for one.

White then sought to point out contradictions between Love's testimony and what he had said at the grand jury proceedings. The contradictions, if they existed, were so minor as to be unimportant. For example, at the grand jury hearing Love had testified that King had staggered toward Powell before Powell struck King in the side. Now he was saying that King rushed Powell and Powell struck King in the chest. It was hardly an impeachment of Officer Love's credibility.

Everybody could see what White was trying to do. It was the prosecution's anemic theory: conspiracy plus code of silence equals cover-up. It wasn't much of a case, but it was the only one the prosecution had at this point.

Love was asked who had called him as a witness, the defense or the prosecution? Initially the prosecution, Love said, but it changed its mind. He was then called by the defense.

We knew what Officer Love would say, and we were not afraid to put him or any other officer on the stand. Good or bad, we wanted the truth revealed. Under questioning, Love said he had related the events to the best of his recollection and that he had not been pressured to testify in any particular way by the defense; he hadn't sold out for a roast-beef sandwich. When asked about discrepancies between his grand jury testimony and trial statements, Love said he guessed it was due to his having been swayed by the video.

Officer Love was right. The video had influenced his memory of the event. It was a phenomenon we planned to have an eyewitness expert explain to the jury. The phenomenon is called created memory. Officer Love was only one example; many officers and witnesses in this case had fallen victim to the same curious experience.[25]

---

[25] It also influenced the opinions of hundreds of millions of people around the world who saw the George Holliday videotape. They have difficulty separating truth and facts from the impressions stamped in memory by the eighty-two-second videotape.

On balance, though, Officer David Love demonstrated considerable courage in testifying at all. He had nothing to be ashamed of, and he had told the truth as he saw it. But this was an emotional, political trial, and emotions and politics often crush truth. The reality of the situation was this: the black community had high expectations for the testimony of Officer Love. They believed his testimony would confirm their version of the incident. They expected him to speak the truth as they saw it. Officer Love did speak the truth. But it wasn't the truth the black community wanted to hear. And so Assistant DA White tried to portray Love as an Uncle Tom who had distorted his testimony to favor four white officers. Love left the courtroom in the unenviable position of having to face unsympathetic friends, black co-workers, and the black community.

Day Eleven of the trial was tiring. The defense had planned to parade before the jury all of the officers who had been at the scene on March 3, 1991. It had been our intention to show the jury that Rodney King's actions were not something conjured out of smoke and mirrors by the defense, but the reality of what had happened.

Anticipating this strategy, Assistant DA White remained seated at the prosecution table in a chair nearest to the defense's side of the room; the prosecutor who conducted cross-examinations always sat closest to the defense table.

Mounger carried his fat notebook to the stand and said he was prepared to call his next witness. Yochelson looked tired, and unsuccessfully tried to suppress a yawn. Mounger said his next witness would be Sergeant Stacey Koon.

Yochelson looked as though he had been dashed in the face with a bucket of ice water. Mounger's tactical move caught Yochelson and White completely by surprise. They almost fell over each other as they switched chairs at the prosecution table.

I would be the first defendant to testify. It had been a long-awaited moment for everybody. The TV audience had been estimated at about 190,000 households prior to my trip to the witness stand. Later, ratings for my testimony projected the television audience at about 390.000 households. I would be on the stand for the rest of Day Eleven and half of Day Twelve. Finally, after more than a year, I was able to tell my side of the story.

DAYS TWELVE AND THIRTEEN

Mounger began by getting biographical data into the record. He had to be careful here, because the prosecution wasn't about to let the character issue be raised; to do so would expose Rodney King's violent nature and conduct.

So Mounger's approach was to concentrate on what my state of mind was on March 3, 1991, which was a legitimate and unobjectionable line of questioning. Of course, in order to understand my state of mind at that time it was necessary to get some biographical information into the record—my age, education, marital status, and almost fifteen-year tenure on the LAPD. In this way, Mounger got the jury to know something about me—the two advanced degrees, my nineteen-year marriage, my five children—that might not have been altogether relevant. But throughout the trial Mounger would stretch the rubber band as far as he could and, if the defense didn't object, he'd keep pulling away.

Mounger then led me back to the night of March 2–3, 1991. He had me describe how I was leaving the Foothill Station when the California Highway Patrol pursuit began, and how I paralleled the route that was being followed.

My testimony led me to Foothill Boulevard, where Rodney King finally stopped. I described the scene when I arrived—the officers with their guns drawn, Rodney King's erratic behavior, and his refusal to comply with orders to get on his stomach and put his hands behind his back. I told the jury about the suspicions I developed that this suspect was intoxicated on PCP and most likely an ex-convict.

I described for the jury why I halted Melanie Singer's approach with a gun and how, afterwards, Officers Powell, Wind, Briseno, and Solano swarmed Rodney King and slammed him face first into the pavement. I told how the situation got more tense and serious, and how my fear started to grow when

Rodney King threw off the four police officers. That was why I escalated the use of force to the TASER, shooting both cartridges into King's clothing and visibly observing their effect.

Then Mounger led me through the George Holliday videotape, almost frame by frame. It was the first time the jury—or anyone else, other than the defense—had had an opportunity to see it in such detail as to prove that Rodney King was always in control of the situation, not the officers. When viewed in detail, not casually in its edited form on the evening news, the tape also proved that Rodney King had deliberately assaulted Officer Powell, that even while on the ground he was constantly rising, constantly threatening officers engaged in the legal performance of their duties. It would be our strongest argument.

Using overlays, I was able to bring the videotape to life in a form never seen before. It was like the animated cartoon that had turned Michael Stone, Powell's attorney, around to an aggressive defense. For the first time, the attention of a viewer of the videotape would be focused on what Rodney King was doing, not on the police batons falling. It would show that Rodney King was a constant threat.

Using the blown-up photos taken from the enhanced videotape and overlays, I outlined for the jury the two-second sequence at the beginning where King, after having been TASED twice, leaps to his feet and in only two seconds collides with Officer Powell.

Why did you think it was an attack? Mounger asked.

Because, using a diagram I clearly showed several avenues of escape existed if Rodney King had been rising to flee, rather than to attack an officer. Using the diagram, I pointed out for the jury at least three directions King could have fled in if he had wanted to. He could have gone to the park, where we were worried about an ambush. He could have fled into the crowd across the street that was watching the scene. He could have run toward the liquor store and gas station. When he chose to accept none of these routes of escape, when he decided instead to go after Powell, all of us had to interpret the movement as an attack, not an escape. The videotape helped us drive home the point.

With this question settled, I went on to explain almost every action captured on the Holliday videotape.

After King ran into Powell and was struck in the clavicle (collarbone) area with a baton, the video shows him slamming face-first into the pavement. Powell is power-stroking him on the arms, shoulder, and chest.

The videotape blurs at this point, but less than eleven seconds later, at minute 3:36:12 on the tape, it clears and shows the officers standing back. They are evaluating the effect of their blows, as they had been trained to do. This explained to the jury the pulsating use of force, the moving in and hitting, then moving back to assess. It showed them that the officers weren't casually taking turns hitting the suspect, but carefully following policies, procedures, and training.

At 3:41:02, the overlay on the photo reveals King suddenly raising himself on his left toes, cocking his right knee, and beginning to rise. Twenty-three hundredths of a second later, he is on his hands and knees and rising. By 3:42:24, he's sitting back on his calves, his arms are free. The jury sees all of this.

Now Powell moves forward to strike King's arms and upper torso. Wind is hitting him in the buttocks. At 3:45:22, Rodney King falls over, turns, and then rises to his hands and knees. For two seconds, I pointed out to the jury, the officers backed away to assess what King was doing, how he was reacting to the power strokes. Was he going to comply and stay down, or get up and attack us again? It was classic LAPD use of force—use the batons, then move back and evaluate. The jurors are transfixed by the scene. It's something they've never seen before.

But Rodney King's not going to stay down. So, at 3:47:10, Powell moves in for more power strokes. He hits King in the left arm and shoulder area. Officer Wind is striking King's upper back. The photo frame from 4:02:16 shows King uncocking his left leg and straightening his body out to a better prone position. It appears as though he's going to comply with our orders. The jury can see that the officers have backed away.

Then at 4:03:20, King begins rolling to the left, lifting his right hip, and cocking his right leg. He's now into the "Folsom Roll," the tactic prisoners at Folsom Prison teach each other to disarm an officer—roll into his legs, grab his gun belt, and then seize his gun while the officer's off balance. Wind recognizes the movement and backs away. Then he moves back in when King stops rolling. Powell is hitting King in the right ankle, Wind is striking his back. The jurors realize that Wind believes he is being threatened by King, and that the threat is caused by King's own actions.

At 4:14:19, King begins to roll onto his back. He cocks his left leg, and his right hand moves to his waist area. King has both knees bent and continues to roll. At 4:20:18, his upper torso is up. The videotape shows me pointing at King. I am shouting at him to get down, stay down, on his belly, hands behind his back.

Despite the orders, five seconds later, Rodney King is rising again. Through the overlays, the jury can see that his left arm is out, his right leg cocked.

But the officers had been led to believe that he was complying, despite the movements to rise. Now the jury can see that Powell is reaching for his handcuffs. Then, at 4:28:20, King has lifted his right hip, his upper torso is raised, and he is drawing up his right leg to rise. Briseno steps forward and delivers a kick—I regarded it as more of a stomp, I told the jury—between King's shoulder blades. King smashes face-first into the asphalt again.

The jury sees that at 4:30:28, Powell and Wind are again striking King's right arm, but two seconds later King is on his hands and knees. The videotape shows that he turns toward Powell. A flurry of blows are delivered on King for the next seventeen seconds. At 4:47:00, King is sitting on his calves, arms at his sides, and the officers have withdrawn to evaluate. Powell hands his handcuffs to Briseno, and at 4:57:00 Briseno begins trying to put the handcuffs on King.

By now we thought the incident was over and that the suspect would comply. We were almost right. Briseno struggled with Rodney King's arms, trying to get them in position behind his back. But I was able to point out to the jury that at 5:01:05, King pulled his left arm away from the handcuffing position. That was when I ordered the final swarm that put Rodney King in custody.

Mounger had me fill in a number of blanks for the jury, explaining our use-of-force policies and how and why the officers did what they did on March 3. And, to get these matters out of the way, I also talked about my log and explained the delay in filing a pursuit summary and use-of-force report.

All of these were important to the case, of course, but the big problem was the George Holliday videotape. We had to turn it around to our advantage, make it our weapon of defense rather than the evidence that could send us to jail. And it worked. The videotape and overlays we had prepared proved devastating to the prosecution. Once the jury understood what had happened, and why, once the videotape had been examined almost frame by frame, a verdict of not guilty was all but assured.

Yochelson cross-examined for several hours. He tried to pick my testimony apart, to show that Rodney King wasn't a threat and that we had overreacted to an innocent motorist guilty of nothing more than speeding and maybe drinking too much. But Yochelson's tactic didn't work. The videotape evidence was too strong.

The PCP issue was not proven, Yochelson contended. He also suggested that I was guilty of trying to cover up the incident by dismissing Rodney King's injuries as "minor" in my log that night. He did his best to try to show that the amount of force was unnecessary. Often, I had to bite my tongue to keep from responding that he obviously didn't know anything about police work, about what a street cop has to face every day.

Near the end of his cross-examination, Yochelson made the mistake I had been waiting for. It made all the tongue-biting worthwhile. He was describing the intense level of force being applied to Rodney King, and how it wasn't necessary to subdue an unarmed suspect. Then he asked the question I'd been hoping for.

"Did Mr. King have any weapons?" the assistant DA asked.

"Yes," I answered. "His body, under the influence of PCP."

Yochelson realized his mistake, and tried to correct it by pointing out that no tests on Rodney King proved the presence of PCP.

It is true that tests did not reveal PCP usage, I answered. But it was my perception and belief that on March 3, 1991, Rodney King's actions strongly suggested PCP intoxication, and that it made him a dangerous felony suspect. Perceptions were what mattered. And my testimony and the videotape provided the jury with a new view of what George Holliday filmed that night.[26]

DAYS FOURTEEN THROUGH TWENTY-NINE

The last half of the twenty-nine-day trial was important, but not as dramatic as the first half. The first fourteen days of testimony featured most of the stars in this drama, except the one in the title role: Rodney King. He wouldn't testify, and we wouldn't call him. The prosecution believed it would be unnecessary. We believed it would be unnecessary also. We were already blowing the prosecution out of the water. They knew it. We knew it. The courtroom spectators knew it. The media knew it. Everybody except the millions of people who'd seen the Rodney King videotape and not heard the courtroom testimony knew it.

But even without King, we wanted to nail the case shut. We put on a succession of police officers who were at the scene and did not believe the force used was excessive. We had our two LAPD use-of-force experts, Sgt. Charles Duke and Capt. Robert Michael, describe how what happened was well within the accepted guidelines, that the officers' actions didn't even

---

[26] During breaks in my testimony, the media observers and commentators made much about how I must have had a great deal of experience in testifying, because I was coming across as an expert witness. That's untrue. I can count on the fingers of one hand the number of times I've been on a witness stand. If I came across well—and the jury's verdict suggests that I did—it was because I was being truthful and had no reason to hedge.

bump against the limits of policy but followed the rules as written.

Another defense witness who seemed to impress the jury was Dr. Dallas Long, who had earned medical degrees in both medicine and dental science after winning an Olympic gold medal as shot-putter in 1964. Dr. Long was able to tie up all of the medical questions—the extent of Rodney King's facial injuries, the characteristics exhibited by somebody on PCP, whether a TASER leaves a burn as evidence of its use (Rodney King had no burn; a TASER dart doesn't leave one)—that might still be confusing the jury.

One witness we had hoped to get on the stand didn't make it. That was Prof. Elizabeth Loftus of the University of Washington. She had been on the faculty at the school in Seattle since 1973, and had bachelor's, master's, and doctoral degrees in psychology. Her area of expertise was memory and how it worked, and she had written sixteen books and more than two hundred articles on perception.

Had she been allowed to testify, she would have demonstrated to the jury that what you see isn't necessarily what actually happens. She had research proving that memory can be manipulated by questions and how they're asked, by conversations, by peer-group pressure, and—most significantly—by the media. We especially wanted her testimony out in the open, hoping that it might get through to some people who weren't being given an accurate picture of what was happening at the trial. But Judge Weisberg ruled that her testimony would be too time-consuming and would contribute little to the process, and so she was not allowed to take the stand. It was the second procedural defeat we suffered during the trial (the first being when Judge Weisberg cut out the daily news conferences—or at least strongly suggested as much).

It was also during the second half of the trial that the Briseno defection became complete. Briseno testified that he had sought to stop the beating, that he had tried to prevent Powell from using his baton on Rodney King. He said Powell's continued blows to King were unnecessary. But the arguments wouldn't wash. We proved that Briseno's warning came at about the time I was shooting the remaining current from the second TASER cartridge, and that when Briseno sought to restrain Powell by holding up a warning hand, it was to prevent Powell and Wind from touching King while the TASER was still active and being zapped with the current, too. And more: If Briseno were trying to prevent Rodney King from being hurt, why did he step forward and kick King in the back? The jury understood common sense.

Something else addressed during the trial's second half was Powell's state of mind when the Rodney King incident occurred. The prosecution made a big point of his "gorillas in the mist" comment before the King arrest. It seemed that Powell and Wind had answered a domestic disturbance call involving a black couple shortly before midnight on March 2. Afterwards, Powell had sent a message to the effect that the scene was right out of *Gorillas in the Mist*, a motion picture that had just been released. It was a movie about wild gorillas in their natural habitat. It may have been stupid of Powell to make the reference after answering the domestic disturbance call, which involved a black couple. But was it racist?

Moreover, whether it was a racist comment or not is somewhat beside the point, or should be. Powell did not force Rodney King to drink beer and speed that night. Powell did not initiate the pursuit of Rodney King. He did not begin beating Rodney King without cause. He was assaulted by Rodney King, and he then tried to protect himself. After that, everything he did was according to my orders. Whatever Larry Powell's views on race might be, they did not enter into the situation on March 3, 1991.

Finally, after twenty-five days of testimony, the last witness was heard. Before the closing arguments, the prosecution made a motion that encouraged us to believe they knew the case was lost. The DA's office moved to charge us with lesser offenses, in addition to the felony charges. What did this mean?

It meant that the prosecution had been in such a hurry to hang the presumed guilty that they had accused us of only felony crimes. Now they wanted to alter the indictment to include misdemeanor charges. To us, that meant they knew the jury wasn't about to send us to prison, but might be willing to slap our wrists with lesser crimes. But the prosecution showed its ineptness here, too. In order to change the indictment, they needed our approval. And there was no way we were going to agree to lesser charges, because we knew we were innocent and had put on a strong case. We were certain we would be exonerated. If you truly believe in your case, in your innocence, and we did, then you force the jury to make a hard decision. It's a felony or it's nothing. A gamble? Not in our view. We knew the prosecution would not be able to prove its case beyond a reasonable doubt and moral certainty. So we turned the prosecution down. Judge Weisberg was disbelieving that we'd take such a risk. In open court, he sought a personal waiver from each defendant rejecting the prosecution offer.

After hearing both the defense and prosecution wrap the case up in closing arguments, the jury retired to deliberate. They would study the evidence for seven days.

At 3:15 P.M. on April 29, the jury returned not guilty verdicts on all counts against me, Briseno, and Wind. The jury couldn't decide on one count against Powell, voting eight to four for acquittal.

Throughout the trial, the media had been reporting only one side of the story. Minority leaders had been warning that if the verdict was not guilty, riots were inevitable. The media faithfully reported the rumors. An hour after the verdict, a helicopter traffic reporter for a Los Angeles radio station reported the story before it happened, telling viewers that "we don't see any fires yet."[27]

But they didn't have long to wait. A self-fulfilling prophecy was about to come true. By nightfall on April 29, 1992, only hours after the verdict, Los Angeles was in flames.

---

[27] *Time* magazine, May 11, 1992, p. 43.

6

Tragic Consequences

Three hours and ten minutes after the Simi Valley jury returned its verdicts, the first person to die in the Los Angeles riot of 1992 was killed at the corner of Vernon and Vermont Avenues. His name was Louis Watson Fleming. He was waiting for a bus when someone shot him in the head. He was a young black man. According to his friends and neighbors, Louis Fleming was a responsible youth who had changed high schools several times to avoid involvement with gangs. He was twelve days shy of his nineteenth birthday when he died.

Moments later, Dwight "Fishman" Taylor, a forty-two-year-old black seafood cutter whose nickname derived from his occupation, needed to buy a half-gallon of milk for his family. He left his job to walk across the street to a supermarket in the 400 block of Martin Luther King Boulevard. "Fishman" never made it. Someone shot him in the neck and chest as he walked across the supermarket parking lot. Witnesses said they didn't see the assassin. According to a neighbor who rushed to his aid, Taylor's final words were, "Go back and tell my wife I love her. I know I'm not going to make it."[1] He didn't.

By late afternoon on May 1, forty-eight hours after the jury's

---

[1] *New York Times*, May 4, 1992, p. B-8.

verdict was announced, thirty-eight people were dead in Los Angeles. Of these, more than a third—fifteen—were black. The media were reporting that another 1,419 were injured, four thousand people had been arrested, and the Los Angeles Fire Department had responded to 3,767 fire calls associated with the disorder.

In the five days following the Simi Valley verdict, until order was restored, the grisly body count would rise . . . Matthew Haines, a thirty-two-year-old white man pulled from his motorcycle and shot in the head in the Belmont Shores neighborhood of Long Beach . . . Juan A. Tineda, a nineteen-year-old Hispanic shot to death on Thursday, April 30, for no apparent reason . . . Dennis Jackson, a thirty-eight-year-old black male killed in a gun battle at Nickerson Gardens when snipers fired on Los Angeles police officers . . . Edward Lee Song, an eighteen-year-old Korean-American shot to death . . . The list would continue with dreadful regularity, almost like the casualty reports during the North Vietnamese Tet offensive at the height of the Vietnam War in the early months of 1968.

And so it would go in Los Angeles until sixty people were dead, more than two thousand others injured, bandaged, and hurting with physical pain, some of them crippled by emotional wounds that will stay with them for life. More than $800 million in property was lost through looting, fires, and wanton destruction. It made the 1965 riots in Watts look like a minor street disturbance.

People rushed to assign blame almost as soon as the first fires were set, the first store-fronts smashed and liquor stores looted, the first bullets fired. The cause was years of neglect to inner cities, according to some urbanologists; the grim desperation of life in an economic ghetto without hope of improvement, said some politicians, sociologists, and many newspapers. All of this could be true. In fact, based upon my experience, it probably is true. But almost everybody agreed that the Simi Valley verdicts provided the fuel that sparked and fed the explosion.

To the nation's media, of course, the culprits responsible for the mayhem and devastation in Los Angeles were clearly identifiable. They were the "guilty" cops and the Simi Valley jury.

Newsweek magazine, for example, said in its first report on the riots:

"Out of a city endlessly burning, out of the heart of Simi Valley and the soul of South-Central Los Angeles, a verdict *seen as a miscarriage of justice*[2] induced a convulsion of violence that left 44 dead (at the time of publication), 2,000 bleeding and $1 billion in charred ruins. The 56 videotaped blows administered by Los Angeles police to Rodney King last year had landed hard on everyone's mind. But they fell like feathers on a suburban jury that acquitted the cops of using force. . . ." (emphasis added).

The media were simply emphasizing and enlarging on the story they had etched on the public mind through endless replays of the edited eighty-two-second videotape. At a press conference a day after the riots began, Los Angeles Mayor Tom Bradley said, "Today the system has failed us. . . . The jury's verdict will never blind us to what we saw on that videotape. The men who beat Rodney King do not deserve to wear the uniform of the LAPD." Never mind the facts seen and heard by the jury or other testimony. Look again at what Mayor Bradley said: *"The jury's verdict will never blind us to what we saw on that videotape"* (emphasis added).

Presidential candidate Bill Clinton, the governor of Arkansas, on his way to the Democratic nomination, simply said, "I don't understand the verdict." It was the most moderate statement made by a political figure during those charged few days.

President George Bush also indicated that the videotape was more important than the evidence presented at the trial, evidence that proved innocence. President Bush, the leader of the free world, the chief executive of the nation, said, in effect, that proof was less important than the videotape. His words: "Viewed from the outside, it was hard to understand how the verdict could possibly square with the video." Then he made sure that the nation understood that this was a family response, not a presidential directive. The president added that

---

[2] By whom? *Newsweek*? It certainly wasn't a "miscarriage of justice" to the jury, which heard all of the facts. *Newsweek* magazine, May 11, 1992, p. 30.

he, his wife Barbara, and his children were "stunned" by the verdict.[3]

The ultimate media establishment voice, the *New York Times*, made its judgment on May 1, two days after the verdict. Of course, this meant the editorial was written within twenty-four hours of the Simi Valley decision, since the *Times'* deadline schedule cannot accommodate instant response. And, again, that judgment was based on the videotape—to their minds, the only evidence—and not on the evidence presented during the trial, which the nation's newspaper of record had presumably covered.

On Friday, May 1, the *Times* said that the George Holliday videotape "made the verdict rendered Wednesday by the Rodney King jury doubly shocking. It found the four defendant policemen to be not guilty of brutality that millions of Americans, the other jury, thought was indisputable. And far from discouraging uncontrolled police brutality, the trial jury's actions seemed to *validate* it" (emphasis in original).[4]

The only hero during the riots, suggested *Newsweek* competitor *Time* magazine, was Rodney King.

"For more than a year he had been a writhing body twisting on the ground under kicks and nightstick blows in what may be the most endlessly replayed videotape ever made," *Time* said. "Then on Friday afternoon TV finally gave Rodney King a face and a voice—a hesitant, almost sobbing voice that yet was more eloquent than any other that spoke during the terrible week. 'Stop making it horrible,' King pleaded with the rioters who had been doing just that in Los Angeles—and, to a lesser degree in San Francisco, Atlanta, Seattle, Pittsburgh and other cities."[5]

It is necessary here to dwell on Rodney King's "writhing" on the ground under "kicks and nightstick blows." The evidence

---

[3] Transcript of televised speech by President Bush, May 1, 1992.

[4] As noted, Rodney King was not on trial. Police officers were on trial. Rodney King never was called to account for his conduct in the early morning hours of March 3, 1991. The *New York Times*, May 1, 1992, p. A-34.

[5] *Time* magazine, May 11, 1992, p. 20.

clearly shows that the "writhing" was repeated attempts to get up in order to assault a police officer. He wasn't feeling pain. Nor did he suffer major injuries. All of the proof presented at the trial validated that point. Even the prosecution's proof conceded that point.

Was he being kicked? Yes, at least once. For the rest, they weren't kicks so much as efforts to keep a dangerous felony suspect down on the ground, to keep his hands out of pockets we hadn't yet had an opportunity to search. Did the kicks hurt Rodney King? No. Did they keep him from assaulting an officer again? We'll never know. All we know is that he didn't have another chance to attack an officer.

Was he being beaten? Absolutely. That's because we had exhausted every tool we had available short of shooting the suspect. And we didn't want to shoot him, we didn't want to kill him.

It is not frivolous, I think, to dwell for a short time on the "eloquence" that *Time* ascribed to Rodney King. It is worth a moment to question whether a dangerous drunken driver, parole violator, and aggressively violent felony offender has earned noble, even heroic, status for repeatedly violating the law and resisting arrest. And it is worth another to observe that Rodney King's "hesitant, almost sobbing" eloquence referred to by *Time* magazine might have been, as *Vanity Fair* later suggested, due more to being tranquilized by modern drugs and the prospect of collecting on a $56 million lawsuit than a result of any other factor.

The reason for mentioning these matters is that of all the victims of the violence, Rodney King was not one of them. Indeed, he and his attorneys may be the only winners in the entire affair. Rodney King stands to collect millions of dollars in ransom from the city of Los Angeles because he got drunk and violently resisted arrest on March 3, 1991. He also may get millions of dollars more by selling T-shirts and other collectibles bearing his name. As evidence can demonstrate, in today's society, the criminal can extract ransoms and make the law enforcement community the bad guy. Rodney King and his promoters reportedly are peddling a life story and a movie script lionizing him as a courageous champion of civil rights somewhere in the midst of the passive resistance of Martin Luther King, the militant activism of Malcolm X, and the political savvy of Nelson Mandela.[6]

Still, Rodney King is a victim in one sense. His life has changed forever. He will always be a symbol, although not necessarily a wholesome one, to minority activists.

That's criminal, in itself, especially when so many more honorable symbols of minority success and achievement exist in our multicultural society. Compare Rodney King, for example, with people like New York City Mayor David Dinkins, former U.S. Representative Barbara Jordan of Houston, Joint Chiefs of Staff Chairman General Colin Powell, Virginia Governor Douglas Wilder, former San Antonio Mayor Henry Cisneros, and even LA Mayor Tom Bradley, not to mention Magic Johnson and Michael Jordan and the thousands and thousands of black, Hispanic, and Asian attorneys, doctors, entertainers, scientists, cops, firefighters, state legislators, U.S. representatives, and other public officials.

But as time dims passions, as the George Holliday videotape fades from memory, the civil rights movement will be less kind to Rodney King than the present one has been. Let's add to Abraham Lincoln's observation by noting that not only is it impossible to fool all of the people all of the time, you can't fool all of them endlessly. If not today, then someday, the record doubtless will be reviewed with more objectivity. Then Rodney King will be relegated to the minor footnote of history that he and his actions deserve.

But even if you regard him as the first victim, Rodney King

---

[6] It will be interesting to see how Rodney King's encounters with the law will be treated in his announced autobiography. Especially the two occasions of alleged spousal abuse and the time he was arrested after picking up a transvestite male prostitute and then tried to run over vice squad officers with his car. A sexual preference for cross-dressing male whores invites both attention and explanation.

was the least victimized of all. That's certainly true when you compare the profits he stands to reap from his actions on March 3, 1991, with the price paid by the people who died and were hurt in the riots, those storekeepers who lost their shops and livelihood, the workers whose jobs vanished in the smoke of flames from the riots.

But let's begin with the Simi Valley jurors. They are most certainly victims. According to press reports, since the trial some have been menaced by death threats from anonymous callers. All have suffered abusive criticism from the media for their verdicts of not guilty. They have become outcasts in their own communities. Some have had children threatened. Others have lost friendships. The media have reported that one woman juror fears for her job. All of the jurors were deeply affronted by communications from the Ku Klux Klan, notifying them that they had been made members of the KKK and that the right-wing lunatic fringe "stands ready to defend you at a moment's notice."[7]

This dubious compliment from the KKK right-wing wackos is in sharp contrast to the absence of support from the court system for the bravery of the jurors' actions and verdict, their willingness to judge a case on facts, evidence, and law and not on the emotional politics of media-fed passions. After the trial, the jurors were abandoned by the court without even the customary expression of appreciation for their service. According to *Los Angeles Magazine*, the jurors suffer many of the same symptoms of stress and tension experienced by war veterans. Not surprisingly, they have formed a mutual support group that meets occasionally to offer comfort to one another.[8]

And what about the cops who were found innocent? Even before the spurious charges of violating Rodney King's civil

---

[7] *Los Angeles Magazine*, July 1992, p. 62.

[8] Quoting alternate juror Lindy Miller's husband Paul, *Los Angeles Magazine* reported that the jurors " 'were squeezed to the point of mental exhaustion and then they were thrown to the wolves. It's like Vietnam—they went to war together, and when they came home nobody liked them. No wonder they're clinging to each other now.' " Ibid., p. 63.

rights that a federal grand jury returned on August 5, 1992, it was disturbing to see what had happened to the officers who were doing their duty on March 3, 1991. This is especially true when you compare their experience with Rodney King's apparent reprieve from parole violations that would have returned him to prison, and his efforts to gouge millions of dollars from the city of Los Angeles.

Tim Wind, Ted Briseno, and Larry Powell have been doing odd jobs since going on unpaid suspension in April 1991. These three trained, dedicated police officers have had to spend most of their time preparing for the defense of a criminal trial, a federal trial, and subsequent internal administrative hearings that have yet to be scheduled. The three have been able to pick up some cash by helping the police league move its offices, working as part-time security guards, and doing other routine blue collar work. But none has been able to find a full-time job. No employer is going to hire somebody whose time is being taken up defending against criminal charges, even if an employer could ignore the massive publicity attending those charges.

Even after the federal civil rights suit and LAPD trial boards are concluded, their careers on the Los Angeles Police Department are effectively over. However unjust it might be, Wind, Briseno, and Powell will always bear the stigma of having been involved in the Rodney King affair.

Tim Wind may be able to return to police work, perhaps in his native Kansas. Let's hope so. He is a competent, dedicated, and idealistic police officer who truly believes in the contribution he can make to society through law enforcement work. Larry Powell may undergo the ordeal of another trial, and his future in police work is uncertain.

Ted Briseno might be able to continue in a law-enforcement career somewhere, but not in Los Angles, where his nickname among LAPD street cops is now "Benedict" because of his defection at the Simi Valley trial. There, he testified that he saw something no other police officer at the scene witnessed and contradicted a former statement of his saying he agreed with the way the matter had been handled on March 3—not exactly the "one-for-all and all-for-one" attitude attributed to coppers. This is not to say that Ted Briseno perjured himself. It is to say that Ted Briseno was looking out for his own interests, and he decided that those interests did not coincide with those of his fellow officers. I can excuse him for that. But some of his colleagues might not.

Like me, Wind, Powell, and Briseno have had their legal expenses paid by the Los Angeles Police Department Protective League. Without that financial assistance they doubtless would be in bankruptcy. My legal bills alone have exceeded $100,000, and without the league's help I would have been insolvent long ago. Here is a bitter irony: at the same time the city of Los Angeles negotiates a huge ransom for Rodney King, city officials have steadfastly refused to approve any assistance to their police officers. The city has done nothing to assist us with legal costs or medical expenses.

For example, one of the four of us—not I, and no purpose is served by saying who—has required extensive medical care following the March 3, 1991, affair. And for one simple reason: no ordinary human being can endure being called a racist street thug day after day, on international television and in the nation's leading newspapers, without suffering some psychological harm. This is especially true when the reason for the condemnation comes from having done a job to the best of his ability, within the legal guidelines prescribed by officials, and then being found innocent of wrongdoing.

Yet the city of Los Angeles turned its back on this officer, and the rest of us, and declined to pay the bills for the care required. As a result, this officer's psychiatrist discontinued treatment.

As for me, you may recall that I mentioned at the beginning of this book that I was the best possible person to handle the Rodney King arrest. That's not just because of my training, educational background in law enforcement, and thirteen years of experience on the street. It's also because of my personal situation.

I am also fortunate in being sufficiently well educated to embark upon a second career. I am considering returning to college to earn a PhD in criminal justice, then seeking a teaching position at the university level.

Whatever happens, I know that I cannot return to police work as a street cop. This realization has been perhaps the most crushing blow of all. I love police work. Being a street cop is my career. Putting bad guys in jail is all I have wanted to do since entering the Los Angeles Police Department Academy in August 1976.

After finally accepting that I could no longer be a street cop, I spent many nights pondering the past. I recalled the Police Academy and its rigorous physical training. Still fresh is the memory of being a probationer in Van Nuys, and of such experiences as the time my training officer showed me how to kick through a door. A caller had reported a woman screaming. We arrived at the scene. My training officer pounded on the door. There was no answer. So he told me to stand back, he'd show me how to open a locked door. He kicked, and his foot went right through the flimsy, hollow wooden panel. But the now-open door got stuck on his foot. A naked woman rushed to the door, and we could see a naked man inside—the woman had been screaming in the throes of passionate coupling. As the nude woman looked wonderingly on, and as my training officer kept apologizing while struggling to remove his foot from the door, I innocently asked, "Just so I've got it straight, is that how I'm to kick in a door?" You don't want to hear the training officer's answer.

There were good times and bad. I remember my first murder call, the first time a training officer told me, "There ain't going to be no medals of valor[9] in this black-and-white, kid. Medals of valor are for officers with a momentary lapse of sanity." It was a lesson I recalled the night I faced down the suspect with an AK-47. I didn't want a medal of valor. All I wanted was to stay alive, for my partner to stay alive, to do my job.

I learned both on the street and in the classroom, progressing to sergeant, and I gained great personal and career satisfaction

---

[9] The highest award for personal bravery that the LAPD bestows upon an officer.

in being able to share what I had learned with younger officers. It is my fervent hope, as well as firm belief, that the institutional memory of being a street cop that I have passed along will someday save lives—the lives of not just officers but civilians, too. Even civilians like Rodney King, whose life I saved on March 3, 1991, by not escalating to deadly force when I had every justification for doing so.

You see, there are two reasons why I cannot be a street cop again. The first is that even if I rejoined the LAPD after being found innocent by an administrative tribunal, the department would not permit me to go back to the war zone. Sgt. Stacey C. Koon has embarrassed the department. That is the unforgivable sin on the LAPD. So the department could not allow me back on the streets, which would mean more bad publicity for the department. Instead, I would be assigned to do administrative work where I would be a target for all of the management sycophants looking for a chance to take pot-shots at an easy target, pot-shots that would help them ride a rocket to the top.

The second reason I cannot be a street cop is more personal and much more serious. It is because I now question my judgment.

Those questions of judgment aren't the result of how the Rodney King arrest was handled: I know it was done properly, according to policies, procedures, and training.[10] I know it was done with minimum levels of force, and that we saved lives on the night of March 3, 1991.

No, the reason I question my judgment is because I cannot trust my superior officers to support good-faith decisions made in accordance with accepted instructions and guidelines, decisions that must be made in fractions of seconds, not minutes, if lives and property are to be made safe.

---

[10] Some critics might ask: Isn't this like being a good Nazi, just carrying out orders? Not at all. The orders and guidelines for using force were conceived and approved by the Los Angeles Police Commission, the LAPD itself, and the Los Angeles City Council, in accordance with the demands of minority critics of police procedures. Please review Chapter 2 if this question occurs to you.

I believe in what I do, that what I did on March 3, 1991, was proper. But if I returned to the streets, second-guessing my superiors and allowing that lack of trust to intrude upon my decisions, as it surely would, somebody might get killed. I might get killed. That is a consequence I wish to avoid. Worse, if one of my officers got killed because of my indecision, I would regret it for the rest of my life.

But you've probably read enough about me. And besides, I'm not a victim so much as a survivor. I shall survive. English students please note the imperative, "shall." I "shall" survive. But others affected by the Rodney King affair may not be so confident about the future as I.

Ira Reiner, for example, had a political career. It's over. He may not know it now, but he will. You can't lose "easy" cases like the LAPD Four and get reelected. That's as it should be, but not because he lost the case, but because he shouldn't have let the case progress to the point that it did in the first place. He should have short-circuited the case before it ever went to trial. But Reiner and the Los Angeles political establishment, which includes the LAPD, had to push the case to a conclusion that couldn't be won. We are all now paying the price for that political expediency. The ultimate price was paid by the people who died in the riots and their survivors who loved them.

Then there's former Chief Daryl Gates. His controversial career was over when he turned his back on his street cops. Daryl Gates was a good cop in his time and, as chief, he began some worthwhile initiatives, especially in combating drug abuse among young people. He could have done more. But he lost it. If he had stayed with his street cops, if he had tried to protect us for doing our jobs as we had been taught with the same fervor he used to guard his own career, his street cops would have followed him forever. But he didn't, and he lost us. Now he is gone.

And Mayor Tom Bradley? Politics is more important to Mayor Bradley than truth. He knows, perhaps better than anyone else, how Los Angeles political leaders and their minority-community allies imposed unrealistic rules of force on the LAPD. He knows that these rules made it inevitable that what might appear to be a brutal beating would someday occur. Yet he blames the police, not the policies. Hypocrisy isn't pretty.

Don't forget the liberal community and their spokesfolks, Zev Yaroslavsky, former Councilman Robert Farrell, the Los Angeles chapter of the American Civil Liberties Union, and all of their allies. They're the ones who said that money was more important than black people's lives. They're the ones who said the city budget would be better off by beating suspects with a PR 24 baton than by using a chokehold and paying off lawsuits. They may try to deny that now, and doubtless will do so. But the record is clear: these are the people who imposed the rules on police officers, rules that we have tried conscientiously to follow. And now they are leaders of the mob trying to lynch cops for doing what they've been ordered to do. Reiner, Gates, Yaroslavsky—all of these people could have done the right thing by supporting the rules they approved. But they chose to pervert the truth to save their own skins.

These are just some of the tragic consequences of the Rodney King affair, just some of the casualties.

Yet the incident is not a total loss. Oddly enough, the justice system is one of the winners from this episode. Or at least it has been so far. That's because the Simi Valley jury that found me and my officers innocent on most charges performed their duty in accordance with the highest moral standards of justice upon which this nation was established. The Simi Valley jury, despite overwhelming media opposition and public opinion conditioned to a presumption of guilt by the media, did its duty by finding us not guilty, a verdict based upon the law, facts, evidence, and truth.

Therein can be found the most lamentable casualty of the Rodney King Affair: Truth.

Truth has been lost in this affair. Truth is the real victim of how the episode was first revealed and how it continues to be explained to the American people by the news media. As in war, truth has been the first and most serious casualty of the Rodney King affair.

7

The Media's Responsibility

A. J. Liebling, the distinguished World War II correspondent and press critic for the *New Yorker* magazine in the 1940s, 1950s, and 1960s, once compared journalism to cheap-shot guerrilla warfare.

Journalists, Liebling said, were people who hid up in the hills and waited until the battle was over. Then they would come down to the deserted battlefield and shoot the wounded.

At the time, Liebling was referring only to editorial writers, but he could as easily have been describing today's reporters. Because, since the early 1970s and the Watergate episode, reporters and editors have taken upon themselves the responsibility to determine the proper standards of social and political behavior, a responsibility that goes far beyond what the Founding Fathers anticipated when the First Amendment guaranteed freedom of the press. And all too often these standards have been established without a thorough examination of facts that might lead the media to a different conclusion.

The Rodney King affair is a classic example. If ever there was a case of instant trial and conviction by the media, particularly television, this was it. Some background is necessary here to understand why and how the media conditioned the American people to presume guilt on the part of police officers in the arrest of Rodney King, despite overwhelming evidence to the contrary.

First, it should be noted that I do not believe a media conspiracy existed to blame the cops rather than the proper culprits— primarily the inadequate use-of-force policies adopted by Los Angeles officialdom in the early 1980s. The media are altogether too diverse, too diffused, for such collusion. It is silly to suggest that thousands of editors, reporters, and television and radio commentators conspired to convict me and my officers in the court of public opinion on a presumption of guilt created by an incomplete and usually edited eighty-two-second videotape. An intrigue this widespread would be even more difficult to organize and sustain than the alleged "conspiracy" to beat Rodney King that the Los Angeles DA's office and others have tried to hang on my officers and me, the CHIPs, and the Los Angeles Unified School District police. No, instead of a media conspiracy, at least four other factors were at work here.

The first was the media's self-assumed role as a watchdog to sniff out official wrongdoing and bring it to public attention. This is a laudable goal, but it was not envisioned by the framers of the Constitution when they wrote the First Amendment guaranteeing a free press. The media and its leading spokesmen and spokeswomen would have you believe this, but it is not true. As I have learned from my journalist colleague who assisted with this book, for most of the nation's early years newspapers were largely journals of partisan political opinion with no allegiance to either the truth or the broad public interest. It was only in the 1840s that the press began to adopt the role of advocate of the public interest.[1] Over the years, this role,

---

[1] You can almost put a date on it. James Gordon Bennett was a Washington, D.C., publisher who had supported Andrew Jackson. Jackson's protégé, Martin Van Buren, promised Bennett some lucrative government printing contracts, then reneged on the deal. In retaliation, Bennett established the *New York Herald* as a "voice of the people," beholden to no political philosophy or partisan cause. And he made a pile of money selling papers for two or three cents to hundreds of thousands of the people. Other editors soon awakened to the profit potential in being a "voice of the people." Thus was nonpartisan, anti-establishment journalism born. It was not a noble search for the truth. It was a desire to make money. Which is, of course, in the finest traditions of American business and journalism.

largely worthwhile, has become institutionalized. There's no question that aggressive media attention to official wrongdoing has uncovered many sins by appointed and elected officials and others in authority. The abuse of public trust by the railroads in the nineteenth century, the muckraking exposés of oil cartels and beef trusts, and, of course, Watergate leap immediately to mind.

But when the media's suspicions of fiendish official behavior become paranoid and they accept facts without examining the evidence, the media's own sins can be far more dangerous than wrongdoing by government. Look at the LA riots, for example. More than fifty people dead, thousands injured, almost $1 billion in property destroyed. Whatever the underlying social and economic causes for the discontent, you can make a good case that the riots were prompted by the media's unwillingness or failure to report facts during the Simi Valley trial that would have cast legitimate clouds of doubt over a presumption of guilt. But these facts would have intruded upon a good story, and they were not reported. And so, by omission, the media prepared the public for guilty verdicts. Just recall some of the reactions to the Simi Valley verdicts of innocence:

"I was stunned," said Mayor Tom Bradley. "I was shocked. I was outraged. I was speechless when I heard that verdict. Today this jury told the world that what we all saw with our own eyes was not a crime. The jury's verdict will never blind the world to what we saw on the videotape. Nobody could have anticipated this verdict."[2] Benjamin Hooks, executive director of the NAACP, told the *Los Angeles Times* that the acquittals were "outrageous, a mockery of justice." Hooks insisted that "given the evidence [presumably the George Holliday videotape], it is difficult to see how the jurors will ever live with their consciences."[3] Bradley's and Hooks's reactions were typical. Condemnation of the verdict poured from every quarter.

Yet the verdicts of innocence were almost a foregone conclusion from the moment the trial began. For one simple reason:

[2] *Los Angeles Times*, pp. A-1, A-23, A-24, April 30, 1992.

[3] Ibid., p. A-24.

the facts, evidence, and law demanded a not guilty finding, although you never would have believed it from reading news accounts or watching TV news. By the time of the trial, of course, the George Holliday videotape had been shown so often that it would have been difficult for the media to stand back and say, "Hey, folks, maybe there's more here than what we've been showing you for a year." As Jonathan Alter said in a postmortem in the May 11, 1992, issue of *Newsweek*: "A fire needs oxygen. . . . From the very beginning, the oxygen that has given life to the Rodney King story is television."[4]

Even more to the point was a piece by Thomas B. Rosenstiel of the *Los Angeles Times* on May 3, 1992. He wrote: "In the Rodney King case,[5] several experts said that during coverage of the trial, television stations, always eager for the most compelling picture, would replay the [George Holliday] videotape rather than show the more mundane images from the courtroom itself. While that does not mean the verdict was correct, it may help explain why it seemed so shocking to the public." Rosenstiel went on to report a wonderful example of how television can casually distort in its effort to add graphic drama to ordinary words. He noted that on Cable News Network, "one jury member's explanation that [Rodney] King was in control at all times and that the force used against him was reasonable was shown . . . written in text across the bottom of the screen while the pictures of the beating played above it."[6] Presumed guilty? Media distortion? You decide.

Moreover, there's a strange contradiction in the media's First Amendment rights, one that works against private citizens who become unwilling objects of harmful reporting. In the

---

[4] *Newsweek*, May 11, 1992, p. 45.

[5] Sic. You see, it's still the Rodney King case, even though he was not on trial. Had he been on trial for drunken driving, felony evading, resisting arrest, and parole violation, the evidence would have convicted him. This is a curious situation, where the case is misnamed and a guilty verdict regarded as the only possible outcome. Who created the situation? It's an easy question to answer. You can start with the media.

[6] *Los Angeles Times*, May 3, 1992, p. A-7.

1964 *Sullivan* decision, the courts generally held that it is difficult to libel a "public person." And how does somebody become a "public person"? By media publicity, of course. So the media have the power to make me and my officers "public" people, and then can report almost any inaccuracies without fear of penalty. For example, *Time* magazine said on May 11 that Rodney King sustained "half a dozen blows to the head from Koon alone. . . ."

Where *Time* got this information is a mystery. At no time did I physically strike Rodney King (unless you regard using the TASER as a "physical strike"). The Holliday videotape shows no blows to Rodney King's head, and certainly none delivered by me. It is clear that I am removed from the center of activity, directing my officers from about five feet away. Yet I am a "public person," made reluctantly so by the LAPD's unauthorized release of my name to the media as soon as the Rodney King affair got hot. So I had no recourse against *Time* except to ask for a correction (which the magazine made in a later issue).

The second factor is a news-gathering socialization process that makes reporters and editors suspicious of officialdom and, since at least the 1960s, particularly distrustful when cops and civil rights are involved. This socialization process means that journalists become clones of one another, at least intellectually. Although reporters and editors like to regard themselves as fiercely independent chroniclers of the truth and facts, it has been my experience that they tend to think very much alike. (This is true of cops, too. In fact, it's true of almost all professions.) This explains the "pack" mentality that you see in journalism today—one newspaper reporter or TV cameraman comes up with a story, and all the others rush to report it so they won't be left out. You see the pack mentality at work in journalism every day. It is most evident in politics.

And there's another contradiction here as well. Right along with being suspicious of officialdom, journalists tend to rely heavily on official pronouncements, to treat them as facts that require no examination. This explains the curious spectacle of reporters obediently parroting the words of an allegedly wronged citizen (in this case, Rodney King, with help from his lawyer), then finding official confirmation of those allegations (from the Los Angeles district attorney's office, along with comments by Mayor Bradley and members of the Los Angeles City Council and Police Commission). These reports are dutifully conveyed to the public without any probing scrutiny or examination of conflicting positions to determine whether the statements are truthful or irresponsible, self-serving lies. In short, reporters like to run with the hare and hunt with the hounds. They try to have it both ways, and they often succeed.

A third factor that influenced the imbalanced coverage of the Rodney King affair is simply that the media have become big business. And, like all big businesses, the profit motive is paramount. So it's in the media's best interest to be as sensational and controversial as possible in order to build ratings for the evening news and sell newspapers and magazines.

Once the media jumped on the Rodney King story, no detail of the affair could be ignored, regardless of its relevance to the events of March 3, 1991. One evening, for example, I received a telephone call from a *Los Angeles Times* reporter who seemed reluctant, almost embarrassed, to ask her question. She said she had heard that I had a close relative who was openly gay, and she wanted to know if the rumor was true. Yes, I said, it was true, although I failed to see what the lifestyle of someone I love, a lifestyle that I don't approve of but that does not intrude upon my feelings for the person, has to do with the arrest of Rodney King. The reporter didn't print the information; presumably the editor decided that it was not exactly a matter of burning public interest. Yet the media could and did intrude upon an innocent third party's privacy in their restless pursuit of any fact or detail that might add drama to the Rodney King incident.[7]

The fourth and final factor involves the nature of television.

---

[7] Although, in fact, many pertinent details of public interest could have been dredged up about Rodney King and given wide publicity. His arrest record before and after March 3, 1991, is a good example. But, of course, that sort of background didn't fit the stereotype of an innocently wronged black man, so it was only occasionally mentioned, and almost never in context with the George Holliday videotape.

Television is a news medium that is visual and visceral, not given to thoughtful analysis or explanation of facts that might detract from the theatrics of news-as-entertainment. The main interest of television news is to portray an incident with as much drama and controversy as superficial facts allow.

The Rodney King affair was perfect for television: cops cruelly beating a black man. And if that incident could be presented in a fashion that could resurrect the images of Old South police brutality, so much the better. Then television would have not only drama and controversy, but a rich mixture of official wrongdoing, the social and historical drama of the civil rights movement, and rogue Los Angeles cops out on an orgy of savage behavior, all in one juicy morsel.

That's why it was inconvenient for television to include the first two seconds of the George Holliday videotape. Those were the two seconds that showed Rodney King rising from the ground to attack Officer Powell—deliberately. Those two seconds did not reveal police batons swinging on a helpless black man, writhing innocently on the ground. Never mind that he was neither helpless nor harmlessly squirming to avoid getting hit; those crucial first two seconds impaired the drama of the videotape because police batons weren't falling.

So most viewers of the Holliday videotape never saw (and still haven't seen) the attack on Officer Powell. Neither were they told that Rodney King earlier had thrown off four police officers who had swarmed him in an unsuccessful effort to put him in handcuffs. Nor was it commonly reported that Rodney King had overcome two blasts of fifty thousand volts each from my TASER. All of these facts, you see, did not conform to the image of police officers brutalizing an unoffending black man. And that was the image that played well on television.

A thorough analysis of how the media covered the Rodney King affair from the beginning to the present would require enough research to earn a doctoral degree in mass communications.[8] So far, the media's introspection has been confined to

---

[8] Hopefully, that project will someday be undertaken. It could be an instructive tool for the media to analyze their own power.

looking at its failure to anticipate the Los Angeles riots in terms of social issues and rap fast-talkers. The prestigious *Nieman Reports*, for example, published by the Nieman Foundation at Harvard University, is widely regarded as the media profession's journal of intellectual opinion. It is to journalism what the *New England Journal of Medicine* is to doctors— widely read, widely quoted, and a molder of professional thought and conduct.

Yet in a report on how the media failed in its responsibilities in the Rodney King affair, the 1992 summer issue of *Nieman Reports* proclaimed: "We Weren't Listening—By Not Tapping Into Rap's Message of Violence [the] Media Failed to Prepare Public for Rampage." The article, by Pulitzer Prize-winning journalist Harold Jackson of the *Birmingham News*, noted that the media hadn't taken care to listen to the rage growing within Los Angeles's black community, rage that was expressed in rap music but ignored by more establishment minority leaders. "The media are no longer trusted to tell the whole story of the neglected communities where violence is most likely to occur," Jackson concluded. "The media must regain that trust."

Journalist Jackson's contention that the media are not listening to outrage in the black community is doubtless true. That the media have lost trust is certainly true. But you can make an equally good case that the way the media have treated the Rodney King affair, especially television's repetitive replays of an incomplete and edited videotape, did indeed "prepare the public for rampage" as much or more than had it taken heed of rap musicians.

Absent a thorough academic study of just how many times the George Holliday videotape was replayed on national and local television outlets, let's look at just a few specific examples of how the media distorted the story.

On April 30, with the riots twenty-four hours in progress, ABC ran the Rodney King videotape three times on the World News Tonight, according to Accuracy in Media (AIM). AIM quoted Howard Rosenberg, the Pulitzer Prize-winning television critic for the *Los Angeles Times*, as saying that television had "fanned the flames" by continuing to show the video.

But TV kept the fans churning. For example, on May 3, Sam Donaldson of ABC was on "This Week With David Brinkley." Donaldson said: "There the man [Rodney King] was on the ground, covering up toward the end, being beaten into insensitivity [sic], and this all-white jury decided the police were the good guys. Now, I don't want to be too hard on those twelve people because I think that's very indicative of what happens all across the country. We do have a society which is still racist, and in the case of the police, a society which wants to forgive them any transgression as long as they are not breaking into our house or beating our children. . . . The message it sent is very dangerous. . . . We are all at risk from that type of action."[9]

As one of television's foremost news reporters and commentators, Donaldson's comments are worth some analysis. Yes, Rodney King was on the ground. No, he wasn't "covering up toward the end," but constantly rising to threaten the officers. And, no, he wasn't being "beaten into insensitivity" or even into insensibility. The jury never heard testimony to that effect, and Donaldson either was speaking from ignorance or deliberately distorting the truth.

The medical reports introduced as evidence in the trial clearly show that Rodney King was never unconscious, that he was alert and aware at all times, and that the preliminary diagnosis of his injuries at Pacifica Hospital were PCP overdose and superficial facial lacerations. All of that information was publicly introduced in the trial, and Donaldson should have known about it. About the only thing Donaldson said that might be true is that "We are all at risk from that type of [police] action."

As a veteran street cop, I can assure you that anyone who gets drunk and leads police officers on a 7.8-mile chase at speeds of up to 115 miles an hour at midnight, then tosses four

---

[9] Quoted by Accuracy in Media in the May 1992 AIM *Report*.

cops off his back, then absorbs two blasts with a TASER, then attacks a cop, all the while refusing to obey police commands to be handcuffed is, indeed, "at risk."

Time magazine's report on the Simi Valley verdict refused to concede that justice might have been served, not betrayed, by the jury's not guilty verdicts on most counts. Instead, *Time* blamed an inept prosecution. "With race the ever present issue in the case—King has claimed that he was taunted throughout the beating with racial slurs—the prosecution did little to bring home its significance to the jury."[10] Maybe that was because Rodney King himself had said in a videotaped interview only a couple of days after the incident that race was not a factor, and perhaps the prosecution wanted to avoid explaining that annoying little contradiction.

Time went on to say that the race issue "will now be central to the civil rights investigation the Justice Department is still pursuing." Well, it may be central to *Time* magazine, but it's not to the Justice Department. In the indictments handed down August 5, 1992, the Justice Department specifically said race was not an issue. That's because it isn't. Rodney King was subdued and arrested because he was a felony evader, not because he was a black man.

Finally, *Time* concluded that the acquittal "cannot have provided much satisfaction to many who watched the beating of King or the televised rioting that broke out once it was announced. . . . And the videotape will go on to haunt the nation with its scene of what still looks like sanctioned sadism. For most Americans, no legal argument about the stages of police procedure can explain away those images, though legal argument may have worked for 12 jurors in Simi Valley who were disposed to heed it. To most Americans, black and white, in this case good lawyering triumphed over justice itself."[11]

Time's reaction was painfully characteristic of how the

---

[10] *Time* magazine, May 11, p. 31.

[11] Ibid., May 11, 1992, p. 33.

mainstream media reported the verdict and the reasons behind it. Only smaller, more targeted publications have sought to unravel the truth about the incident and why the Simi Valley jury returned the verdict it did. Accuracy in Media, for example, attempted to place a full-page advertisement in the *Houston Post*, defending the jury verdict and advertising its analytical report on the trial proceedings. According to AIM editor Reed Irvine, the ad was rejected.

Perhaps the most thoughtful analysis was made in the June 1992 issue of the *American Lawyer*. Roger Orloff, described by *American Lawyer* Media President Steven Brill as "a careful, liberal-leaning lawyer," provided a devastating critique of how the mainstream media summarized the trial in reports following the verdict. Orloff, having carefully followed the trial in its entirety on the Courtroom TV Network, concluded that "The defense case I saw was plausible; indeed, many of its most significant points were essentially undisputed."[12]

Orloff went on to say that news accounts of the trial verdict published by the *New York Times* omitted some of the "significant points" that apparently influenced the jury. Dissecting the *Times'* analysis of the defense case, he noted that:

• While the *Times* accurately reported the defense contention that batons were used "in response to 'aggressive movements and postures by the mostly prone Mr. King,' " the *Times* failed to point out that King had already been TASED twice and had attacked Officer Powell.

• While the *Times* also accurately reported the defense claim that the officers had to use all but deadly force to prevent King from rising from the ground, Orloff added, "Yes, but can the reader appreciate the strength of that argument without understanding *that King had already twice risen from the ground and advanced upon the officers?*" (emphasis in original)

• And, third, while the *Times* characterized King's injuries

---

[12] Reprinted in *Legal Times*, June 8, 1992, p. 23.

as "not as serious as the prosecution contended," that wasn't quite true. The defense argument, Orloff continued, was that King's injuries were not the sort someone would expect to see if King had been hit repeatedly in the head with power strokes from a police baton, "the crime most of the nation's population assumes was committed [by the officers]."

In his analysis, Orloff admitted to his concern about defending the Simi Valley verdicts, adding that he feared "the reactions of people I work with who will see this article's headline and byline and never read the rest." Orloff concluded: "And I am terrified at the prospect of quotation out of context. After all, imagine if the media were to summarize this article the way they summarized the trial."[13]

But Orloff's work has largely been either ignored or not seen by the nation's mainstream media, nor, indeed, by even the specialized professional publications. Orloff's conclusions cannot be shunted aside simply because the media continue to portray the Rodney King affair in the most dramatic—not the most truthful—terms possible.

For example, following the August 5, 1992, indictment of me and my officers on federal civil rights charges (a development that will be discussed in the epilogue) wire service stories continued to refer to Rodney King as a "motorist," without noting that in leading officers on an almost eight-mile chase at speeds of more than one hundred miles per hour he hardly qualified as a simple "motorist." Even the ABA *Journal*, the legal profession's most influential publication, continued to perpetuate that myth in its August 1992 issue. In an analysis of whether a different jury would have reached a different conclusion from the one voted by the Simi Valley panelists, reporter Mark Hansen of the ABA *Journal* wrote: "King, as everybody knows by now, is the black motorist whose beating last year by

---

[13] With apologies to Mr. Orloff, the summary of his article in this book is not intended to be complete. But I hope that I have in no way distorted the intent of any of his comments quoted here.

four white Los Angeles police officers was captured on video-tape for all the world to see."[14]

But perhaps the most egregious example of how the media continue to distort the truth and inflame public passion by incomplete reporting was provided by *USAToday* on August 6, 1992, in its report on the federal indictments. On page one, the national weekday newspaper described Rodney King simply as a "black motorist." Any uninformed reader could conclude from that article that King was stopped just for being black and driving. But *USAToday* wasn't quite through with its advocacy journalism under the disguise of fair reporting. In an inside-page article, "Catching up with the central figures," *USAToday* said of Rodney King:

"King, 27, is still struggling to recover from a concussion, several head fractures, and a shattered eye socket and cheek-bone from his beating. The former construction worker has been picked up by police three times since the beating, the latest on suspicion of drunk driving. He suffers from post-traumatic stress syndrome, his lawyers say, and spent the last year secluded and heavily medicated."[15] The capsule-sized news bite went on to reveal how King made a plea for calm during the riots and how he was negotiating a settlement with the city of Los Angeles.

If ever distortion existed, this is it. It's true that he had a cheekbone fractured, but there was no proof offered at the state trial that it was a result of a beating. Proof *was* provided, however, that the fractured cheekbone came from smashing face-first into the pavement three times. As for "concussion" and "several head fractures," no evidence was ever submitted to sustain any such claims.

Nor is *USAToday* to be complimented for pointing out that King has been arrested three times since March 3, 1991, "the latest on suspicion of drunken driving." It glibly ignores the

---

[14] In all fairness, the ABA package of stories on the trial and its impact on the legal system tended to be balanced and equitable.

[15] *USAToday*, August 6, 1992, p. 8-A.

other arrests that suggest something about Rodney King's character—a complaint of physical abuse filed by his wife and the Hollywood charge, later dismissed, of allegedly trying to run down two vice squad officers after King picked up a transvestite male prostitute; he then tried to flee from officers because he said he feared that he was being pursued by gang members, according to newspaper accounts.

It is also reportedly true that since the incident King has "spent the last year secluded and heavily medicated." But the implication from *USAToday*'s article is that the medication was required for injuries sustained at the hands of police on March 3, 1991, not, as *Vanity Fair* reported, to keep him sedated so he wouldn't blow a multimillion dollar lawsuit.

Now, contrast that with how *USAToday* characterized "The Four Officers." Laurence Powell "hasn't been able to work . . . basically doing nothing," the newspaper quoted a friend as saying. Tim Wind was fired, *USAToday* reported, failing to note that he had been reinstated. Ted Briseno was accurately identified as "the only officer to break ranks during the trial and blame the others for the beating." The newspaper said I "was trying to sell a 275-page manuscript entitled *The Ides of March* to potential publishers in which he [the author] describes police work and jokes about using force against minorities."[16]

The point here is that *USAToday*'s treatment of Rodney

---

[16] It is unfortunate that this subject has to be addressed, but the "manuscript" story has gotten some publicity all by itself and needs to be explained. "The Ides of March" was not a manuscript. It was nothing more than a collection of notes I had made about my life in police work and submitted to several publishers as a basis of consideration for a more polished manuscript. It was, indeed, a therapeutic exercise, and represented a finished manuscript no more than a reporter's rough notes constitute a completed news story. How many reporters would permit their notes to be published as representative of their work? I recall newspaper and TV reporters and editors filing suit frequently to prevent disclosure of their rough notes or unused "outtake" film. That same courtesy should also be extended to others, especially when the subject is one so volatile as race, and no evidence has ever been presented that race was a factor in the Rodney King incident.

King, when not an outright distortion, was true, but in a positive, laudatory way. *USAToday* ignored broader negative truths about King. In contrast, what was reported about the status of the officers was negatively true, while ignoring broader positive truths. This is not an unimportant distinction. It is the way public opinion is formed. One can only conclude that *USAToday*, like most of the rest of the mainstream U.S. media, is sympathetic to Rodney King and hostile to me and my officers.

That's the media's right. But it shouldn't be presented—or misrepresented—as fair and objective journalism. It isn't. Worse, even as I write, they continue to do their best to convince people of our guilt before our second trial even begins. And therein lies the problem. We made every effort to inform both television and newspapers of the facts as they unfolded. Both media consciously chose to ignore these facts. Let me be specific here: the *Los Angeles Times* reporters who covered the trial were routinely informed of the strategy, tactics, and facts of the defense argument. We also made a specific point of telling these reporters to improve the coverage they gave to the trial. But they either chose to ignore these summaries, or their editors elected to prevent their publication.

A presumption of guilt, when proven false, can result in an explosion of unimaginable fury. We've seen it happen. And we almost certainly will see it happen again if another trial finds me and my officers innocent.[17]

And this because the basic lessons of the Rodney King affair have not yet been absorbed. In this case, to paraphrase Liebling, the media came down from the hills to shoot the wounded before the battle was even over.

What propelled the riots was the media reporting. By ignoring one side of the story, the media misled the public. Then,

---

[17] This is a very real danger. It is likely a federal jury will review the same evidence seen by the Simi Valley jury and come to the same conclusion of innocence. What will be the response then?

when the jury delivered its opinion, everyone was surprised. The question must be asked: if the facts had been reported from the beginning, would people have been outraged by the decision? The obvious answer is no. But the media failed in their responsiblity, and the city of Los Angeles, and the nation, paid the price.

8

Lessons Unlearned

In the turbulent wake of the Rodney King affair, Los Angeles city officials scurried to repair the damage. Damage control was the foremost consideration.

The first step was to make certain the officers in the Rodney King affair—the presumed guilty—were indicted and thrown into the legal system that knew the officers were innocent of the charges, or had plenty of reasons to believe so. But the knowledge of innocence notwithstanding, the presumed guilty had to be prosecuted to pacify an inflamed public that had been deceived by the media.

And what was the next step? It was predictable. As officials are inclined to do, the city appointed a study commission. The commission's job was to patch the holes in the road.

As most have surely observed, study commissions are perhaps the most useless of official bodies. That's certainly true at the bottom of the police food chain, where all study commission reports on police misdeeds eventually land. What happens is this: study commissions identify problems everybody knows exist, provide whatever obvious evidence can be accumulated, and then make recommendations that are useful but are either already in place or subsequently ignored.

The Christopher Commission study that followed the

Rodney King incident was different for several reasons.[1] But, oddly enough, it was also the same. Let's look first at why it was the same as other study commissions that have examined big city problems.

First, the Christopher Commission found that racism did indeed exist in the Los Angeles Police Department. Well, now, there's a finding calculated to leave one breathless. Especially a Los Angeles street cop.

Of course racism exists on the LAPD, as it does throughout American business and society at large. So does sexism. So does every other kind of "ism" that poisons today's American society seeking to placate every identifiable group that has a complaint. But this doesn't mean everybody is a racist or sexist. This observation is not intended to shrug off the abusive racism that has pervaded the Los Angeles Police Department for years. I am painfully aware of that problem. Again, let me give two examples.

You probably know by now, or at least you should, that my last name is "Koon." It is an honorable name, my father's name, and his father's before him. It is one of which I am proud. Yet you probably also know that "koon," or "coon," is a derisive term that has been applied to black people. To call a black person a "koon" or "coon" is offensive and racist and, to any black person, an unmistakable signal of bigotry.

You can probably see what's coming here. It happened when I was a probationer in Van Nuys. At that time, I worked both P.M. and A.M. watches. The A.M. training officers were older, more laid back, and less inclined to seek trouble than the P.M. training officers, who were generally younger, brasher cops with a gunslinger mentality.

Anyway, while I was a probationer in Van Nuys, the only black area I worked was off Roscoe between Orion and Langdon. There, my training officers had fun with my name,

---

[1] As noted earlier, the commission took as its own the name of the chairman, Warren Christopher, a distinguished Los Angeles attorney and former deputy secretary of state under President Jimmy Carter.

"Koon." We'd go to the black neighborhoods on calls. As expected, as soon as the cops arrived there was an instant crowd. My training officers would put me within shouting distance of themselves, and then one of them would call, "Hey, Koon!"

The citizens would become immediately alert, suspicious. The training officers loved the looks they could generate in a black crowd by simply shouting, "Hey, Koon!" Then they'd deflate the situation. "Hey," they'd say to the crowd that was growing angrier by the moment, "I'm just calling my partner. Oh, you thought it was a racial thing? No, no. Not at all. It's my partner's name."

The blacks would look at me. They'd look at my name tag, at the name "Koon." Then the tension would subside. The citizens would smile. We'd smile. It was all in good fun. But it really wasn't. It's the sort of thing that builds tension, and unnecessarily. The sort of thing over which I had no control. Racism on the LAPD? You'd better believe it.

Then there was the time I got a bad mark on my jacket (reputation). That means I screwed up. It happened in West Valley. I spent about five years in West Valley. It was longer than I wanted, but I stayed for a purpose. I'd been marked as a climber by my supervisors, but I was too educated for my own good, and that's where I made a mistake. It happened with a simple family dispute at an apartment complex, and overcoming that "mistake" was the reason I stayed in West Valley for so long.

Several neighbors had called to report a domestic quarrel at an apartment complex. Arriving at the scene, my partner and I were greeted by a black male. This was kind of unusual for West Valley, since most blacks lived off Roscoe in Van Nuys. At that time, some coppers used the acronym, "NWOB," for stopping a black person in West Valley. That meant, "Nigger West of Balboa" (a major north-south artery that dissected the West Valley's eastern border). In short, a black person wasn't where he or she was supposed to be. The acronym may still be used today. I don't know. I didn't like it then, and I don't like it today.

Anyway, my partner and I detained the black male involved

in this domestic dispute. Then the female made her appearance. She was white. She had a broken jaw. The couple had had a fight, and the suspect had hit her in the mouth with a blunt object. She was afraid of her boyfriend, the suspect, who was on parole for attempted murder. After talking with neighbors on both sides of the apartment, my partner and I decided he was the bad guy. So we hooked him up with cuffs and were about to cart him off to jail when my partner suggested we request a sergeant.

"Why?" I asked.

Well, my partner said, he thought maybe a sergeant should review the circumstances.

"What circumstances?" I asked again. "We've got a legitimate ADW [assault with a deadly weapon charge] here." But I agreed to have my partner call a sergeant. It was a decision I came to regret.

The sergeant arrived and made a cursory inspection. Then he looked at me and asked, "What do you plan on doing?"

"Arrest the suspect," I answered.

"How long have you been on the job?" he asked again.

"Two years," I answered.

The interrogation continued. "Where have you worked?"

"Van Nuys and West Vallcy," I said.

"Have you ever worked the South End?" he continued.

"No," I replied.

The sergeant was contemptuous. "Do you know what you've got here?"

"Yeah, I got an ADW."

"No, you don't," the sergeant said. "What you got here is a nigger and a white woman. And whatever she gets, she deserves."

At that point I made my second tactical career error: I argued with the sergeant. The first was having relented and requested his presence. Upon reflection, the second error was probably because I was dumbfounded by his response. Have you ever argued with a bigot? You can't win. And I didn't. In fact, I lost twice. First, the sergeant made us release the suspect. And, second, he blackened my name with all of the other supervisors. He gave me a marked jacket—I was too educated for my own good.

The point of this is: of course racism exists on the LAPD. But good cops try to work around it. After the Rodney King incident, the City Council didn't need a blue-ribbon commission to confirm racism. Everybody knew it existed. But here's something else, something you should know by now:

Racism had nothing to do with the arrest of Rodney King. Everybody knew that as soon as the facts were uncovered. Even the Christopher Commission couldn't find racism in the King arrest, although they tried mightily. The IAD couldn't find any racial motivation in our stopping or using force to subdue King. The DA and County Grand Jury couldn't find any racial motivation in our actions. And the federal civil rights cops couldn't find a racial motivation in what we did, either.

That's why the prosecutors didn't raise racism as an issue at the Simi Valley trial; racism was a nonissue. The prosecution did have some contradictory remarks made by King, but he wasn't called to testify because those contradictions might have been tough to explain. The prosecution also had an analysis of the George Holliday tape soundtrack done at a retail store, which indicated that the word "nigger" had been used during the King episode. But the defense was able to refute this with a much more sophisticated FBI state-of-the-art analysis of the soundtrack that clearly demonstrated no racial remarks whatsoever were made. In fact, no evidence ever existed that anything more was involved than police stopping a dangerous felon who was under the influence of intoxicants, and then trying to subdue him with minimum force when he resisted lawful efforts to put him in handcuffs.

Even so, the Christopher Commission had to fulfill its responsibility, which was to recognize and confirm what minority critics had been saying for years and thus ease tensions created by the Rodney King affair and cool a community that had the potential to erupt in violent riots. Which, of course, happened.

The Christopher Commission Report was filed on July 9, 1991. Its 228 pages, compiled by a ten-member panel of some of the highest-profile citizens of the greater Los Angeles area,[2] included a number of recommendations that showed nothing so much as commission-study overkill.[3] To an outside observer, this apparently was done for three purposes.

First, a majority of the commission recommendations were already in place, or could be easily implemented. But by having a large number of recommendations that could quickly be adopted, the public was assured that the report findings would result in immediate action. Give the public bread and circuses, never mind that the bread is stale and the circus an illusory magic show. Among such recommendations were those involving equal opportunity for minorities and women, and command procedures to provide more supervision of street cops. These systems were already in place.

Second, the large number of recommendations hid the key proposals, such as the one involving community-based policing. More about this in a moment, because it is an important issue.

Finally, many of the proposals were tossed in for their controversial value; the commissin knew that these ideas would

---

[2] In addition to Warren Christopher, the members were John A. Arguellas, retired justice of the Supreme Court of California; Roy A. Anderson, chairman emeritus of Lockheed Corporation and chairman of La 2000 Partnership; Willie R. Barnes, a partner in the law firm of Katten, Muchin, Zavis & Weitzman and a former California commissioner of corporations; Leo F. Estrada, associate professor at the UCLA Graduate School of Architecture and Urban Planning; Mickey Kantor, a partner in the law firm of Manatt, Phelps & Phillips and former member of the board of the Legal Service Corp.; Richard M. Mosk, a partner in the law firm of Sanders, Barnett, Goldman & Mosk and a former judge of the Iran-U.S. Claims Tribunal; Andrea Sheridan Ordin, former U.S. attorney, president of the Los Angeles County Bar Association, and partner in the law firm of Pepper, Hamilton & Scheetz; John Brooks Slaughter, president of Occidental College; and Robert E. Tranquada, professor of medicine and former dean of the University of Southern California School of Medicine.

[3] Like everybody else, the Christopher Commission presumed the officers' guilt even though no trial had been held or evidence presented. For example, the foreword to the Christopher Commission report had such inflammatory statements as: "Rightly called 'sickening' by President Bush, and condemned by all segments of society. . . ." And it made hasty judgments, such as, "the report of the involved officers was falsified." Presumed guilty?

attract vocal minority support (such as the hiring of homosexuals), yet face a difficult road to approval because they involved collective bargaining issues with the Police Protective League or required approval by the voters at large. Beyond these, the Christopher Commission reported several findings that doubtless reassured the minority community that their outrage over the Rodney King affair was justified. Among the findings:

1. Excessive force was used by many LAPD officers.
2. Racial and sexual bias was reflected in the conduct of many officers.
3. The LAPD command structure failed effectively to monitor, discipline, and control officers accused of improper conduct.
4. Officers abused the computer communication system by making racist and/or sexist remarks without fear of reprimand.
5. There was a lack of accountability on the LAPD to civilian oversight authority.

All of these were true, or at least enough evidence existed to suggest that they were partially true. Let's look, for example, at the first charge involving excessive force.

The Christopher Commission determined that over a five-year period (from 1986 to 1990), allegations of use of excessive force were made against a total of 1,800 LAPD officers. With a police force of about eight thousand cops, this means that about one in twenty officers was accused of using excessive force over the five-year period.

But then the commission gave more details. It reported that only 244 officers had enough allegations against them to warrant serious attention. This means that the percentage of bad cops, as defined by multiple excessive-force reports, drops to only about one-half of 1 percent.

The second charge is that racism and sexism exist on the LAPD. Just look at what I have reported so far in this book and you can determine the truth of that allegation. But the fact remains that racism played no part in the Rodney King arrest.

Third, what about command structure? Well, I've dealt with that, too. The field sergeants and many of the lieutenants, the people who actually work the streets, are good at their jobs and exercise command influence despite—not because of—the captains and their superiors in the management structure.

Example: everything that happened in the Rodney King affair on the night of March 3, 1991, was my responsibility. I was in charge of the officers. I was not in charge of the situation; Rodney King controlled that. The suspect always controls the use of force. The officers under my command should never have been accused of any wrongdoing, because they did only what I told them to do. And I did only what I had been told and trained to do. Do you see the inconsistency here? Lower-level officers are hung out to dry, while the management people in charge protect their own salaries and pensions. It's the double standard at work.

As to the fourth finding—that officers abused the computer communications system with racist and/or sexist reports—I fall back on statistics. Less than one-tenth of 1 percent of the approximately 6 million communications studied by the Christopher Commission are in that category. That's too many, to be sure. But compare it with any other monitored workplace in the United States and I believe it will pass muster. It's never acceptable, but all we can do is to work for zero tolerance towards racism.

Finally, let's look at the fifth conclusion of the Christopher Commission report: more civilian oversight of the Police Department is needed.

To this end, among the specific recommendations made by the Christopher Commission were proposals that would limit the length of time a chief of police could serve and remove the chief of police from civil service protection. These proposals were specifically aimed at Chief Daryl Gates, who had served as chief for fourteen years and gave no sign of wishing to relinquish his authority until he finally stepped down in June 1992.

The minority black and Hispanic communities enthusiastically embraced the Christopher Commission report as confirmation of the evils they believed existed on the LAPD (some of which I readily acknowledge). But, once again, they were being taken for a stroll down the garden path.

There is no question that the LAPD is political and operates with extreme efficiency within the Los Angeles political arena. Look, for example, at the Christopher Commission recommendation for community-based policing. It is a proposal that will come back to haunt the city's leadership.

You see, LAPD already engages in community-based policing. There are a variety of definitions as to what "community-based policing" actually is, and the Christopher Commission version was blurred. The method the LAPD currently utilizes is a hazy mixture of the old concepts of team policing and neighborhood watch groups, and the assignment of a senior officer to be responsible for a given area and maintain liaison with a variety of other city services, such as street maintenance, building inspection, and so on. This program allows citizens to see, and even participate in, neighborhood improvement through such projects as removing graffiti, boarding up or demolishing dilapidated residences, removing abandoned vehicles from the streets, and a host of other community beautification ventures.

Well, things are going to change under the new approach to community-based policing. Police officers are going to get even more intimately involved in neighborhood watch groups. They're going to get even closer to the people whose safety they guard. And that's precisely what the LAPD wants. Do you know why?

Because the concept of close, community-based policing has hidden benefits that the LAPD once enjoyed, but which were eliminated by Mayor Tom Bradley. What it means is political power for the LAPD, political power among the thousands of organized groups—eligible registered voters—who can be mustered and manipulated by the chief of police. Just as they were under Chief Ed Davis.

You see, what the Christopher Commission has done with community-based policing is to reinvent the wheel. In the mid-1970s, Los Angeles was in a financial bind. All of the city departments were fighting for a piece of a shrinking (or barely expanding) municipal budget. It was evident to the LAPD that the days of ever-increasing spending and ever-rising taxes were at an end.

Before Proposition 13 limited tax increases, then-Chief Ed Davis of the LAPD tried an innovative policing system. It was called "team policing," and it worked this way: each of the LAPD's eighteen divisions was broken down into a group of areas and each area was assigned specific black-and-whites and specific officers. The idea was for the officers to become part of the community. They would get to know the people in the area, and the officers would take on a custodial role for the territory. They would be accountable for crime in their area.

Under the concept, the community relations section of each division was substantially increased and assumed an important role in organizing the community. This was done through a program called "neighborhood watch." Police officers and citizens would meet at a host residence in the neighborhood. The police would discuss their role, crime, and how to take common sense security measures for self-protection. The LAPD developed thousands of these neighborhood watch groups throughout the Los Angeles area.

And the program worked, and not only for residents. A side benefit was that the police discovered they had thousands of organized groups of supporters, and these supporters could and would be used to turn out the vote for candidates favorable to the police. They organized phone banks, wrote letters, and applied other means of political pressure. It amounted to an enormous increase in the chief of police's political clout. He could literally make or break candidates, get propositions passed, or acquire more of the municipal budget.

But then Tom Bradley got elected mayor of Los Angeles. Although victorious, he had run into some resistance from the organized groups of voters involved in Davis's "community-based policing." In fact, Davis's organized groups of neighborhood watch groups caused considerable problems for Bradley. Tom Bradley isn't dumb. He understood very well the implications of what was happening—remember, Bradley had been a cop himself—and so he responded by squashing the LAPD's concept of team policing through a series of budget cuts. This was done to cripple the upcoming vote on Davis's proposal for a ten-thousand-officer police force, an increase of more than 20 percent over existing levels.

Bradley was not about to tolerate such a potentially strong opposition, especially in the hands of an enemy. And so it was a smart political move on Bradley's part to crush community-based policing and send to Davis a message about who was going to run Los Angeles. It would be the mayor, not the chief of police.

As a result, Davis quietly left, opening the door to a new chief, Daryl Gates, who had a different style. Gates was as nonconfrontational with the political establishment as Davis had been challenging, until, that is, Gates finally ran afoul of the same system that had nurtured his career. This doesn't mean Gates wasn't empire-building. To the contrary, he was doing precisely that. But he was doing it in a different way. Gates apparently reasoned that the system could be manipulated. And if so, then the benefits to the LAPD—and, not coincidentally, Daryl Gates—could be immense. If the LAPD could discover a problem that inflamed the public, something like gangs or drugs—or, even better, both—then the public would demand that money be appropriated to solve the problem.

Gangs were a perfect starting place. First, they were a real problem. Second, the spin-off crimes were boundless. They included random violence, drive-by shooting, burglary, murder, robbery, and mugging. If the LAPD were to protect the public from gangs, it would need more officers. As a result, Gates asked for and received authorization for a few hundred additional officers.

Gates employed the same concept with the drug problem, and he got the same results. Actually, it was even better because it mixed gangs and drugs, and this ended up in more officers for Gates to command.

Nor was the manipulation limited to hiring more cops. There were major new expenditures for the police department in other areas, too. For example, the LAPD argued, and justifiably so, that gangs and drugs had changed the complexion of modern urban police work. Drug dealers had Uzis and AK-47s. The police were outgunned, and needed additional firepower to put them on an equal footing. Bingo: we got 9 mm. weapons and hollow-point ammunition.

Then the department wanted a new communications system that the existing budget could not accommodate. A tax hike would be necessary to pay for it. Well, citizens had complained for years about police response time, about not being able to get through busy phone lines when police were needed. This was especially true in South Los Angeles, where violence was endemic. So the LAPD exploited the situation. The department produced statistics showing how many calls were being received and the high percentage that were never answered. The department showed the tragic results of calls that weren't answered—the murders, assaults, robberies. And it was all because of an overburdened communications system that hadn't been changed since the 1920s. The news media were brought on board. Political leaders were enlisted. And before you knew it, everybody was demanding a new communications system for the LAPD. The measure was put on the ballot and passed overwhelmingly. Its passage convinced the LAPD of something very important: the public could be effectively manipulated to the department's advantage. This was an astute move. Chief Gates needed to get this done, so he educated everybody. And everybody benefited.

And what makes all of this important to the Christopher Commission report and the Rodney King affair? Just this: the LAPD is intensely political; it operates in a political environment. Under Gates, the department found a way around the loss of the grass roots support it was able to develop through "community-based policing." But now that circuitous route is unnecessary. The Christopher Commission has endorsed community-based policing, and it has been approved by Los Angeles voters. Which means you can expect the LAPD to enjoy even greater political clout than it had in the past.

Whether that's good or bad depends upon how you view the Los Angeles Police Department and its influence over the politics of the nation's second-largest city. From my viewpoint, it's both good and bad. It's good because cops are more in touch with the city than most critics would have you believe. Cops are out there on the streets daily. They have more contact with people than the elected officials who claim to be the people's representatives. But it's bad, too. That's because, in my experience, the police management hierarchy in Los Angeles is too political, too involved in its own empire-building to be truly concerned with what would be best for the people.

On balance, there's no question that the Christopher Commission report helped. It pointed up some problems with racism and command deficiencies that street cops have known about for years. It resulted in a new infusion of federal funds and attention to inner cities that have been neglected for years.

But this is all in the domain of sophisticated sociologists and urban experts. Although well educated in criminal justice and public policy, I am still a street cop. And it is as a street cop that I studied the Christopher Commission report with a growing sense of dismay, because it missed the point when it got down to the guts of the Rodney King affair.

It is all well and fine to analyze racism, sexism, command structures, and communications etiquette. It is worthwhile to recommend more community involvement by police. Spending more money to improve the economic infrastructure of distressed urban neighborhoods may be of some benefit in relieving poverty and indigence among people. However, that's only a partial solution. What's needed is a systemic approach— one that stresses family values, morals, ethics, education, helping people to help themselves.

But from a street cop's perspective, it somewhat misses the point. And that point cannot be ignored when you're out on the streets after midnight, chasing people who don't want to be caught, risking your life every time you stop a speeding motorist, never knowing whether the person you're stopping will greet you with a surly hello or a blast from a sawed-off shotgun.

You see, from a street cop's viewpoint, nothing has changed with the LAPD's rules of when to use force, and how much of it you should apply. A gap still exists between the baton and the pistol or chokehold. It's a gap that could easily be filled. There are all sorts of tools that could be thrown into the breach to prevent another Rodney King affair from happening. But it's a void that has been ignored by the Christopher Commission, the Police Commission, the LAPD, and the City Council.

And that's perhaps the ultimate tragedy of the Rodney King affair. It is that the LAPD still has no new stratagems to employ to subdue a violent suspect, such as Rodney King was in the early morning hours of March 3, 1991.

Just as the Rodney King incident was anticipated in 1982 when the Los Angeles city officials outlawed the chokehold, so can another such episode be expected in the future. That's a street cop's perception. But it's one you can take to the bank. And it's one that will come back and haunt us all at some unknown moment in days to come when a felon under the influence of intoxicants decides to lead LAPD cops on a high-speed chase, then resist all efforts to be put in handcuffs.

Next time, it's likely that even more people will die.

Epilogue

The Rodney King Affair—A Story Still Not Over

On August 5, 1992, sealed indictments that had been returned two days earlier by a Los Angeles federal grand jury were opened. To no one's surprise, the indictments resurrected the charges against Officers Timothy Wind, Laurence Powell, Theodore Briseno, and me for our conduct in arresting Rodney King on March 3, 1991.

Officers Wind, Powell, and Briseno were charged with "willfully" depriving King of his constitutional right to a reasonable arrest by their actions to subdue him. I was accused of "aiding and abetting" an unlawful assault and failing to prevent that assault while King was in custody.

These same basic charges had already been settled by the Simi Valley jury. No matter. The federal government said the Simi Valley decision did not meet the Justice Department's expectations—presumably, a guilty verdict. So under Supreme Court decisions that permit double jeopardy for defendants despite a constitutional prohibition to the contrary, the federal government is allowed to retry the same case again.

233

This latest ordeal is difficult to understand in terms of the criminal justice system. But not from a political standpoint. The lynch mob howling for "justice" in the Rodney King affair has not yet been satisfied, its blood lust not yet satiated. So political capital can be gained from pursuing the "guilty."

This time, Rodney G. King will testify, according to his attorney, Steven Lerman. We'll wait and see. Lerman said King would testify at the first trial. But King, of course, didn't take the stand, for good reasons that have already been outlined. If Rodney King does decide to testify, it will be a surprise, especially if he hasn't yet settled his lawsuit against the city of Los Angeles. A bad showing on the witness stand could damage his chances of collecting ransom.

This time, too, I have no doubt that Officer Briseno will repeat his assertions that my other officers and I were out of control and he, Briseno, sought to stop the violence. That's what Officer Briseno said when the indictments were returned. But again, we'll wait and see how effective his testimony will be. His argument didn't wash with the Simi Valley jury, because the videotape clearly shows Briseno participating in our efforts to put King in handcuffs.

And my case? It will be essentially the same argument. That reasonable force, which fully complied with LAPD policies, training, and procedures, was employed to subdue a violent and aggressive felony suspect. This was the position that prevailed, and rightfully so, in Simi Valley.

Perhaps a new jury will see matters differently. That's a chance that must be taken, since we have no other choice. But I doubt that this will be the case. For one thing, I still believe in the American system of justice. More to the point, the government still has only one piece of evidence to support its fragile contention that Rodney King was treated badly. That evidence is the George Holliday videotape of the incident.

And, ironically, that videotape is our strongest defense, because it proves the truth of our contention that Rodney King attacked a police officer in the lawful performance of his duty. The videotape shows that King resisted all of our best efforts to place him in custody through existing uses of force permitted

by the Los Angeles Police Department. The videotape demonstrates that King was constantly rising either to escape, or to
assault an officer again. The videotape provides conclusive
affirmation that Rodney King was in control until he finally
complied with our orders.

The Rodney King videotape is true. But it is not the truth.
The truth can only be found by viewing the videotape in the
context of everything else that happened when Rodney King
finally stopped his car in Foothill Division of Los Angeles on
March 3, 1991.

APPENDIX A

The Rodney King Affair: Myths and Realities

Myth #1: *Rodney King couldn't have been traveling 115 miles per hour. The Hyundai Excel he was driving doesn't go that fast.*
Reality: The car he was driving does go that fast. CHIP Officer Melanie Singer had the pedal to the metal on her cruiser, which topped out at 115 miles per hour, and couldn't close the gap. For an explanation, please see footnote 15, Chapter 5.

Myth #2: *Rodney King was stopped because he was black.*
Reality: Rodney King was stopped because he led police on a 7.8-mile chase at speeds of up to 115 miles per hour, ignoring flashing lights and sirens. He committed more than fifteen traffic violations, endangering the safety of other motorists, before he finally was forced to stop beside a park that is known as a graveyard for drug deals gone bad. Was he luring us there? That was our state of mind on March 3, 1991.

Myth #3: *It was a case of white officers beating up a black man. No minority officers were present.*
Reality: Officer David Love, a black man, was present at the scene, assisted in cuffing Rodney King, and testified that the force used to subdue King was reasonable (see Chapter 5). Also, Officer Ted Briseno is Hispanic, as is Officer Rolando Solano.

Myth #4: *A conspiracy existed to beat Rodney King.*
Reality: The incident involved more than twenty police officers

from three different jurisdictions, including officers in a police helicopter. Suggesting that they conspired to stop and beat Rodney King isn't just paranoid, it's sheer nonsense.

Myth #5: *The officers were out of control, weren't they? Why was Rodney King beaten so badly? Why couldn't other options be used? Was it to teach him a lesson?*

Reality: King was a felony suspect, resisting arrest, and the LAPD had no other options to take him into custody than the ones used. The available uses of force were: first, physical presence; second, verbal orders; third, a swarm; fourth, the TASER; fifth, the baton. Each of these was used and exhausted. Our final option was deadly force—either a gun or the chokehold. We did not want deadly force. That's why the baton was used. Intermediate tools are available on other police departments, but not on the Los Angeles Police Department. No one was angry with King. We feared him because of his actions.

Myth #6: *With more than twenty officers present, why couldn't you have controlled Rodney King instead of striking him repeatedly?*

Reality: There were eleven officers present. Seven were LAPD, two of them in the helicopter. The CHIPs and school police took the other two suspects into custody. They could not be used to subdue King because they had different training. I did not know how they would react to specific orders, and that can be dangerous. Most of the officers arrived when the incident was almost over. I was in the glare of the helicopter searchlight and was focusing on the event. I did not see the arrival of additional officers. Let me draw an analogy. Stand in a lighted room at night and look out of a window. How much can you see outside the light? That's how much I saw outside of the glare of the helicopter's spotlight while the incident was occurring. At the end of the incident, when Rodney King finally submitted, I was aware of the presence of additional officers and used them to subdue the suspect. This is evident in the videotape.

Myth #7: *Rodney King was reeling in pain from the baton blows.*

Reality: There was no evidence that Rodney King experienced any pain until I ordered the baton power strokes to his joints. That was when he submitted. All medical personnel who examined King at the scene and at Pacific Hospital testified that he was alert and did not complain of pain. No one at the scene heard him complain. All he did was spit blood and curse at officers.

Myth #8: *Rodney King was hit fifty-six times.*
Reality: Not so. Rodney King was struck thirty-three times. The videotape shows that twenty-three of the blows missed him altogether (see footnote 8, Chapter 1). Whatever the number, it is unimportant. He was struck only enough times to force compliance with lawful commands.

Myth #9: *Rodney King was only speeding.*
Reality: He was driving at speeds of up to 115 miles per hour, and chased by police for almost eight miles. He was observed committing fifteen or more major moving traffic violations before he finally stopped. By definition, that made him a felony evader.

Myth #10: *Rodney King was not under the influence of PCP.*
Reality: It is true that blood and urine tests showed no evidence of PCP usage. However, medical testimony by the prosecution's own witnesses proved that the tests were invalid. He displayed all of the characteristics of a PCP-dusted suspect, and police officers had every reason to believe that he was influenced by that dangerous drug. That was because of his strength and ability to throw off four officers, absorb one hundred thousand volts from the TASER in two fifty thousand volt increments, and keep trying to rise. In any event, Rodney King was almost two and-a-half times legally drunk at the time of the incident, according to the prosecution's own stipulation.

Myth #11: *Rodney King could have been subdued with a second "swarm," thus avoiding the use of batons.*
Reality: Again, not so. The Los Angeles Police Department has a specific rule against tying up physically with a PCP suspect. Once the first swarm failed, it would have been dangerous and contrary to policy and a poor police tactic to attempt a second such effort, especially since PCP intoxication provides extraordinary strength.

Myth #12: *Rodney King was submissive, merely rolling on the ground to avoid getting hit.*

Reality: The George Holliday videotape clearly refutes this argument. Rodney King was constantly aggressive, constantly rising, having already assaulted Officer Powell. For example, he performed the Folsom Roll toward Officers Wind and Powell. Only at the end, when he raised his hands and said, "Please stop," was he submissive. And even then he tried to resist being cuffed.

Myth #13: *Rodney King suffered severe skull fractures and other serious head injuries from the beating.*

Reality: All of the available medical evidence provided by the prosecution demonstrated that King's head injuries were minor; he also had "superficial" face lacerations and a fractured cheekbone that did not require treatment. There were no head fractures, nor any evidence of brain damage. The Holliday videotape shows no head blows by police. All available evidence indicates the fractured cheekbone occurred when he slammed face-first into the asphalt on three separate occasions.

Myth #14: *The Simi Valley jury was racist.*

Reality: Race did not enter into the jury-selection process. The site of the trial was chosen by three separate judicial jurisdictions (the state, Los Angeles County, and Ventura County), and the jury was selected in accordance with procedures approved by voters under Proposition 115.

Myth #15: *The force used was excessive and illegal.*

Reality: No. Everything done in subduing Rodney King on March 3, 1991, was strictly in accordance with LAPD policies, procedures, and training. Physical presence didn't work. Verbalization failed to make Rodney King comply with legal orders. A swarm was attempted and failed. The suspect was TASED twice with fifty thousand volts each time. None of these measures had any impact on Rodney King. So my officers and I didn't even bump up against the limits of excessive force. We followed the rules right down the middle. Are the rules wrong? Perhaps so. But that's not what was on trial. Police officers were on trial. And we did precisely what we had been instructed to do, according to guidelines established by the LAPD, Mayor Tom Bradley, the Los Angeles City Council, and the Police Commission, acting on the advice of minority leaders concerned about the excessive use of force.

Myth #16: *Officer Theodore Briseno tried to stop the use of force because he believed it was excessive.*

Reality: Officer Ted Briseno acted in accordance with his instructions. He did not try to stop Officers Powell and Wind from striking Rodney King. He sought to prevent them from being accidentally TASED when I applied the third (or second and-a-half) power burst. His own videotaped actions stomping King to prevent him from reaching for a concealed weapon demonstrate conclusively that he did not disagree with the uses of force being applied.

Myth #17: *The videotape seems clear about what happened.*

Reality: The videotape is a one-dimensional picture of part of an incident. It provides more proof to sustain innocence than it does to demonstrate guilt. That's what the jury found in Simi Valley, and rightfully so. Rodney King was never controlled until he finally complied with our orders. And even then, his compliance was only partial. We had to "swarm" him at the end with multiple officers in order to get him in handcuffs.

Myth #18: *Rodney King was given no chance to comply with your orders, was he? Weren't you beating him when he was down and perhaps willing to give up?*

Reality: The videotape clearly shows the "pulsation" of officers. They would go in to strike the suspect when he would not comply with orders. Then they would back away to see what the suspect's intentions might be. If King had complied with orders, he would have been handcuffed and no further violence would have been necessary. It is appropriate to escalate the force only if the suspect indicates that he is going to rise again. The George Holliday videotape clearly shows officers retreating to evaluate at least eleven separate times.

Myth #19: *The jury failed the justice system.*

Reality: To the contrary, the jury *sustained* the justice system. My officers and I were supposed to be presumed innocent unless found guilty without reasonable doubt. Instead, we were presumed guilty by almost everybody. It is a tribute to the American system of justice that we were found innocent despite the presumption of guilt. If anything failed, it was the expectation of guilt anticipated by the media, the Los Angeles political establishment, the LAPD management structure, and everybody else in the world who saw only snippets of the George Holliday videotape. We were presumed guilty. The justice system worked because of the citizens on the jury.

Myth #20: *The reporting was balanced and factual.*
Reality: This is the most sinister of all the myths. The media reported what was easy and what would sell. Reporters were given facts. Either the media did not pay attention, or they deliberately distorted those facts.

APPENDIX B

The George Holliday Videotape, Second-by-Second[1]

The National Audio Forensic Lab Analysis of the Transcript[2]

THE GEORGE HOLLIDAY VIDEOTAPE

(The time sequence listed is from the videocamera time recorder, beginning with the first two seconds most viewers of the Holliday videotape have not seen.)

3:22:25   Rodney King lifts toes off ground and pushes up from hands and knees.

3:25:05   King is up. He turns 180 degrees with arms out from his shoulders and charges in the direction of Officer Laurence Powell.

Use of force begins

3:25:17   Powell uses power stroke and appears to hit King on the arms and right clavicle, shoulder, and chest area. King falls down hard on his face, possible face trauma from asphalt.

---

[1] Prepared by Capt. Robert Michael, LAPD (Ret.).
[2] Prepared by defense witness Norman Pearl.

3:26:05   Video out of focus, but possibly 12 blows of unknown type to unknown areas.

End of use of force. Officers evaluate.

3:36:12   Video clears. No blows are being struck. King is on his stomach, upper torso raised.

3:40:19   Officer Briseno places hand in front of Officer Powell, who is focused on King with baton raised.

3:41:02   King suddenly raises left toes and cocks his right knee. He begins to rise. Powell sees this action, but Briseno doesn't.

3:41:25   King is on hands and knees, rising.

3:42:24   King sits back on his calves, arms free.

Use of force resumes

3:42:28   Powell strikes King's arms and upper torso.

3:43:05   Wind strokes King near the buttocks and Powell hits King in the upper front torso. The camera wanders momentarily.

3:44:15   Powell strikes King's front upper torso.

3:45:22   King topples over and turns 270 degrees. He rises to his hands and knees.

End of use of force. Officers evaluate.

3:47:10   King is now on hands and knees and is mobile. Powell strikes King in the left arm and shoulder area.

3:48:15   King sits back on calves, arms free.

3:48:24   King raises left knee, as though to rise.

3:48:29   Powell strikes King's left arm.

3:49:11   King drops left knee and raises right knee, turning 90 degrees to his right and away from Powell.

3:49:18   Powell strikes King on left back, while King turns and rises toward Wind.

3:50:02   Powell hits King's left shoulder.

3:50:22   Powell strikes King's upper back area.

3:51:18   King is on his hands and knees, facing Wind.

3:52:00   King raises his left knee and turns back toward Powell. King raises his left arm and is on the rise.

3:52:04   Powell strikes King's left arm.

3:53:07   Powell hits King's left arm, as King lifts up from his knees.

3:53:17   King is on his feet, his right hand on the ground.

3:53:24   Wind swings to strike King's right arm as King begins to fall.

3:54:02   Wind swings where King's arm had been, and King appears to fall, possibly with the right side of his face in the asphalt causing trauma.

3:55:00   King's left knee is cocked. Powell strikes the back of the knee.

3:55:04   Wind strikes King's right shoulder.

3:55:20   King's head and chest are up, his left leg is cocked and hands close to his body. Wind strikes the right side of King's back.

3:56:19–4:01:19   Powell and Wind deliver power strokes to King's upper and lower back, buttocks, and thighs.

4:02:16   King uncocks his left leg and straightens out to a better prone position. No blows are delivered.

End of use of force. Officers evaluate.

4:03:20   King rolls his right heel and begins rolling to the left as he lifts his right hip and cocks his right leg—the "Folsom Roll."

4:05:20   The leg cocking is now extreme and officers resume using force. Powell strikes both of King's legs.

4:06:00   Rodney King lifts his toes off the ground in a rising position.

4:06:29:   King lifts his upper torso.

4:07:12   Powell strikes King's right ankle.

4:08:07   Wind strikes King's back.

4:08:12   Powell strikes King's right ankle again.

4:09:01   Wind strikes King's back.

4:09:12   King continues to roll into Powell's legs and onto his right side. King is doing the Folsom Roll. Officers are evaluating.

4:11:20   King now has his left leg cocked, upper torso raised and his hands in a push-up position.

4:13:05   King rolls to his right shoulder and reaches toward his waistband with his left hand.

4:13:20   Sgt. Koon is standing in front of King, demonstrating with his arms out in the form of a cross—the position he wants King to assume.

4:13:29   Powell strikes King's left leg.

4:14:19   King begins to roll onto his back.

4:16:02   On his back, King cocks his left leg.

4:18:00   Powell strikes King's right hand, which has moved to the waist area, and both of King's hands move out from the side.

4:18:15   King continues the Folsom Roll onto his left side.

4:20:18   King has both knees bent and is continuing to roll. His upper torso is up. His toes are coming off the ground. The officers are evaluating his actions.

4:23:20   Sgt. Koon is talking to and pointing at King, who is facing Koon.

4:24:18   King cocks his right leg. Officer Powell reaches for his handcuffs.

4:25:13   King brings his left arm into a push-up position.

4:25:29   King's left arm is straight out, his right leg cocked as if to rise.

4:26:15   Powell is still reaching for his handcuffs.

4:26:29–4:28:10   King brings his left arm into his body, lifts his right hip, looks to his right, his upper torso is raised, and he is drawing up his right leg.

4:28:20   Briseno delivers a kick to the middle of King's shoulder-blade area. King's head and face go into the asphalt again.

4:28:25   King sweeps his left arm forward in the area of Briseno's left leg.

4:30:08   Briseno points to King.

4:30:28   Powell strikes King's right arm.

4:31:11   Wind hits King's right arm area.

4:32:05   King's upper torso is coming up off the ground.

4:32:12   King's right leg is cocked.

4:32:20   King is drawing up his left leg, as if to rise.

4:32:25   Rodney King is on his hands and knees.

4:33:14   King turns left toward Powell.

4:34:02   Powell strikes King's back.

4:34:08–4:35:19   Wind strikes King's back three times.

4:35:25   King looks at Powell and raises his left shoulder and arm.

4:38:22   Powell strikes King's left arm.

4:38:28   King pulls back his left arm.

4:39:16   Wind delivers right front kick to King's rear shoulder area.

4:39:20   King maintains his balance on his hands and knees.

4:40:02   Powell strikes King's left buttocks area.

4:41:00   Wind delivers a right front kick to King's rear shoulder area. King is still sitting.

4:43:02   Wind delivers another kick to the upper back area. The video is now out of focus.

4:43:16–4:46:18   Video is back in focus. Powell swings blows at King, but the contact area cannot be determined.

4:47:00   King is sitting on his calves, arms at his side. Sgt. Koon is facing and pointing at King. The officers are assessing.

4:52:00   King has his hands on his head. Powell removes his handcuffs.

4:53:05   Powell hands Briseno the handcuffs.

4:57:00   Briseno begins handcuffing Rodney King.

5:01:05   King pulls his left arm away from handcuffing position, renewing the struggle.

5:05:00   Multiple officers with arm and foot pressure overcome Rodney King's resistance, and he is put in handcuffs.

NATIONAL AUDIO FORENSIC LAB ANALYSIS OF THE GEORGE HOLLIDAY VIDEOTAPE TRANSCRIPT

(The time sequence of this record does not correspond with the George Holliday videotape because it was measured in a different way, not according to the sequence of frames on the videotape but according to actual time.)

1.33   "Put your hands behind your back."
3:80   "Hands behind your back."
4:61   "Hands behind your back."
5:86   "Just lay down."
8:64   "Behind your back."
10:15   "Lay on the ground."
13:14   (Unintelligible.)
13:64   (High frequency noise.)
17:42   "You've gotta' put your arms out now."
19:16   "Put your arms out."
20:33   "Get your arms out."
21:81   "Put your arms out."
22:14   "Put your arms out."
25:15   (Unintelligible because of camera sounds.)
25:72   "He's comin' up."
27:02   (High-frequency noise.)
28:23   (Holliday overtalk masks officers' commands.)
29:16   "You're gonna' get shot, you're gonna' get shot."
30:35   "Keep your arms spread out."

32:24   "Stop . . ."
37:63   ". . . Roll over."
39:02   "Get down."
39:74   "Come in from the back."
41:45   "Cuff him."
42:65   (Ambient overtalk masks officers' commands.)
44:63   "Put your hands behind your back."
47:35   "Hands behind your back."
48:54   "Put your hands behind your back, put your hands behind your back."
51:30   "Put your hands behind your back."
53:37   "Put your hands behind your back."
54:63   (Ambient overtalk masks officers' commands.)
55:12   "Look out."
55:28   "Look out."
56:07   "Get down."
57:51–61:87   (Unintelligible.)
68:28   "Take him down."
70:43   "Now."

APPENDIX C

The following documents are Sgt. Stacey C. Koon's log entry for the arrest of Rodney G. King, the Pacifica Hospital Emergency Room record on Rodney King for March 3, 1991, the arrest report filed by Officer Laurence Powell (part of it written by California Highway Patrol Officer Tim Singer), and the use-of-force summary filed in connection with the incident. The prosecution in the Simi Valley trial attempted to show that the officers covered up the incident. But all of these documents demonstrate that there never was an effort to conceal actions taken in connection with the arrest of Rodney King in the Foothills of Los Angeles on March 3, 1991.

Los Angeles Police Department
SERGEANT'S DAILY REPORT

Sergeant....... Stacey C Koon

Division .. FTHL .... Watch .... Am .... Assignment ..... 16A40. .... Date ... 3-3-91

Available Field Time..... 6

Details:

2300 E\C

0100 FOOTHILL/OSBORNE — RESPONDED TO CHP (UNIT 9860) PURSUIT.
CHP REQUESTED LAPD ASSIST, DUE TO (1) NO CHP UNITS AVAILABLE
&(2) W/I CITY LIMITS. 16A23 (POWELL/WIND) CAME UPON THE
PURSUIT AT FOOTHILL/VNY — (1)CHP UNIT & (1) LAUSD POLICE UNIT
WERE IN PURSUIT — THE VEH HAD STOPPED @ THE RED TRLIGHT &
A23 THOUGHT THE PURSUIT HAD TERMINATED — HOWEVER, THE SUSP
THEN IMMEDIATELY RAN THE LIGHT & CHP REQUESTED A23 TAKE OVER THE
PURSUIT — A23 DID SO — TERMINATING AT FTHL/OSBORNE. AN
AIR UNIT HAD BEEN REQUESTED AS SOON AS CHP ADVISED LAPD
THEY WERE IN PURSUIT & AIR UNIT ARRIVED AT PURSUIT'S
TERMINATION. I WAS AT SCENE UPON TERMINATION.
IT WAS IMMEDIATELY OBVIOUS THE SUSP WAS UNDER THE
INFLUENCE OF PCP & OFFS ATTEMPTED TO VERBALIZE WITH
THE SUSP W/O SUCCESS. THE PASSENGER WAS TAKEN INTO
CUSTODY & ISOLATED IMMEDIATELY. THE DRIVER — PCP SUSP—
WAS EXCEPTIONALLY UNCOOPERATIVE — A SWARM PLAN WAS
IMMEDIATELY PUT INTO FORCE — BUT THE SUSP 6:2, 250 (APPROX)
BEGAN TO STRUGGLE & FOUR OFFS WERE UNABLE TO CONTROL —
THE SUSP WAS THEN TASED (BY MYSELF) & HAD LITTLE
IMPACT ON HIS BEHAVIOR — 2ND TASING & VERY LIMITED
REACTION — THE OFFS TEAM OF POWELL/WIND THEN
UTILIZED PR24 & DELIVERED A TORENT OF POWER
STROKES, JABS, ETC TO ARMS — TORSO & LESS — TASER GOING
THE ENTIRE TIME — FINALLY WERE SUSP DOWN & OFFS SWARMED —
WITH CONSIDERABLE DIFFICULTY & WERE ABLE TO CUFF &
CORD CUFF. RA CALLED TO SCENE & TRANS TO SIERRA HOSP —
MT PROVIDED — SEVERAL FACIAL CUTS DUE TO CONTACT WITH
ASPHALT — OF A MINOR NATURE — & A SPLIT INNER LIP — SUSP OBVILIOUS
TO PAIN & STILL HIGH AT HOSP. RE: DOC FROM VTD TO BK
FELONY EVADING — CHP HAD SUSP @ 115 MPH & RAN NUMEROUS
RED LIGHTS — NEAR T/AS, ETC — CHP INITIALLY P/U SUSP AT

Noted by

This log entry, written before Sgt. Koon went off duty at 7:45 A.M. on March 3, 1991, demonstrates that there was no effort to "cover up" the incident. The report clearly states that force was used on King, and that King's injuries were minor in nature, as shown by the Pacifica Hospital ER report, which was all the evidence Sgt. Koon had to work with at the time. Please note the conclusion of Sgt. Koon's log, regarding use of force on PCP suspects.

Los Angeles Police Department
SERGEANT'S DAILY REPORT

2/2

Sergeant.......... STACEY (KOON)

Jivision.... FTR   Watch.. AM   Assignment.... 16L140   Date.. 3-3-5

Details: Available Field Time.... 6

PAXTON/ETHL — SUSP BKD AT LACUSC DUE TO RCP STATE
BY A23.

AT SCENE, I DISCUSSED HOW CHP WANTED THE
INCIDENT HANDLED — & DUE TO RCP STATE OF SUSP &
LIMITED CHP RESOURCES AVAILABLE & DUE TO THE
FACT LAPD WAS PRIMARY WIT @ TERMINATION &
SOLELY INVOLVED IN USE OF FORCE — IT WAS DECIDED
WE'D HANDLE BOOK-MT & ARREST & CHP HANDLED
IMPOUND & OFCRS SERVED AS WITS.

USE OF FORCE & PURSUIT WILL BE COMPLETED BY
SGT. DISTEFANO UPON COMPLETION OF REPTS BY
POWELL & WIND

@ IMPORTANT NOTE FOR OIC TRAINING, — ALWAYS HAVE
A B/U PLAN WITH A USE OF FORCE — IT DOESN'T
ALWAYS WORK THE WAY YOU'RE TRAINED — TASER
DOESN'T ALWAYS IMMOBILIZE — PR24 DOESN'T ALWAYS
CRIPPLE, ETC. IF YOU DON'T HAVE A FRAME OF
REFERENCE — OFCR TEND TO PANIC — WHEN THINGS
DON'T WORK THE WAY THEY'RE SUPPOSED TO — A B/U
PLAN PREVENTS PANIC — & IT DON'T HURT TO HAVE
LOTS OF B/U — ESPECIALLY WITH PCP SUSPS —

HAVE
SGT KOON
DISCUSS
AT R/C.

0745 EOW

Noted by
Watch Commander..................   Signature

Please note the bottom left-hand corner, where the attending physician's diagnosis of Rodney King's injuries was "PCP overdose" and "facial lacerations, superficial." The bottom right-hand corner shows that King "walked" to his transfer to LACUSCMC, and his condition on discharge was "fair."

The following pages are the arrest report filed by LAPD officer Laurence Powell, with an addendum by California Highway Patrol Officer Tim Singer. If the officers had attempted to cover-up the incident as the prosecution charged, why was a report written by prosecution witness Tim Singer attached at the time of arrest?

ARREST REPORT

ARRESTEE'S LAST NAME: KING FIRST: RODNEY MIDDLE: GLENN

ADDRESS: 1550 N LINCOLN AV ALTADENA

SEX: M DESCENT: B HAIR: BLK EYES: BRO HEIGHT: 603 WEIGHT: 225 BIRTHDATE: 040265 AGE: 25

AKA LAST: KING FIRST: GLENN

BIRTHPLACE: LA PROB. INV. UNIT: US 26

DIVISION AND: 4216 DETAIL ARRESTING: A DATE ARRESTED: 030391 TIME ARR.: 0100 TIME BKD.: 0417

LOCATION OF ARREST: OSBORNE FOOTHILL BL

CHARGE & CODE: F 2800.2VC DEFINITION: EVADING

DR: 2006709K
CII: 507490672
MAIN: 01235600

ADMONITION OF RIGHTS (WHEN APPLICABLE)

THE FOLLOWING STATEMENT WAS READ TO THE ARRESTEE.
"YOU HAVE THE RIGHT TO REMAIN SILENT. IF YOU GIVE UP THE RIGHT TO REMAIN SILENT, ANYTHING YOU SAY CAN AND WILL BE USED AGAINST YOU IN A COURT OF LAW. YOU HAVE THE RIGHT TO SPEAK WITH AN ATTORNEY AND TO HAVE AN ATTORNEY PRESENT DURING QUESTIONING. IF YOU SO DESIRE AND CANNOT AFFORD ONE, AN ATTORNEY WILL BE APPOINTED FOR YOU WITHOUT CHARGE BEFORE QUESTIONING."
THE ADMONITION WAS READ TO THE ARRESTEE BY: NOT GIVEN

LOCATION CRIME COMMITTED: SAA
RESIDENCE PHONE NO.: 1655 797-3670

EMPLOYER / SCHOOL: DODGER STADIUM

CLOTHING WORN: BLK SHT. WHT SHT. GRY PNT. BLU SHS

EXACT LOCATION / DISPOSITION ARRESTEE'S VEHICLE: BLK WHT TOW (CHP IMPOUND)

LIST CONNECTING RPTS BY TYPE & IDENTIFYING NOS: USE OF FORCE

VEHICLE USED (YEAR, MAKE, MODEL, TYPE, COLORS, LIC. NO, ID MARKS): 88 HYUNDAI EXCEL 2DR WHT PASSENGER: 2

COMPLAINTS / EVID OF ILLNESS / INJ-BY WHOM TREATED: MT LKOJHILL WARD

DRIVING VEH (DIRECTIONS & NAME OF STREET) AT OR BETWEEN STREETS: SB FOOTHILL BL AT OSBORNE ST

INVOLVED PERSONS Code: V: VICTIM W: WITNESS P/A: PRIVATE PERS R: PERSON RPTG 459: P-PERSON SECURING D-PERSON DISCOVERING JUV: F-BOTH PARE G-GUARDIAN

COMBINED CRIME REPORT

COMBINED EVID. RPT.

APPROVAL / REPORTING OFFICERS

REPORTING OFFICER(S): POWELL +G SERIAL NO.: 25440 DIV. & DETAIL: G 4216 23
(P.P. ARREST OFCR. BKG. EVID. IF LISTED ON THIS PAGE): WIND +G 27745 FL 23

JUVENILE DISPO. Petition Request: □ DETAINED □ RELEASED □ NON-BOOK □ NON-BOOK & WARR.

70-06.01.2 (REV. 5-90)   ARREST REPORT

PAGE NO. 2/7	TYPE OF REPORT ARREST				BOOKING NO. 238 1167	DR NO. —	
ITEM NO.	QUAN.	ARTICLE	SERIAL NO.	BRAND	MODEL NO.	MISC. DESCRIPTION (EG. COLOR, SIZE, INSCRIPTIONS, CALIBER, REVOLVER, ETC)	DOLLAR VA.

DEFT KING, RODNEY GLENN   CHG 2800.2 VC FEL EVAC

SOURCE OF ACTIVITY

ON 3-3-91 AT APPROX 0030 HRS OFCR T WIND #27745
AND I. L POWELL #25440, ASSIGNED 16A23 FTML PA-
WERE RESPONDING TO ASSIST CHP OFCRS M G SINGE
#12403 AND T J SINGER #9301, UNIT 98-60 VERCUGO
HILLS OFFICE, WHO WERE IN A VEH PURSUIT OF
A 'RECKLESS' DRIVER SB GLENOAKS BL FROM FFX-2.
BOTH POLICE VEHS WERE MKD BLK/WHT VEH'S WITH
EMERGENCY LIGHT BARS ON ROOFS. ALL OFCRS WERE IN
FULL UNIFORM.

USE OF FORCE

OBSERVATIONS

OFCRS SINGER AND SINGER WERE WB I-210 FWY
APPROACHING SUNLAND BL WHEN THEY OBS DEFTS VE
APPROACHING THEM FROM THE REAR AT A HIGH RAT-
OF SPEED. DEFTS VEH PASSED THEIR PATROL CA
THEN SLOWED. OFCRS SINGER AND SINGER EXITED THE
FWY AT SUNLAND, THEN IMMEDIATELY RE-ENTERED IN AN
ATTEMPT TO PACE DEFT'S VEH. DEFT WAS DRIVING
A WHT 88 HYUNDAI EXCEL 2DR LIC '2KFM102' WHEN
THEY GOT BACK ON THE FWY THEY OBS DEFT'S VEH AS A
TRAVELLING AT A HIGH SPEED APPROACHING WHEATLAND.
AV. THEY WERE ABLE TO OVERTAKE DEFTS VEH AS IT
PASSED 'THE OSBORNE EXIT AND PACED THE SPEED
AT 110 TO 115 MPH USING THE #1, #2 AND #3 LANES
WHEN THEY WERE W OF OSBORNE, OFCR SINGER ACTIV-
THEIR VEH EMERGENCY LIGHTS AND SIREN. DEFTS VEH
SLOWED TO 80 MPH CONTINUING TO THE PAXTON ST
EXIT. DEFT FAILED TO STOP AT THE STOP SIGN A-
THE END OF THE OFFRAMP WHICH WAS APPROX S-
W FROM THE END OF A BLIND CURVE, ENDANGER IN

PAGE NO.		TYPE OF REPORT				BOOKING NO.		OR NO.	
4 / 7		ARREST				2381162			

ITEM NO	QUAN.	ARTICLE	SERIAL NO.	BRAND	MODEL NO.	MISC. DESCRIPTION (EG. COLOR SIZE INSCRIPTIONS, CALIBER, REVOLVER ETC)	DOLLAR ...

USE OF FORCE

OBSERVATIONS (CONT.)

FELONY STOP PROCEDURES. BOTH PASSENGERS EXITED IN PASS SIDE OF DEFTS VEH. COMPLIED WITH SINGER'S ORDERS AND WERE TAKEN INTO CUSTODY WITHOUT INCIDENT. DEFT HOWEVER DID NOT COMP WITH SINGER'S ORDERS. DEFT AT FIRST WOULD N EXIT VEH. AFTER SEVERAL MORE ORDERS OVER PA DEFT EXITED HIS VEH, THEN GOT BACK IN, AND THEN EXITED AGAIN. DEFT FAILED TO PUT HIS HANDS ON HIS HEAD INSTEAD PUTTING HIS LT HAND IN PANTS POCKET AND PLACING HIS RT HAND ON THE ROOF OF HIS CAR. WE CONTINUED ORDERING DEFT TO PLACE HIS HANDS ON HIS HEAD AND LAY DOW ON THE GROUND. DEFT FINALLY LAID DOWN ON THE GROUND AND I APPROACHED HIM TO HAND CUFF HIM. DEFT THEN STARTED TO RAISE UP AND I PLACED MY KNEE ON HIS BACK TO PREVE THIS MOVEMENT. DEFT CONTINUED TO TRY AND RISE UP CAUSING ME TO LOSE MY BALANCE AN FALL OFF. DEFT STARTED TO TURN AND CHARGE TOWARDS ME. I BACKED AWAY AND SGT KEC #71667 FIRED A TASER AT DEFT STRIKING H IN THE BACK AND TEMPORARILY HALTING DEFT'S ATTACK. DEFT RECOVERED ALMOST IMMEDIATELY AND RESUMED HIS HOSTILE CHARGE IN OUR DIREC OFCR WIND AND I DREW OUR BATONS TO DEFEND AGAINST DEFT'S ATTACK AND STRUCK HIM SEVERAL TIMES IN THE ARM AND LEG AREAS TO INCAPACITATE HIM. DEFT CONTIN RESISTING. KICKING AND SWINGING HIS ARMS AT US. WE FINALLY KNOCKED DEFT DOWN HE WAS SUBDUED BY SEVERAL OFRS USING TH SWARM TECHNIQUE. DEFT CONTINUED STRUGGLING WHILE ON THE GROUND AND THEN STARTED LAUGH AND MAKING INCOHERENT STATEMENTS. DEFT CONTINUED STRUGGLING AND I WAS SPITTING AT OFCRS AND PARAMEDICS EVEN AFTER BEING TOLD TO:

CONTINUE ON REVERSE SIDE.

CONTINUATION SHEET

PAGE NO.	TYPE OF REPORT				BOOKING NO.	DR NO.
7/7	ARREST				2381162	—
ITEM NO.	BRAND	ARTICLE	SERIAL NO.	BRAND	MODEL NO.	MISC. DESCRIPTION (EG. COLOR, SIZE INSCRIPTIONS, CALIBER, REVOLVER, ETC.) DOLLAR

OBSERVATIONS (CONT)

ANY TRF WB ON PAXTON WHO COULD NOT HAVE STOPPED IN TIME TO PREVENT A T/A. DEFT DROVE WB PAXTON AT 45-50MPH FAILING TO STOP AT THE RED TRI-LIGHT AT FOOTHILL BL. CAUSING NB AND SB VEHS TO YIELD TO AVOID T/A'S. DEFT ACCELERATED TO APPROX 80 MPH WB ON PAXTON'S TO SB GLENOAKS BL. DEFT CONTINUED AT APPROX 80MPH IN 35MPH ZONE PASSING OTHER VEHS. AND PEDS ON THE SIDEWALKS, WHO WOULD BE INJURED IF DEFTS VEH HAD CAUSED A T/A. DEFT DROVE THROUGH THE RED TRI-LIGHT AT GLENOAKS BL AND VAN NUYS AT APPROX 35 MPH, CAUSING SEVERAL EB AND WB VEHS TO SLAM ON THEIR BRAKES TO AVOID T/A. WE CAUGHT UP TO THE CHP UNIT AND DEFTS VEH. AT THIS POINT, ACTIVATED OUR EMERGENCY LIGHTS AND CONTINUED IN THE PURSUIT TO ASSIST THE CHP. WE OBS DEFT AND 2 MB PASSENGERS TURN AND LOOK BACK TOWARD THE PURSUING UNITS SEVERAL TIMES. DEFT CONTINUED DRIVING EB AT APPROX 65MPH PASSING OTHER VEHS IN A 35 MPH MOSTLY RESIDENTIAL AREA. DEFT RAN THE RED TRI-L AT VAN NUYS BL AND FOOTHILL BL CAUSING A SB VEH TO SKID TO A STOP TO AVOID T/A WITH DEFT OR POLICE VEH'S. DEFT CONTINUED SB FOOTHILL AT APPROX 60 MPH /35MPH ZONE. DEFT DROVE THROUGH THE MID PHASE RED TRI-LIGHT AT TERRA BELLA AT APPROX 60MPH. ANY VEHS EB ON TERRABELLA WHO VIEW OF THE INTERSECTION WAS LIMITED DUE TO B INGS ON N SIDE WOULD NOT HAVE BEEN ABLE REACT AND STOP TO AVOID A T/A. DEFT STOPP SUDDENLY FOR RED TRI-LIGHT AT OSBORNE ST AND FOOTHILL JUST BARELY AVOIDING A BROADSIDE TA WITH AN E VEH. DEFT THEN PROCEEDED SB #2 LN AND STOPPED JUST SHORT OF HITTING A TRUCK THAT WAS YIELDING TO OUR LIGHTS AND SIRENS. OFCR T SINGER ORDERED ALL PERSONS OUT OF VEH USING

CONTINUE ON REVERSE SIDE.   CONTINUATION SHEET   15.09C

5 7	TYPE OF REPORT ARREST					BOOKING NO. 2381162		DR NO.
ITEM NO.	QUAN.	ARTICLE	SERIAL NO.	BRAND	MODEL NO.	MISC. DESCRIPTION (IE, COLOR, SIZE, INSCRIPTIONS, CALIBER, REVOLVER, ETC)		DOLLAR

OBSERVATIONS (CONT)

DEFT WAS TRANSP TO PACIFICA HOSP FOR INITIAL MT THEN TO LACO USC MC JAIL WARD FOR BOOK. WE DETECTED A FAINT ODOR OF ALCOHOL AND A C... ODOR ON DEFTS BREATH. DEFT WAS UNABLE TO ANSW. QUESTIONS ABOUT WHAT HAPPENED AND HIS HOSTIL AGITATED DEMEANOR CONTINUED FOR APPROX AN DEFTS SPEECH WAS HURRIED AND USUALLY WOMEN AND HIS MUSCLES WERE EXTREMLY RIGID. DEFT WAS POSSIBLY UNDER THE INFLUENCE OF A L...   DRUG, PROBABLY PCP, BUT DUE TO HIS INJURIES WE WERE UNABLE TO EVALUATE - AFTER ABOUT 1 HR, DEFT WAS SEMI-CO-OPERATIVE AND STATED HE THEN REMEMBERED FIGHTING WITH C...

ARREST
DEFT WAS ARRESTED 2800.2VC FELONY EVADING.

BOOKING
DEFT WAS BKD 2800.2VC AT LACO USC MC JAIL WAR BKG WAS APPROVED BY SGT TROUTT #15392 UTD L

MT
DEFT WAS MTD FOR ABRASIONS AND CONTUSIONS ON HIS FACE, ARMS, LEGS AND TORSO AREAS.

ADDITIONAL
DEFTS LICENSE STATUS WAS SUSPENDED. DEFT WAS ON PAROLE FOR 211 PC CDC #E48354 AND A PAROLE HOLD WAS PLACED ON HIM.

CONTINUE ON REVERSE SIDE.   CONTINUATION SHEET   15.090

NARRATIVE/SUPPLEMENTAL

DATE OF INCIDENT OCCURRENCE	TIME (2400)	NCIC NUMBER	OFFICER ID	NUMBER

"X" ONE	"X" ONE	TYPE SUPPLEMENTAL ("X" APPLICABLE)		
NARRATIVE	COLLISION REPORT	SA UPDATE	FATAL	HIT & RUN UPDATE
SUPPLEMENTAL	OTHER	HAZARDOUS MATERIALS	SCHOOL BUS	OTHER

CITY/COUNTY/JUDICIAL DISTRICT — REPORTING DISTRICT/BEAT — CITATION NUMBER

LOCATION/SUBJECT — STATE HIGHWAY RELATED: YES / NO

1. CHP OFFICERS: M.G. SINGER #12403 (DRIVER) VERDUGO HILLS AREA
2. T.J. SINGER #9301   2130 WINDSOR ALTADENA
3. SUMMARY:
4. CHP VEH. (M. SINGER) DRIVER WAS W/B I-210
5. APPROACHING SUNLAND BL. WHEN SUBJ. VEH. (S/V) WAS
6. FIRST OBSD. APPROACHING FROM THE REAR AT HIGH
7. SPEED. S/V OVERTOOK & THEN SLOWED IN FRONT
8. OF THE PATROL CAR. THE PATROL CAR EXITED THE
9. FWY. AT SUNLAND BLVD. & IMMEDIATELY RE-ENTERED
10. IN AN ATTEMPT TO PACE THE VEH. WHEN WE
11. GOT BACK ON THE FWY. S/V WAS AGAIN TRAVELLING
12. AT A HIGH SPEED AND APPROACHING WHEATLAND BL.
13. WE WERE ABLE TO OVERTAKE S/V AS IT PASSED THE
14. OSBORNE EXIT. A PACE INDICATED S/V WAS
15. TRAVELLING AT 110 TO 115 MPH. (USING THE #1, 2
16. AND 3 LANES). W/OF OSBORNE ST. EXIT THE
17. PATROL CARS EMERGENCY LIGHTS WERE ACTIVATED
18. & SIREN TURNED ON. S/V SLOWED TO APPROX.
19. 80 MPH BUT FAILED TO YIELD CONTINUING TO THE
20. PAXTON ST. EXIT. S/V ROLLED THROUGH THE
21. STOP SIGN AT THE BOTTOM OF THE OFFRAMP &
22. DROVE W/B ON PAXTON. S/V RAN THE RED
23. LIGHT AT FOOTHILL BL. AT APPROX 45-50 MPH.
24. L.A.P.D. ASSISTANCE WAS REQUESTED DUE TO NO CHP ASSISTANCE AVAIL
25. S/V CONTINUED W/B REACHING APPROX. 80
26. MPH. BEFORE SLOWING & TURNING LEFT ON
27. GLEN OAKS BL. AS S/V DROVE S/B ON GLEN
28. OAKS IT AGAIN ACCELERATED TO APPROX. 80
29. MPH S/V SLOWED FOR A RED LIGHT AT
30. VAN NUYS BL. AND THEN DROVE THROUGH IT
31. AT APPROX. 35 MPH. TURNING LEFT (E/B).
32. BY NOW ADDITIONAL UNITS WERE WITH THE

PREPARER'S NAME: T.J. SINGER   ID NUMBER: 9301   05-03-91   REVIEWER'S NAME

CHP 556 (Rev. 7-87) OPI 042

NARRATIVE/SUPPLEMENTAL

| DATE OF INCIDENT OCCURRENCE | TIME (2400) | NCIC NUMBER | OFFICER ID | NUMBER |

"X" ONE: ☐ NARRATIVE ☐ SUPPLEMENTAL
"X" ONE: ☐ COLLISION REPORT ☐ OTHER
TYPE SUPPLEMENTAL ("X" APPLICABLE): ☐ SA UPDATE ☐ HAZARDOUS MATERIALS ☐ FATAL ☐ SCHOOL BUS ☐ HIT & RUN UPDATE ☐ OTHER

| CITY / COUNTY / JUDICIAL DISTRICT | | | REPORTING DISTRICT / BEAT | CITATION NUMBER |

LOCATION / SUBJECT | STATE HIGHWAY RE... ☐ YES

1.
2. PURSUIT AS IT CONTINUED E/B AT SPEEDS 45
3. TO 65 M.P.H. S/V TURNED N/B ON
4. FOOTHILL BL. & ACCELERATED TO APPROX.
5. 60 M.P.H. RUNNING A RED LIGHT AT
6. TERRA BELLA AS IT APPROACHED OSBORNE ST
7. ST. S/V SLOWED TO A STOP FOR A RED
8. LIGHT IN THE #1 LN. WHEN THE LIGHT
9. TURNED GREEN S/V PULLED OVER TO THE
10. RIGHT N/OF THE INTERSECTION. CHP OFFICER
11. T. SINGER ATTEMPTED TO GET SUBJ. DRIVER
12. OUT OF THE VEH.. USING FELONY STOP PROCEDURE
13. BUT HE WAS UNCOOPERATIVE AND FAILED TO
14. OBEY VERBAL COMMANDS AS HE EXITED THE
15. DRIVERS SIDE DOOR AND STOOD IN THE STREET
16.
17. THE TWO PASSENGERS COMPLIED WITH THE
18. FELONY STOP ORDERS AND WERE TAKEN OUT
19. ON THE R/SIDE OF THE VEH. AND PLACED
20. ON THE GROUND. LAPD UNITS HANDLED
21. THE SUBDUING & ARREST OF THE DRIVER.
22. BOTH PASSENGERS PRODUCED GOOD 'ID'
23. AND WERE RELEASED WHEN IT WAS DETERMINE
24. THE VEH WAS NOT STOLEN.
25.
26.
27.
28.
29.
30.
31.
32. REVIEWER'S NAME: T. J. SINGER STO ID NUMBER: 9301 MONTH/DAY/YEAR: 08-08-91

CHP 556 (Rev. 7-87) OPI 042

The following two pages are the use-of-force reports filed in connection with the arrest of Rodney King. The first shows that the officers correctly reported that the suspect was "swarmed by numerous officers" after attacking an officer, but that he continued and, in fact, increased his resistance. The second reports the use of a TASER twice on Rodney King by Sgt. Koon from a distance of about five feet.

LOS ANGELES POLICE DEPARTMENT
USE OF FORCE REPORT

DATE: 3-3-91   TIME: 0030   LOCATION OF OCCURRENCE: OSBORNE - FOOTHILL BL   DR: 1655

SUSPECT'S NAME (LAST, FIRST, MIDDLE): KING, RODNEY GLENN   BOOKING NO.: 2381162   CHARGE: 2800.2 VC

SEX: M   DESCENT: BLK   HEIGHT: 603   WEIGHT: 225   DOB: 4-2-65   AGE: 25   CONNECTING REPORTS: ARREST

SOURCE OF ACTIVITY:
— OBSERVED   X RADIO CALL   — CITIZEN CALL   — STATION CALL   — OTHER

CONDITIONS (CHECK ALL THAT APPLY):
— PCP   — MENTAL   — FOOT PURSUIT   — FAMILY DISPUTE   X ASSAULT ON OFFICER
— OTHER DRUG   X DUI   X OTHER TRAF. VIOL.   — BUSINESS DISPUTE   — ASSAULT ON CITIZEN
X ALCOHOL   X VEH. PURSUIT   X 415   — NEIGHBOR DISPUTE   X OTHER: POSS UI UNK DRUG

TYPE FORCE (CHECK ALL THAT APPLY):

PHYSICAL FORCE
BATON SAP   PAIN COMPLIANCE
— STRAIGHT   — TWIST LOCK
X MONADNOCK   — WRIST LOCK
— KUBATON   — OTHER: SPECIFY
— SAP

MOTION USED: UPPER BODY
X STRIKE   — CAROTID
— BLOCK   — MODIFIED CAROTID
— CONTROL   — LOCKED CAROTID

OTHER
X KICKS
— PUNCH
— MARTIAL ART TECHNIQUE
— MISCELLANEOUS PHYSICAL FORCE
— OTHER: SPECIFY

CHEMICAL SPRAY
NO TIMES SPRAYED
TYPE SPRAY USED (BRAND)
MODEL NO.:   EXPIR. DATE
DISTANCE FROM SUSPECT
1 FT.   2 FT.   FT.
DURATION OF SPRAY
1 SECS.   2 SEC   3 SECS
WAS SPRAY EFFECTIVE? YES NO
IF NO, REASON (STATE IF UNK.)

SHADE AREA(S) SPRAYED

TASER
TASER SERIAL NO
NO. OF CASSETTES FIRED
DISTANCE TO SUSPECT
1
2
3
DID DARTS PENETRATE
SKIN? YES NO
WAITING TIME FOR TASER
TO ARRIVE MINUTES
WAS IT EFFECTIVE?
— YES NO
IF NO, REASON
(STATE IF UNK)

ENTER THE ONE LAST TYPE OF FORCE THAT FINALLY CONTROLLED THIS SUSPECT.
SWARMED BY NUMEROUS OFCRS

EFFECTS (Check all that apply)   WAS SUSP. INCAPACITATED? YES X NO   TIME REQUIRED TO INCAPACITATE SUSPECT: ___ SECONDS
— NONE APPARENT   — CHOKING   — FELL TO GROUND   X CONT. SOME RESISTANCE   — STOPPED RESISTANCE
— EYE CLOSURE   — COUGHING   X ATTACKED OFCR.   X INCREASED RESISTANCE   — OTHER:

RESIDUAL EFFECTS ON OFFICERS: X NONE   — CHEMICAL   — ELECTRICAL SHOCK

INJURIES RESULTING FROM USE OF FORCE   TYPES: A - MAJOR (USUALLY HOSPITALIZED)   B - VISIBLE (NOT HOSPITALIZED)   C - COMPLAINED OF ONLY   N - NONE

LAST NAME	TYPE INJURY	BRIEF DESCRIPTION OF INJURY	HOSPITALIZED YES NO	OFF YES NO	HIGH YES NO
OFCR. POWELL LARRY	N	NONE	X	X	X
OFCR. WIND TIM	N	NONE	X	X	X
SUSP. KING, RODNEY	A	CONTUSIONS - ABRASIONS	X		

ADDITIONAL (USE OF OTHER DEVICE; I.E., FIELD TEST, ADDITIONAL OFFICER INJURED; SUSP. INJURIES UNRELATED TO USE OF FORCE, ANY OTHER PERTINENT INF)

INVOLVED OFFICERS	SERIAL NO.	SEX	DESCENT	DIVISION: DETAIL	ON-DUTY?	IN UNIFORM?
WIND	27745	M	WHT	FT 16	YES X NO	YES X NO
POWELL	25490	M	WHT	HL 23	YES X NO	YES X NO

DATE AND TIME REPRODUCED   DIVISION   CLERK   INVESTIGATING SUPERVISOR   SERIAL NO.   DIV..DETAIL   W C OR OIC APPROVING   SERIAL NO.

DISTRIBUTION: 1 - ORIGINAL, COMMANDING OFFICER, PERSONNEL & TRAINING BUREAU; 1 - EMPLOYEE'S COMMANDING OFFICER;
1 - EMPLOYEE'S BUREAU COMMANDING OFFICER; 1 - COMMANDING OFFICER, TRAINING DIVISION
(ATTACH A COPY OF ALL RELATED REPORTS)

USE OF FORCE REPORT

DR

DATE	TIME	LOCATION OF OCCURRENCE		RD
3-3-91	0030	OSBORNE - FOOTHILL BL		1655

SUSPECT'S NAME (LAST, FIRST, MIDDLE) KING, RODNEY GLENN   BOOKING NO. 2381162   CHARGE 2800.2 VC

| SEX M | DESCENT BLK | HEIGHT 603 | WEIGHT 225 | DOB 4-2-65 | AGE 25 | CONNECTING REPORTS ARREST |

SOURCE OF ACTIVITY

___ OBSERVED   X RADIO CALL   ___ CITIZEN CALL   ___ STATION CALL   ___ OTHER

CONDITIONS (CHECK ALL THAT APPLY)

___ PCP	___ MENTAL	___ FOOT PURSUIT	___ FAMILY DISPUTE	X ASSAULT ON OFFICER
___ OTHER DRUG	X DUI	X OTHER TRAF. VIOL.	___ BUSINESS DISPUTE	___ ASSAULT ON CITIZEN
X ALCOHOL	X VEH. PURSUIT	X 415	___ NEIGHBOR DISPUTE	X OTHER: POSS W/ UNK DRUG

TYPE FORCE (CHECK ALL THAT APPLY)

PHYSICAL FORCE

BATON SAP	PAIN COMPLIANCE
___ STRAIGHT	___ TWIST LOCK
___ MONADNOCK	___ WRIST LOCK
___ KUBATON	___ OTHER: (SPECIFY)
___ SAP	

UPPER BODY

(MOTION USED)
___ STRIKE   ___ CAROTID
___ BLOCK   ___ MODIFIED CAROTID
___ CONTROL   ___ LOCKED CAROTID

OTHER
___ KICKS
___ PUNCH
___ MARTIAL ART TECHNIQUE
___ MISCELLANEOUS PHYSICAL FORCE
___ OTHER: (SPECIFY)

CHEMICAL SPRAY

NO TIMES SPRAYED ___
TYPE SPRAY USED (BRAND) ___
(MODEL NO.) ___   (EXPIR. DATE) ___
DISTANCE FROM SUSPECT
1 ___ FT. 2 ___ FT. 3 ___ FT.
DURATION OF SPRAY
1 ___ SECS. 2 ___ SECS. 3 ___ SECS
WAS SPRAY EFFECTIVE? ___ YES ___ NO
IF NO, REASON (STATE IF UNK.)

SHADE AREA(S) SPRAYED

TASER

TASER SERIAL NO. 09
NO. OF CASSETTES FIRED 2
DISTANCE TO SUSPECT
1 5 FT
2 5 FT
3
DID DARTS PENETRATE
SKIN? X YES ___ NO
WAITING TIME FOR TASER
TO ARRIVE 0 MINUTES
WAS IT EFFECTIVE?
___ YES X NO
IF NO, REASON (STATE IF UNK.)
UNK

ENTER THE ONE LAST TYPE OF FORCE THAT FINALLY CONTROLLED THIS SUSPECT.

SWARMED BY NUMEROUS OFCRS

EFFECTS (Check all that apply)   WAS SUSP. INCAPACITATED? ___ YES X NO   TIME REQUIRED TO INCAPACITATE SUSPECT: ___ SECONDS

| ___ NONE APPARENT | ___ CHOKING | ___ FELL TO GROUND | X CONT. SOME RESISTANCE | ___ STOPPED RESISTANCE |
| ___ EYE CLOSURE | ___ COUGHING | X ATTACKED OFCR. | X INCREASED RESISTANCE | ___ OTHER: |

RESIDUAL EFFECTS ON OFFICERS: X NONE   ___ CHEMICAL   ___ ELECTRICAL SHOCK

INJURIES (RESULTING FROM USE OF FORCE)   TYPES: A - MAJOR (USUALLY HOSPITALIZED)   B - VISIBLE (NOT HOSPITALIZED)   C - COMPLAINED OF ONLY   N - NONE

	LAST NAME		TYPE INJURY	BRIEF DESCRIPTION OF INJURY	HOSPITALIZED YES / NO	OFF DU YES / NO	
OFCR. Sgt.	KOON,	STACY	N	NONE		X	X	X
OFCR.								
SUSP.	KING	RODNEY	A	CONTUSIONS - ABRASIONS	X			

ADDITIONAL (USE OF OTHER DEVICE; I.E., FIELD TEST; ADDITIONAL OFFICER INJURED; SUSP. INJURIES UNRELATED TO USE OF FORCE; ANY OTHER PERTINENT

INVOLVED OFFICERS	SERIAL NO.	SEX	DESCENT	DIVISION/DETAIL	ON-DUTY?	IN UNIFORM?
		M	WHT	FT 16	YES X NO ___	YES X NO ___
				C 140	YES ___ NO ___	YES ___ NO ___

DATE AND TIME REPRODUCED   DIVISION CLERK   INVESTIGATING SUPERVISOR   SERIAL NO.   DIV./DETAIL   W C OR OIC APPROVING   SERIAL NO.

DISTRIBUTION: 1 - ORIGINAL, COMMANDING OFFICER, PERSONNEL & TRAINING BUREAU; 1 - EMPLOYEE'S COMMANDING OFFICER; 1 - EMPLOYEE'S BUREAU COMMANDING OFFICER; 1 - COMMANDING OFFICER, TRAINING DIVISION (ATTACH A COPY OF ALL RELATED REPORTS)

Index

Page references followed by an n refer to footnotes.